The Disney Fetish

The Disney Fetish

Seán Harrington

British Library Cataloguing in Publication Data

The Disney Fetish

A catalogue entry for this book is available from the British Library

ISBN: 9780 86196 713 1 (Paperback)

Published by
John Libbey Publishing Ltd, 3 Leicester Road, New Barnet, Herts EN5 5EW,
United Kingdom
e-mail: john.libbey@orange.fr; web site: www.johnlibbey.com

Direct orders: **Marston Book Services Ltd:** direct.orders@marston.co.uk

Distributed in Asia and North America by **Indiana University Press**,
Herman B Wells Library – 350, 1320 E. 10th St., Bloomington, IN 47405, USA.
www.iupress.indiana.edu

Printed and bound in China by 1010 Printing International Ltd.

Contents

	Preface	1
	Acknowledgements	4
	Introduction	5
Part One	**The Homunculus**	**13**
Chapter 1	A Theoretical Context	15
Chapter 2	Psycho-mythology	29
	Walt Disney	35
	Alice in Cartoon-land	37
Chapter 3	The Phallus and Disney Animation	39
	Oswald the Lucky Rabbit	40
	Mickey Mouse and Donald Duck, the Ego Ideal and the Id	43
	Steamboat Willy	45
	The Duck	48
	Analysis	53
Chapter 4	The Conceptual Homunculus	57
	Fetishism	59
	Anality and Rivalry in the *Silly Symphonies* series	61
Part Two	**The Regressive Apparatus**	**65**
Chapter 5	Disney Character Tropes	67
	Mass Appeal and Regression	68
	A Disney Apparatus	70
	Snow White	72
	Disney Character Tropes	81
Chapter 6	The Industrial Process and the Father	89
	A Lexicon of Regression	89
	Absent Fathers: Disney and the Real Boy	93
	Malevolence and the Castrating Fathers	99
	Threat to the Homuncule Body	104

Chapter 7	*Fantasia* and Eroticism	107
	Fantasia's Utopia	108
	Pastoral Symphony	111
	The Sorcerer's Apprentice	114
	Death of the Dinosaurs	115
	A Night on Bald Mountain	116
Chapter 8	Regression and Jouissance	121
	The Regressive	121
	The Law and the Primordial in Regression	123
	Dumbo: Regressive Narratives	124
	Ugly Children	125
	Bambi: Death of the Mother and Jouissance	130
	Violence and the Cartoon Body in *Bambi*	137
Part Three	**The Hybrid Utopia**	**143**
Chapter 9	Hegemony	145
	Unionisation and the Disney Strike	146
	Films Made in Studio During the Strike	148
Chapter 10	Disney's 'Good Neighbour'	157
	The Three Caballeros: Hyper-real Sexuality and Cartoon Jouissance	158
	Communist witch-hunts and red fear	165
Chapter 11	World War II and Propaganda	169
	The Production of Canadian Propaganda	172
	The United States Enters the War	176
	Donald gets Drafted	177
	The Cartoon Body: Sadism, Exaggeration and Manipulation	183
	Propaganda, pornography and utopia	189
Chapter 12	The Consumerist Utopia	193
	Television and Disneyland	198
	Feature-length Films of the 50s and 60s: Familial Sexuality	201
	Walt Disney's Death and Walt Disney World	206
	Conclusion	208
	Future Research and End Notes	216
	References, Filmography, Studios, Digital Rights	221
	Index	231

Preface

In picking up this book, one might be curious about the slightly provocative title. Perhaps more specifically: what is the Disney Fetish? Those for whom this may suggest that this book will include latex Mickey Mouse costumes, or perhaps furries or paraphillic infantalists that *really* enjoy their Disney films, I can only offer apologies, as you are partially correct. While these excitingly prurient elements are absent from this book, I will be addressing the more abstract and structural questions of Disney as a fetishistic practice and more specifically what composes the fetish in structure and form. To best accomplish this I have endeavoured to paint a picture of Disney based on a selection of the multitude of signifiers which compose Disney as the vast socio-cultural institution we know today. The Disney 'Thing' within this text is formed of pseudo-mythical psycho-biography, film analysis and critical theory. It is a frozen image of Disney's classic era, its foray into propaganda and its industrial disputes. While any attempt to distil such an established institution as Disney will be left invariably incomplete, this book attempts to synthesize a perversely delimited entity that we can refer to as Disney for our purposes. In doing so it seems that this research has inadvertently created a fetish of Disney itself; a simplified and seemingly encompassing form that at times disavows a more expansive irrefutable reality. So for those that are curious as to what the Disney Fetish is, we can surmise that this book is itself a Disney fetish. Vulgar pretensions and perverse disappointment aside, this book is essentially an attempt to address how we consume mass media and the broader question of whether our consumption of media is itself problematic.

This text seeks to provide an account of the subject as a consumer of mass-media. Within this consumption it is argued that this consumer must interact with commercial entities (the producers of mass-media) as socio-cultural institutions. These commercial entities provide media that in turn enables a self-administration of gratification. In this context it is argued that the Walt Disney Company is structurally perverse, that the gratification of the Disney consumer is achieved at their expense, and that this expense is to the benefit of Disney commercially and structurally as a major socio-cultural institution. This text makes use of Lacanian psychoanalytic theory, film and cultural studies, and the industrial-organisational history of the Walt Disney Company to create an account of the subject's interactions within the apparatus of Disney media. The account of consumerism constructed by text is organised by a synthesis of several theoretical constructs: the animated homunculus, the regressive cinematic apparatus and the Disney consumerist utopia.

In attempting to study Disney it has been necessary to constitute and delimit an object of study: a concept of Disney that is made up of various theoretical accounts, biographical mythologies and established commercial physicalities (media and corporate practice). In wishing to study a concept of Disney it has been necessary to create one in smaller form, much like the homunculus is a smaller copy of the human being; an embryonic image of itself, scaled by an alchemic practice of psychoanalytic and critical theory. This alchemic rendering of Disney in theory and practice mirrors the process of 'Disneyification': the simplification of texts, concepts and images in order to make them mass consumable to a wide family-friendly audience. While I feel assured that children will not be read this book as a bed-time story, I am concerned that the rendering of so many areas of thought and realms of information may mislead the reader to believing that this text somehow summates the entirety of 'Disney studies'. Rather this text stands with many others in attempting to critique and complicate our 'common sense' notions of family entertainment and Disney media. The many other texts and articles that compose contemporary Disney studies (at least in part) are mentioned through-out this text.

It is my hope that this attempt to create a homuncule image of Disney has not come too close to 'Disneyifying' Disney studies (and indeed psycho-analysis), but it is important for the reader of this text to be aware of this tendency. In attempting to study and render a cultural entity in all its complexities and nuances, simplifications and reductions are perhaps an inevitability. Thus what has been developed in this text should be understood in these terms, it is an attempt to delimit a vast, over-determined and complex set of images and practices from a social, cultural and corporate institution which has been over 80 years in development. This is essentially why I claim that this text creates the object of study, in doing it is hoped that an image of Disney will emerge that will in part account for the contemporary consumer's complex relation to media, fetishism and mass consumption.

Acknowledgements

I would like to take this opportunity to sincerely thank Dany Nobus and Tanya Krzywinska for their enthusiasm and support. I would also like to thank those at DBS-Arts who initiated me into my cult-like interest in Lacanian psychoanalysis, namely Rik Loose, Aurélie Olivier, Patricia McCarthy and Stephen Costello. A special thanks to Parveen Adams for helping me consolidate and develop my understanding of psychoanalysis in the context of contemporary society. Special thanks to Bruce Gilchrist and Jo Joelson, the work of whom inspired me to begin my research into Disney as a socio-cultural institution, and to Camille Rose Garcia whose work so perfectly encapsulates the essence of our consumption of Disney.

This book has been expertly illustrated by two exceptional graphic artists: Paul 'Poncho' Byrne and Rupert Norfolk. Thank you for all your hard work.

Lastly I would like to thank my family and friends for all their support, without which this work would not have been possible, and to my father, whose presence, laughter and encouragement I miss terribly.

Introduction

Since the 1930s cultural theorists have been taking note of the changes in consumerism that the industrialisation of the West had produced. People were now confronted by a world where material and mental comforts were becoming more readily available. In his text *The Delay of the Machine Age*, Hanns Sachs (1933) describes the potential consequences that the creation of the free market and mechanised industrialisation pose for modern man, specifically in the use of machines as supports of gratification. For Sachs, what became troubling in the growing dependence on machines was not the automated assembly-lines that created vast redundancies, but the machines that provide the individual with an escape from the difficulties and complications of conscious life. These are the machines of play, the machines that offer a reprieve from daily life and immersion in fantasy. Sachs refers this to an automatic marionette theatre, in which mechanised puppets would dazzle audiences by performing popular stories. Crucially, he noted that it was the mystery of the automation itself that made the marionette theatre such a spectacle.

Fritz Mollenhoff (1940) would later draw the comparison between Sachs' discussion of the automatic marionettes and the escapist joys of Disney cartoons, which by the 1940s had become a global phenomenon. Mollenhoff suggests that the cartoon's image is a functional artifice that functions as yet another machination. In similar discussions, Walter Benjamin (1936) saw Mickey Mouse as a unique balancing of machination and fantasy. This was a dynamic which he saw as crucial to the problems the contemporary subject faced in situating themselves within a relation to technology and nature.

What interested Mollenhoff, Benjamin and Sachs was the increasing dependence on both real and imaginary machinations. Imaginary machines take the form of cultural facilities that support the subject's fantasy life by way of enjoyment, just as manufacturing machines offer physical support in the real. Cartoons thus have the capacity to provide an imaginary support to the subject by enabling and supporting a fantasmatic gratification.

Mollenhoff and Sachs were keen to emphasise that a machine's sole purpose is to act as a support. For Sachs, the machines of leisure are a projection of an excessively loved ego, an "ego simulacra" (Sachs, 1933, p418). They form a projection of an idealised possibility: an image of solidity and enablement. Their purpose is thus to support the ego, the subject's imaginary construction of self.

The consequences of becoming dependent on machines that offer physical and real support are obvious: people lose skills and become alienated from the world they inhabit. The contemporary subject is also dependent on machines of fantasy, yet the consequences of this dependency on machines of leisure are less obvious.

This book is an exploration into the ways in which machines of leisure have affected the subject, in particular the manner in which they enable gratification. This text offers an analysis of the place that these fantasy machinations have in contemporary society; how they are marketed and sold to the consumer, who now depends on their little piece of supportive fantasy. It shall be proposed that the consequences of the consumers' relation to manufactured fantasy have the potential to alter the subject's structural relation to gratification and enjoyment.

There is no better subject for analysis than that which Mollenhoff chose to discuss over 60 years ago. The Walt Disney Company is perhaps the most iconic media empire in the world. The Disney Corporation is at its base an industry that exports a relatively homogeneous product across the world. It provides a perfect example of how media can interact with society and influence culture. This base relation to society shall be elucidated through the discussion of a number of theoretical concepts which shall present a structural account of the company's mediation of the subject's gratification.

So far there have been few psychoanalytic studies that have tried to capture and describe the essence of Disney as an object of study (see Berland, 1982 and Berger, 1991). While some have made passing reference to Lacanian theory (Hansen, 1993), none have extensively drawn on Lacan and contemporary psychoanalytic conceptions of addiction and perversion in understanding the consumers relation to Disney as an institution. There have been relatively few engagements with Lacanian theory in the broader field of animation studies, and while there have been several psychoanalytically informed texts that have discussed animation (Cholodenko 2007a, Pilling 2012), there has been little structural discussion of the gratification the viewer derives from their engagement. Pilling's recent edited work *Animating the Unconscious* (2012) discusses several animated short films in terms of desire, yet these analyses remain largely descriptive. Indeed the one essay that goes beyond psychoanalytically informed description does so via the voice of a psychiatrist, whom applies several concepts pertaining to object relations (Roy, 2012). While the essays within this edited volume are authored by several persons, they share the task of vocalizing that which is inexplicit within the animated texts, their *magnitude* (Hayes, 2012, p208): that which is emotive and beyond the exposition. This is likewise the project of this book; it is an attempt to account for an engagement beyond direct text, the sub-textual desire which drives the viewer to look.

While the contributors of Pilling's text demonstrate a limited engagement with psychoanalysis, the recent work of Cholodenko attempts to synthesize several psychoanalytic concepts into discussions of the affect of the animated body on the viewer. In particular, his description of animation as *implicitly uncanny* is provocative. He situates the uncanny as the teetering point of transition between living and the animate thing, which he exemplifies in Maxim Gorky's early experience of cinematic form. Cholodenko describes this encounter as a "primal experience of cinema, a shocking, traumatic experience of animation, of reanimation" (Cholodenko, 2007a, p10). While Cholodenko's monologue surrounding the uncanny is densely descriptive, the relation of the uncanny as an intrinsic value underlying the cartoon body is crucial. Collision with this body will be seen to represent the complex engagement with animation as form.

While the focus of this text is the analysis of Disney, the concepts synthesised within it shall provide the means for further study into the institutions that regulate contemporary society and culture. It is important to note that the methodology of this text is in no way limited to Lacanian theory, although Lacan does form the core of all discussions. Freudian theory is of course the basis of Lacan's theory itself and shall be continually referenced in discussions of analytic theory and concepts. As socio-cultural mediation is also discussed within this text, the work of post-Marxist authors shall be discussed. Featured most prominently is the work of Adorno and Gramsci.

Lacanian psychoanalysis has been chosen in this instance for several reasons. As a methodology, psychoanalysis allows for in-depth discussions pertaining to the gendering (or in this case pre-gendering) of subjective experience. It allows for the inclusion of sexuality as a contextualising value for the subject's experience of gratification. The relation to gratification in the following discussions attempt to map out the subject's relation to desire and the centrality of desire in mass appeal.

Lacan's revisiting of Freud introduced two important threads in psychoanalytic discussion. First, the erotic value of the semiotic, and second: relating desire to wider systems of culture through an understanding of structuralism. Lacanian theory has not evolved in stasis and there have been many revisions and criticisms levelled at Lacanian theory as a theoretical framework. Lacan has been criticised by some for further repeating the patriarchal valuation of the phallus and thus perpetuating an inequality in the gendering of the subject (Rose, 1982). However this does not fully appraise the transgressive value of Lacanian discourse, which specifically points to the fallacy of these inequalities which are rigidly entrenched at the level of culture. Lacanian theory has been somewhat contemporized within this text through the engagement of several writers who incorporate Lacanian theory in light of developments in the field of critical theory and gender studies (namely Adams (1996), Andre (2006), Cowie (1984) and Modleski (1991)). While it this work is not claiming to encompass these fields (post-feminism and gender-studies), it does base its theoretical framework on contemporary theory that is in the very least part of these fields.

This text is not attempting to be exclusionary of other methodologies and discourses but rather welcomes their critiques and illuminations on Disney as a subject, as understood within a Lacanian methodological framework.

The current task is thus to develop a structural understanding of how gratification operates within Disney media. To accomplish this, it is necessary to provide an account of the Disney consumer: the Disneyified subject, who will be demonstrated to exemplify the contemporary subject in its self-administrative consumerist position. When discussing Disney, several things are referenced simultaneously: the Walt Disney persona/company, a media product and a utopian vision. These three aspects of Disney represent the three objects of study in Parts One, Two and Three of this text, respectively.

The purpose of Part One is the theoretical synthesis of Disney as an object of study. This conception of Disney acts as a functional artifice: an illustrative diagram of the subject as consumer, enmeshed within the artificial prosthesis of the cartoon and the ideological context of the Disney studio. The term *homunculus* shall be used to describe this core of the subject and its dynamic relation to gratification within the Disney entity. The homunculus is also an apt metaphor for the object of study in Part One: Disney itself. This image of Disney that will be constructed is part theory, biographical subject and cartoon. It is a construction of the Disney Company, mainstream media and Disney studies. Part One introduces the first component of the aetiology of the contemporary consumer, the basis of which shall be a theoretical account of contemporary society and the institutions that mediate it. There exist a number of theories regarding society's defining characteristics. Part One offers a fusional account of several of these models, among which are cultural narcissism, social addictification and organisational perversion. It shall be argued that contemporary culture enforces a narcissism that the structure of the perverse organisation manipulates to produce consumerist dependency, which manifests itself as an addictified society. Perversion is considered by psychoanalysis to be a component of normative sexuality and thus the propensity to perversion can be seen to be present in all people (Nobus, 2006). This is also the case for the concept of addiction, which can be understood as a structural difficulty in relation to gratification (Loose, 2011). Part One discusses aetiological factors contributing to perversion and addictification. It also approaches how these problems become manifest and exacerbated at the level of the subject's relation to society and culture, and how the subject derives gratification within this structure and context.

Part Two disentangles the dynamic between subject and object by providing an account of Disney's genre and narrative conventions that demonstrate the viewer's position within a regressive cinematic apparatus. This apparatus represents the basic unit of the subject's engagement with Disney from which the subject derives gratification. The purpose of Part Two is to analyse and clarify the concept of spectatorship and its role in the subject's relation to gratification. If the object of study for Part One is the homunculus, then the object of study in Part Two is the screen, as the screen has the capacity to stage the desire of the subject. To make an account of what exactly is staged within Disney films, Part Two will provide a detailed analysis of Disney narrative and stylistic conventions. Part Two shall analyse what can be considered as the most influential Disney films, those that make up the studio's 'classic' era in film-making (1937–1942). These analyses will offer detailed textual readings guided by Lacanian theory and supported by psychoanalytically informed film studies. What emerges from the analysis of the screen is a concept of cartoon aesthetics that constructs and elaborates the homunculus and its relation to the cartoon body.

Part Three connects the cinematic apparatus to the wider struggle for hegemony, which will be argued to be in service of a consumerist utopia. The purpose of this conceptualisation is to situate an account of consumer gratification within a greater historical context that demonstrates a progression to the contemporary subject. Part Three discusses hegemony as illustrative of the dynamic proposed in Part One, the mechanisms of which are discussed in Part Two.

While Lacanian theory provides a complex and adaptable account of the formation of the subject, there is also a need to move beyond Lacanian theory within Part Three, which will draw on post-Marxist cultural studies. The argument shall be made that the contemporary subject as consumer is the product of a capitalist utopian vision that came to maturity in the United States of the 1950s, and was the project of political propaganda during the Second World War. This utopian construction shall be shown to provide an ideological core for the contemporary subject, for whom it exists as a structural disposition demonstrated in societal addictification to consumables.

To summarise, it is the position of this text that there exists an archetypical consumer who is situated in a regressive apparatus of a mass media institution. This apparatus is the expression of its greater context: an addictified society mediated by perverse institutions. The ideological structure underlying this context is the product of a utopian ideal held by Disney and other companies taking the Fordist model. Disney shall be shown to exemplify the attempt to actualize this utopia, as will be evidenced in Part Three's discussion of Disney in the 1950s and 1960s.

A Note on the Disney Audience

In examining a genre and indeed a paradigm in the manufacture of media, it is difficult to create an idea of a generalised audience response. While film genres can be seen to be internally homogeneous, audiences are varied and in flux across time periods, social strata and ethnicity. Before beginning this text, there is a need to delimit what is denoted by 'the audience' and to discuss the different modes by which this audience engages with the medium.

Eisenstein commented that "Walt Disney's work is the most omni-appealing I've ever met." (Eisenstein, 1941–1946, p41), statements such as this point to an interesting quality of the Disney target audience: the Hollywood conception of the family. Disney media has been consistently described as family entertainment. This is distinct from children's entertainment in that it has traditionally targeted the family as a unit. The family is composed, as a popular company slogan maintains, by "children of all ages" (Wasko, 2001, p185). The Disney audience is diverse and yet uniform, in that all viewers are engaged and addressed as children by the Disney film-makers. There is appeal to both the real child and the 'child' within the adult psyche. While some suggest that Disney altered the medium of cartoons to explicitly target children (Smoodin, 1994), it shall become clear in the following analyses that the regressive quality of the medium renders it cathartic and gratifying for children and adults alike, thus rendering it to be a 'family-friendly' indulgence.

Disney perceived a need to bring the family as a unit into a happy and care-free image of childhood and child-like pleasures, to create an innocuous brand of fun that the family can enjoy in unison, while maintaining a homogeneous response across different reading strategies. Despite the possibility of differential readings of the Disney text, the elements within Disney films are uniform in their capacity to be found enjoyable by adults and children alike, thus precipitating the potential for consistent responses across a diverse range of audiences. The family audience is thus the audience at its widest possible generalisation.

Hibernator: Image of the Disney Chimera
(Gilchrist & Joelson, 2007)

Part One:
The Homunculus

As stated, the first part of this book shall be given over to discussion and analysis of the artificial man, the alchemical homunculus. It shall endeavour to create an account of the homunculus as the core of engagement within the Disney apparatus, and the following chapters shall be structured by the creation of a homunculus as an analogy for Disney itself. Thus, the homunculus as a concept is the theoretical construction at the core of the subject's engagement, and the analogical homunculus acts as a metaphor for the structure of part one itself, which seeks to provide a functional model of Disney with which to begin this study. To clarify:

1. The *conceptual homunculus* is the concept related to the cartoon body and is the essence of this body's appeal to the subject. It is the homunculus as gratifying artifice and is central to the discussion of subsequent parts of this text.

2. The second homunculus referenced is a functional artifice. This functional artifice takes the homunculus as an analogy to structure Part One and thus the concept of 'Disney' within this text. This *illustrative/analogical homunculus* is both Disney as an object of study and the structure of Part One itself. It is a synthesis of a theoretical base and a biographical subject, intertwined with images from the screen.

The theoretical base of Part One thus functions as the foundation for situating the functional myth of Walt Disney, as progenitor of Disney as a socio-cultural institution. This mythic image of a biographical subject shall be combined with a thing of its creation. The boundaries between man and mouse (or even man, mouse and duck) are indiscernible in many critical texts (Schickel, 1968, Elliot, 1993, Watts, 1997). Most authors attempting pseudo-psychoanalytic accounts of Walt Disney's life seem to agree that Walt strongly identified with Mickey Mouse and Donald Duck. The identification with Mickey was thought to have been consciously pursued so as to enjoy the mouse's popularity, but the duck's similarities with the mythological Walt appear far more accidental and provocative. The purpose of this overlapping analysis of Walt, the Disney Company and its product (Mickey and Donald) is to emphasise their continuum within Disney as a homuncule object of study. Analysing a singular aspect of Disney in isolation omits the capacity for the Gestalt outcomes of a more encompassing study.

The composition of this homunculus is directly inspired by the *Hibernator* project by London Fieldworks (Gilchrist & Joelson, 2007). To illustrate the cultural pathogens initiated by the socio-cultural institutionalisation of Disney, London Fieldworks created an animatronic Disney chimera. This chimera was tripartite in both form and concept. The machine itself was built with a prosthetic face and head of Walt Disney, the torso and front legs of a realistic Bambi and the hind legs of Thumper the rabbit (see image on page 12).

The chimera was stationary and lifeless until it was connected to a small solar panel that powered its movements. It was then filmed moving against a green screen, after which animators set to work situating the chimera in a computer generated post-apocalyptic environment, set to a surrealistic biographical narrative. Thus the chimera (the hybrid of Walt and animated character) is put in context (of research, abstract theory) to create a concept called Hibernator. It is this concept which is instructive in addressing Disney as a cultural institution that is at its core pathogenic, mutant and transgressive. The psychoanalytic homunculus created herein shall take similar steps, fusing man, cartoon character and theory.

Thus the mythology of Walt shall be situated in a theoretical base of addictification, narcissism and perversion. This image will be blended with the cartoon character as fetishistic object. Only then will the functional artifice of 'Disney' be established for further exploration in Parts Two and Three of this text. From this point onward Walt Disney the biographical subject is refereed to simply by 'Walt', whereas the term 'Disney' shall refer to the functional artifice under construction; it is both Walt Disney the figure, Disney the company and Disney the cultural product. Disney is an object of study in itself, one that is composed of many often intangible parts.

Chapter 1

A Theoretical Context

The following theoretical framework that forms the basis of this discussion is constructed by synthesising several theoretical positions, and is composed of concepts from Sigmund Freud, Jacques Lacan, historian Christopher Lasch and several psychoanalytically oriented theorists: Susan Long and Rik Loose. The last three of these authors share a common field in their discussion of the socio-cultural changes that have occurred in Western countries in the course of the last century. These discussions aim to produce a theoretical diagnosis of society based on trends in contemporary culture and psychopathology. Each of these authors seem to suggest that the contemporary subject exists in a pathologised society, though each uses a different term and concept in making their diagnosis. It is suggested by Lasch, Long and Loose respectively, that the subject exists in a narcissistic, perverse and addictified society. It is the position of this research that all of these diagnoses are linked via a process that occurs between organisations, mass communication and the subject. These diagnoses represent different aspects of the same problem, one that has its origins in collective and individual fantasy.

The concept of a narcissistic society is best associated with Christopher Lasch's text *The Culture of Narcissism* (1979). Lasch suggests that in the last half of the 20th century wealthy Western nations have developed increasingly egotistical societies: "To live for the moment is the prevailing passion – to live for yourself, not for your predecessors or posterity" (Lasch, 1979, p5). Lasch posits that the success of the individual has become paramount, while that of the collective has become secondary. In these societies the subject interacts with others in an instrumental manner; the other becomes a tool for achieving one's own gratification.

Narcissism, as Lasch uses the term, originates in Freud's paper *On Narcissism*

(Freud, 1914). In this text Freud proposes two types of narcissism: primary and secondary. Primary narcissism involves a libidinal investment in the ego, which in turn becomes objectified for the subject. Primary narcissism is an ego libido which operates internally for the subject, for whom the ego becomes gratifying in itself. In Lacan's discussions of the *mirror stage* (Lacan, 1954b) he proposes that the ego becomes a fantasmatic façade that allows the subject to imaginarily constitute itself in the world, in order to create a sense of their body as a point of identification. This image is essentially dysfunctional as what is constituted is not a holistic image of the subject itself, but rather a reflection based on the other as mirror; it is the look of the other that enables to subject to consolidate their sense of self. Thus, the object of the ego libido is not the reflected image of the subject, but a fantasy image of the subject as a consolidated whole. The mirror stage shall be discussed in further detail in Chapter 4.

Secondary narcissism is a pathological state, marked by the withdrawal of libidinal investment in the social realm in favour of the ego libido. The ego becomes central to the subject's sexual economy and offers a simplified gratification (Freud, 1914). The ego itself bears a similar role to a loved object, as both are attempts to cover up the subject's own intrinsic lack (Lacan, 1954a). This lack is constituted when the subject is separated from the Other (as mother) in the Oedipus Complex and forbidden to return to this state by the Law of the father. In attempting to fill the gap left by the Other the subject will always desire something more, as there exist no adequate substitute that entirely encapsulates the Other. Thus, narcissism becomes a defence against this lack, as it seeks an internal solution based on a fantasy of the ego as an entirety in itself.

The Lacanian subject is defined by a lack that motivates desire and speech. Speech becomes a function of desire, as the capacity to enunciate a need directed at the Other. Desire is bound by the rules of language and language itself stems from the same roots as desire (Lacan, 1958b, p525). Thus, narcissism is a tendency to side-step the complications of desire in favour of an intra-subjective attempt to cover up lack. This expresses itself at a societal level as a highly competitive, selfish and individualistic culture. The collective, as expressed in the symbolic, becomes secondary and the individual's need for gratification becomes paramount.

It is important to note that the narcissist will always strive to maintain the Law, but despite this adherence to the Law their primary concern is getting what they want. The Law, Lacan (1953, p230) posits, is synonymous with

16

the Law of the father and is central to the subject's achievement of the symbolic function. The Law embeds the individual in language which provides a platform for discourse with the other. Law creates and shapes desire, and both operate within the realm of the symbolic. Through its subjective interpretation and internalisation into the super-ego, the Law restricts and imposes boundaries on the subject from within. While desire always seeks gratification, it does so within the confines of the Law. When desire transgresses the boundaries established by the Law the gratification that is had is not pleasurable, but painful. In the course of this text the Law will be frequently mentioned. 'Law' is capitalised to emphasise that it does not refer to a specific set of laws but rather a Lacanian conception of the Law of the father.

The term *jouissance* is used by Lacan to indicate an excessive form of gratification. The concept itself is opposed to pleasure and is used to describe a gratification that exists beyond the pleasure principle (the boundary established by the paternal metaphor); where pleasure becomes painful (Lacan, 1966, p694). The introduction of the subject into language is initiated by the Law of the father, which along with the pleasure principle imposes restrictions on the subject's gratification. In a sense, it is a Law that forbids the subject to access the 'too much' of gratification. The narcissist's drive for selfish gratification is supported by fantasy, which is intimately connected to desire (Lacan, 1958b). Fantasy is the imaginary stage upon which the subject can enact their desires and satisfy demands. Fantasy can be thought of as the "*mise-en-scène* of desire" (Cowie, 1984, p159); it represents the staging of wish fulfilments. It is a malleable psychical element that allows the subject to attain the object of their desire in an imagined entirety; the most basic of fantasies is that the Thing desire will in some way complete you.

A narcissistic society is a society defined by secondary narcissism. It is a society in which self improvement and individualism are of ultimate importance. In Lasch's (1979) opinion, individualism has become the dominant and most problematic characteristic of American, and in turn Americanised Western culture. Individualism holds many positive connotations for Westerners, but it is essentially a prerogative for the subject to enjoy *en masse* but in isolation. Cinema is a particularly relevant institution within this dynamic. As Laura Mulvey (1975) notes, the darkened auditorium of the cinema positions the subject in a self-contained space where enjoyment of the object becomes visually accessible and voyeuristically gratifying. The distance between the viewer and screen allows for a very individual and private gratification. While the viewer is surrounded by others, the darkness enables an imagined privacy. The gratification of the viewer is no longer dependent on the others; the enjoyment is collective, yet isolated and alienated within the auditorium. The screen provides the illusion of connection to the Other (Other as the psychical schemata of otherness) from the comfort of the cinema seat. For the narcissistic society alienation becomes a paradoxical norm, in which the members of a population join in separate pursuits of individual gratification. This is closely related to Susan Long's discussion of the role of perverse organisations (Long, 2008).

The argument made by Long (2008) in *The Perverse Organisation* is that contemporary society is mediated by perverse institutions. Perversion should not be confused with the more visible practices of individual perverts, but rather as a power-relation that exists between people. These institutions have developed a perverse logic that regulates interpersonal relations. It is within these relations that the subject's personal gain becomes central, even when this gain is at the expense of others. This logic puts the primacy of the subject's narcissistic gratification over the laws of social conduct. As this logic governs the institution, it provides the persons within the organisation a safe platform to engage perversely with each other.

In the context of perversion Long discusses what has now become the world's most dominant organisational institution: the modern business corporation. In recent times corporate institutions have been seen to usurp the economic influences of religion, monarchy and in some cases democratic government (Bakan, 2004). The individual is forced to engage with corporations as consumer, and consumerism itself has become an integral part of Western society and culture. Without consumption of goods and technologies an individual cannot successfully engage with mainstream culture. Without this consumption the subject is left lacking in signifiers: the linguistic material the subject utilises in their engagement with the other.

There is an increasingly dependency on external institutions for social interaction. Telecommunications companies provide the means with which the individual can communicate with friends and family, via telephones and the internet. That is not to say people lacked contact with their friends and family before the invention of telecommunications, yet now people are wholly dependent on corporations that facilitate and provide communication services. Social relationships have become dependent on technologies which are owned, distributed and made accessible by corporate institutions.

Thus the corporation's influence goes beyond the realm of economics: it influences the subject's engagement with the Other, yet despite this access to many new forms of communication, contemporary society has become increasingly defined by its alienation and mass isolation (Schickel, 1968).

Joel Bakan (2004) suggests that this enforced symbiosis between consumer and product is the result of the creation of vast mega-corporations, whose influence is entirely inescapable. These companies have absorbed many other subsidiary businesses and form corporate empires. These conglomerates are so vast that it becomes nearly impossible for consumers not to engage with them. This becomes evident in the assimilation of most forms of mass media and mainstream news reporting by umbrella organisations such as News Corp. or Time-Warner. It is claimed by some that fewer than a dozen corporations control all American news and television stations (Giroux, 2000). This invites the question: if contemporary corporate organisations mediate society and these organisations are theoretically regulated by perverse logic, what are the consequences for the Lacanian subject as a consumer? Before discussing Long's conception of the perverse organisation, it is necessary to relate a psychoanalytic understanding of perversion.

The concepts of perversion and the 'pervert' are best understood as a dynamic between people. A neurotic or psychotic person can take on a perverse role in relation to another person, or indeed an organisation can fulfil a perverse role in relation to the persons that interact within it. At the base of the perverse is the transgression of the Law through the corruption of an other. The pervert's relation to the other is defined by a lack of mutuality, a need to gratify the self at the other's expense. Although this is similar to the subject's relation with the other in secondary narcissism, it is different in respect of the pervert's relation to the Law. The pervert positions him or her self as the object of the drive: the provider of the other's jouissance (and vicariously the Other's jouissance). As mentioned, jouissance is by its nature transgressive, corrupt and painful; the perverse position is thus inherently sado-masochistic.

The pervert disavows the Law of the father, acknowledging the Law but simultaneously denying its existence. The pervert is embedded in the realm of language and as such is dependent on symbolic relations and thus desire. But the pervert also acts as if the Law that structures desire is not present (Andre, 2006). The pervert suffers a splitting of the ego much like the narcissist, yet what is at stake is not self-love but rather a drive toward gratification in the absence of the Law, coexisting with an awareness of

19

symbolic interactions and subservience to the Law of the father (Long, 2008). The other is an accomplice for both the narcissist and the pervert, but the other takes on a different role in perverse and narcissistic scenarios. The narcissist requires that the other be a mirror to reflect back an image of their being, to facilitate a transient sense of a completed self, while the pervert requires the other to help satisfy their fantasies (of being object of the drive, enabler of jouissance). Where these two structures converge is that both the narcissist and the pervert seek self-sufficiency in their relation to gratification, in which the other is instrumentalized.

The pervert's relation to fantasy is particular in both its fixity and enunciation. While neurotics will sheepishly hide their fantasies, the pervert needs to vocalise a fetishistic scenario in an attempt to corrupt the other. As Serge Andre (2006) notes, it is impossible to separate perversion from fantasy. Indeed all fantasy is basically perverse in that it disavows the Law as embodied in the paternal metaphor. Fantasy is fixed to a simplistic goal, and serves to guard against anxiety (Dor, 1999). The root of this anxiety lies in the subject's castration, which becomes a great ordeal for the pervert. Castration is here not the literal act but rather a metaphoric and psychical process. In the Oedipus Complex the child is bound to the mother in an incestuous union. This mother does not have to be the biological or legal mother (the Real mother), rather she is the Other of the subject: the template of otherness that exists before the child recognises the existence of the other as a separate person (Lacan, 1938). The father's role within this dynamic is to separate the child from the mother; he does this through the imposition of the threat of castration. Castration as it evolves from Freudian to Lacanian theory becomes instrumental in the separation between the child and mother.

According to Freud (1913) leaving the mother is the prerequisite for maturation, as society itself is founded on the incest taboo: the Law that forbids the child and the mother's love. It is not the penis that is at risk in the castration complex, it is the phallus: the signifier of that which the mother lacks. Thus the phallus is the signifier that has the capacity to hide the lack of the Other, which for Lacan (1958a) is synonymous with the Other's desire. What becomes significant in castration is the lack of the Other. It is the trauma of the desire that separates the child from the possibility of union with the Other: the realisation that the child cannot give the mother what she lacks and therefore wants.

The child must realise that the mother lacks; that she too represents a partial object and that her desire cannot coincide with its own. This realisation that the child is not the centre of the Other's universe forms the epicentre of a trauma that forces the child into the symbolic order; the realm of signification, of desire and of *others* (Lacan, 1958a).

For the pervert, the lack of the Other will always be problematic as they have both accepted and denied castration by accepting and denying the Law of the father. The ego of the pervert is essentially split, they engage with the Other metaphorically within the symbolic realm of desiring others, while simultaneously denying that the Other has a desire that does not coincide with their own. The pervert only requires the Other to confirm their fantasy; as a result the desire of the other becomes a complication to this relation. This is why the pervert needs to corrupt an other: to move them to corroborate their fantasy. This corruption of the other concerns how the other enjoys: the pervert must convince the other that they can enjoy free of the Law, just as the pervert would like to believe. The pervert is ultimately selling the other an illusory access to jouissance, access that the pervert accepts and denies the possibility of, just as they accept and deny the Law that forbids it. Thus the pervert seeks to redirect the gratification of the other.

Desire is fundamentally problematic for the pervert as they both refuse and accept the fundamental rules of the symbolic (that which the Law of the father brings). For the Lacanian subject, it is the symbolic that moderates enjoyment and creates desire. The pervert differs from the neurotic, who is entrenched in desire but finds enjoyment problematic. Thus the pervert seeks to convince a neurotic other that they can have a direct route to enjoyment, free of the complication of desire and language (Andre, 2006). The pervert does not need to believe the line that they are selling; the fact that the other believes it will provides the gratification they seek, as the pervert will have succeeded in making themselves the object of the other's drive (and therefore fantasmatically centre of the Other's desire). The other's compliance itself satisfies the pervert; this allows the pervert to maintain the fantasy that their desire alone holds primacy. The pervert acknowledges the desire of the Other but at the same time denies it. Thus the situation with the other as accomplice lends strength to the fixity of the pervert's fantasy. In this way the pervert uses the other to stave off the anxiety that desire brings.

Long (2008) uses psychoanalytic conceptions of perversion to understand how the subject interacts with a corporation. Long references Lacanian, Freudian and Kleinian theory to illustrate that differing accounts of perversion as a concept will produce the same conclusions on contemporary business practices. To clarify the dynamic between the subject and the commercial organisation, Long uses a number of case studies of organisational perversion and the narcissistic use of these organisations for personal gain. The Enron scandal being a prime example, in which traders knowingly broke the law (judicial law, a manifestation of the Law of the father) but were comfortable that their trading was within organisational logic and thus acceptable.

In *The Perverse Organisation,* Long suggests five criteria that demonstrate the prevalence of this perverse logic:

1. That the individual seeks pleasure at the expense of the other.

2. The co-existence of the acknowledgement and denial of reality.

3. The other becomes used as an accomplice in perverse power play.

4. The abundance of instrumental relations in society.

5. The abusive cycle of the perverse encouraging further perversion.

The first of these criteria is an obvious aspect of commercial organisations. Corporations are structurally bound by law to make the acquisition of wealth (growth) their primary objective (see Bakan, 2004). All other considerations are secondary, such as the general well-being of their employees and consumers. Obviously there are external laws in place which protect consumers and employees from physical and mental harm, but these are ultimately viewed as variables rather than core values for positive corporate practice (Bakan, 2004). In this profit-oriented dynamic the individual is rewarded for their ability to outdo the other. Facilitating financial growth becomes the subject's primary motivation. In the highly competitive corporate world this often occurs at the expense of the employees themselves or even the company's customers (Long, 2008). As UBC professor of law Joel Bakan (2004) notes, corporate abuse is not a matter of a few exceptional cases; it is symptomatic of a greater problem that has infected many economic systems. This profit-at-expense dynamic mirrors the power relation that defines the pervert, where the expense of the other is a necessity for gain.

The second of Long's criteria concerns the pervert's ability to deny and accept reality. This is clearly illustrated in the contemporary business environment, which contains many examples of executive fraud and immoral trading (Long, 2008). The acquisition of capital becomes a ground for an ambiguous relationship between those operating within the corporation and the external society. For these people, the corporation that employs them has provided the perverse context that is abundant with predefined and delimited roles; these roles allow the individual to operate within perverse scenarios.

The pervert needs an accomplice but not at the level of socialisation. The other becomes instrumentalised in the context of the corporation, which relates to Long's third and fourth criteria. The prevalence of instrumental relations can be viewed as a symptom of perverse organisational logic. In a society mediated by perverse organisations there should theoretically be an increase in alienated individuals interacting with others as instruments of their gratification. In the perverse society that Long describes, instrumentalisation forms a necessity for the individual's survival. The corporate-individualist world is highly competitive. Ruthlessness rather than altruism becomes an essential and socially sanctioned tool for survival. This establishes social consideration as subservient to self-gain and ego-libido. This dynamic often becomes imbalanced, to the point where ego-libido becomes transgressive to the Law, in a sense becoming a law in itself. This new law drives the subject to enjoy trangsressively in isolation. The 'old' Law is essentially dependent on the interaction with others, and is mediated by the symbolic order so as to enable a gratification that is dependent on others.

The narcissistic society under discussion is homogeneous in the sense that the individuals within it seek to gratify themselves without the complication of socialisation. Although this is supposedly a society of law-abiding narcissists, the organisations that regulate discourse will inevitably become tools of perverse gratification. Organisations such as these provide a platform to stage a fantasmatic scenario that can be seen to step around the Law in all its manifestations.

In a large organisational entity the consequence for action is diffused throughout the organisation and lies in the ether. This allows the subjects within to gratify themselves without deliberately breaking the law, even though they are aware that the law is in existence and that they have indeed broken it. This creates what Long describes in her final criterion: an endlessly repeating culture of perverse transgression: a cycle of abuse. The outcome of this process is a gradual erosion of the law: the cultural manifestation of the Law of the father which curtails gratification. Consumerist and corporate institutions have developed ways around the complicated symbolic paths to enjoyment. This becomes manifest in what has been termed the *law of jouissance* (Loose, 2011, p27).

The law of jouissance represents a prerogative to transgress the Law, to gain access to jouissance, thus defying the Law of the father and the pleasure principle (Dean, 2000). The transgression of the Law is uniquely tied to the realm of fantasy. Fantasy is essentially beyond the reach of any law and has an enveloping appeal (one which disavows lack) that language cannot afford. It is the only capacity at which the subject can enjoy without the complications posed by social interaction. The subject is driven to transgress, thus the law of jouissance is not a real law but an anti-law, a tendency for which the perverse caters for. As described above, a perverse society evolves a 'me first!' mentality that develops a law of its own. This law better resembles the anti-law of jouissance, which transgresses the Law of the symbolic and the social. But what is the result for the subject who is part of this society? Where does this law of jouissance lead? Rik Loose (2011) suggests that the law of jouissance is the basis of addiction.

Loose (2002) uses Lacanian theory to conceptualise addiction as a problem of administration. The subject will seek to administrate over their own enjoyment at the expense of the Laws of the world. Addiction is a-dictive, meaning it is without or opposed to speech and therefore the symbolic order. The addicted subject is the subject for whom speech, as the discourse of and with the Other, has become secondary. The symbolic order thus becomes a tool to use in relation to other people, for selfish gain. The others become instrumentalised and subservient to the addiction. For the addict, the symbolic world is forsaken for a world mediated by the addictive item or practice, which is directly controlled by the addict; who has become the administrator of their own gratification. It is an operant hypothesis of this research that this is a lesson learned from perverse institutions that the subject interacts with in the socio-cultural realm; that the engagement with these institutions creates the structural disposition towards addiction.

The perverse itself does not accept the anti-law of jouissance, any more than it accepts or denies the Law of the father. This is the meaning of disavowal, the essential structure of perversion. If the pervert convinces their victim of the possibility that they can enjoy in isolation, it does not mean that the pervert can enjoy this way themselves. It is the Law of the father that keeps the subject from the painful destructive boundaries of jouissance, thus the addict's path will always lead to their own subjective destruction, their expense to the pervert's benefit.

To summarise the theoretical basis of this work in a sentence, it could be said that the pervert convinces the narcissist to break the Law and this has the potential to institute a structural disposition towards addiction. The pervert and the addict both seek gratification via a transgression of the Law.

The crucial difference between the two is that the pervert will rely on fantasy and manipulation of the other to achieve gratification, whereas the addict must interact with a Thing or process in the Real. This is why the addict needs a Thing; a part of the Real that can enable jouissance (see Lacan, 1959).

The pervert lives vicariously through the other's transgression while the addict must transgress the Law themselves. Thus the second point to this theoretical base is that the perverse organisation (in this case the corporation) takes the role of convincing the subject (the consumer) that they can administrate over their own pleasure. And why would a corporate entity engage in this dynamic? The answer is simple: to produce capital and growth; as Bakan (2004) notes this is the fundamental logic behind corporate discourse. The corporation must convince the subject to consume; this is the drive that structures the organisation. The persons who make up the organisation come together with the goal of producing capital. This is achieved at the expense of an externalised other who is turned into the one who buys; the *dupe who accepts their place in this dynamic* (Loose, 2011). This company interacts with the outside world, just as the individual pervert does with their accomplice. The end result of such a structure is that the company encourages a dependence on the same fantasy that the pervert sells and controls. This fantasy becomes embodied in the Thing that the company sells. As the perverse is the simplest and most fundamental stage of libidinal development, it is perhaps the most basic and unifying means with which the subject can sexually relate to an other. Politicians simplify a message into polemics of right and wrong so as to win over and influence the most people. This is also true for the entertainer, who must refine entertainment to the simplest aspects of enjoyment. This is the key to mass appeal.

Long (2008) provides examples of corporate organisational life affecting various individuals and encouraging transgression of the Law. These case studies illustrate her point in an extreme; i.e. when the persons participating in the perverse organisational structure cause obvious harm to others and break the Law. Long explains that these cases are the symptoms of a greater underlying structure. To conceptualise and substantiate this structure it is necessary to analyse the outward expressions and products of these companies. It is for this reason that this research will analyse film in Part Two. As Althusser (1971) proposed, an industrial product can be seen to bear the ideological finger-print of the industry that produced it. As with most mass media corporations the Walt Disney Company survives on its ability to sell a product to consumers. Thus the product should be the key to exploring commercial perversion as it interacts within society via its ideological imposition. The process of this imposition is the subject of Part Three of this text.

A fast food company can be easily shown to profit at the expense of the consumer. Food is produced that is pleasant-tasting and addictive but holds little nutritional value; in many cases fast food can be carcinogenic and unhealthy for the consumer. It is however less obvious in a corporation like Disney, whose product is intimately connected with popular culture. Disney holds a unique position in the corporate world in that its name is predominantly associated with clean, innocuous fun and (to an extent) high moral values. For many consumers it is a brand name that can be trusted. Yet if Disney's organisational structure fits Long's model and is perverse in nature, then what benefits the company's commerce will perhaps be at the expense of the consumer within society.

Disney has had such wide reaching popular success that it has become part of popular culture, not just in the West where it originated, but across the world. It has become part of a new global mythology, and the company's virtuous image has become intertwined with that mythology (Giroux, 2000). The company is not just selling a product, but an ideology, a perspective on life and childhood that is clean, safe and sanitised for general consumption. The Disney product, imbued with its values and cleanliness, has something which appeals to people *en masse*. This is what is significant in the choice of the Walt Disney Company for this analysis. By illustrating that the ideology implicit in its product is fundamentally perverse, it will be possible to lend support to the hypothesis that the corporate institution seeks to convince the consumer that they can administrate their own gratification; in this sense it can be said that the perverse organisation seeks to *addictify* the consumer.

The perverse organisation supports and initiates the culture of addiction that is prevalent in contemporary society. Disney provides an iconic example of this perverse dynamic between corporate entities (as structure) and the consumers and employees that interact with these entities (as subject). This analysis will therefore discuss Disney as exemplifying perverse organisational structure and discuss its possible influence on the realm of the socio-cultural. The next chapter shall discuss the inception of Disney and its organisational structure. This structure shall be shown to be composed of Walt Disney the man, the Disney company and the company's product. This shall establish a construction of 'Disney' as an organisational entity and structure. It shall be illustrated that the products of the perverse organisation (company and mythic figure combined) are its means of reaching out to the subject and exploiting the collective other as an accomplice (via its product as a form of enunciation to the consumer as other, and thus vicariously to the Other). For the corporation to grow it must exploit a need in the consumer, just as the pervert uses the other to attain gratification. This discussion will begin by examining Walt Disney himself, as the instigator and figurehead of the perverse organisation that shall be shown to demonstrate a structural parity with accounts of his life.

Chapter 2

Psycho-mythography

This chapter shall begin by providing an account of Walt's biographies and shall then proceed to outline chronologically the growth of the company and its structural parity with its figurehead and product. The purpose of this pseudo-biographical section is to produce an image of the man that will ultimately be shown to be indistinct from the organisation of Disney itself, the films it produced and its place in contemporary culture. Discussions of authorship in film are complicated by the dynamic nature of the production process. Many persons are involved in the inception of a film and this is even more obvious in studio made animation. Paul Wells (2002) suggests that Walt Disney moved from one mode of authorship to another. Having started as an artist involved in making the cartoons themselves, Walt took a more production-based role as the studio expanded. Walt, by his own admission, took an editorial and organisational role in film-production (Schickel, 1968). While this role may sound administrative in nature, it was in fact crucial to the creative process that can be defined as specifically 'Disney'.

Initially Disney was a collaborative effort between Walt and Ub Iwerks, a key artist during Disney's inception. With Walt's rise to becoming the head of a large studio, his role becomes that of an auteurial editor; the films were influenced by an aesthetic specific to his tastes. Walt considered himself "author of the process" (Wells, 2002, p82) which by proxy can be said to position him as the auteur of Disney as an institution. As a creative autocrat, Walt could administrate a product made to his tastes.

If the definition of an auteur is a person who executes the styles and narrative conventions of film, then after Walt's death 'Disney' could be seen to become an auteuristic autonomous industry. Walt's name and image became synonymous with all things Disney. Continual discussions of Walt's "vision" (see Barrier, 2007, p124) dissociated the image of the man from his ideological template. Under the title of 'Disney' the studio process itself becomes an autonomous producer, as informed by the ideology of a mythology surrounding Walt Disney. Thus the project of this chapter is to establish this myth and situate it within the theoretical context thus far outlined. As stated before the purpose of Part One is to create a homunculus; an artifice composed of the different concepts, facts and fictions discussed in these chapters. The theoretical base established in chapter one can be seen to form the dynamic internal structures of this homunculus. Its skin shall be drawn from the animated character as fetish, which will be discussed in chapter three. The company and Walt are thus left to contribute its soul; its internal energy and drive.

It is the position of this research that discussing Walt Disney is integral to a discussion of Disney as a major socio-cultural institution (note that Walt shall be used to reference the man and Disney the homuncule institution constructed within Part One). However, such a discussion must take a particular form to be of value to this analysis. Wells (2002) warns that biographically informed readings of film have a tendency not to appreciate the complex and dynamic process of animation production itself. It also remains unclear to what extent biographical information can actually be of service to understanding film, as the idea of personality, or indeed uncon-scious particularities, surviving the industrial process is doubtful. Despite these reservations it is still evident, from various biographical and psychobi-ographical sources (Barrier, 2007 and Schickel, 1968), that Walt was instru-mental in shaping what would eventually be called Disney, and that the internal processes of the company were intimately connected to Walt Disney the man. To the extent that for years after Walt's death the company would maintain the ideological position of its product. In a sense, Walt became the brand.

There are also many difficulties in the attempt to provide a psychoanalytic reading of biographical authorship. Facts are often unreliable and the biog-rapher may manipulate the story to suit their own subjective presuppositions. The validity of this information in the context of production is questionable, as the idea of an absolute auteur is also a gross simplification. In his psychobiography of Leonardo De Vinci, Freud (1910) warns that the psychobiographer inevitably risks either idealising or pathologising his or her subject, a risk that Freud himself falls prey to in the paper (McAdams, 1998). It is perhaps inevitable given the nature of psychobiographical study that this occurs, as what is analysed is not a living, speaking subject, but rather an image constructed from various accounts blended with a few established facts. Thus what is examined within psychobiography is a narrative rather then a person's life in stasis.

The idealisation of the biographical subject is inevitable, as the biographical text will contain the projections of those that provide the accounts of what becomes a pseudo-mythical subject. There is an implicit lack within psycho-biographic text that enables a projection of desire and fantasy; a projective identification that takes place. The subject of the biography is pathologised for the same reasons as it is idealised; it creates a space in which the author can stage their own problematic subjectivity. The gaps in the story allow the subject as reader to fill the space with their own significations. This is ultimately why psychobiographies become relevant to psychoanalysis, as they provide the ground with which the subject can negotiate their own problematic relation to desire.

By gathering and collating various biographical and documentary accounts of a figure it becomes possible to construct a mythology of the original subject; one that both Walt and the company's marketeers were instrumental in creating. This 'Walt' has likewise been the result of the critical discourse of Disney studies. As Michael Barrier notes: "Disney seems no more real in the growing body of academic critiques of the man and the company that bears its name" (Barrier, 2007, p124). This mythology is of particular interest in the discussion of Disney, as the man and the company become indistinguishable in critical and public perceptions. Thus the psychobiography of Walt Disney provides a narrative that enables this discussion to begin conceptualising the archetypical consumer, the essence of the contemporary addictified subject. The company and the figure of Walt become exemplary within the dynamic context of the perverse organisation and the subject. The biographical information regarding Walt Disney is thus used to illustrate an understanding of organisational-auteurism within corporate media and so exemplifies the manner in which the contemporary subject interacts with organisations as the staging grounds for perverse fantasies.

By analysing the story of Walt Disney the person, it becomes possible to situate the subject in an analysis of the organisation and the product created. In attempting psychomythographically to understand the complex dynamic which affected Walt as a fantasist, a consumer and (as reported by some) an addict, it may be possible to map the subject who engages with Disney and their relation to Walt's pseudo-auteurised products. Walt Disney's life was typical of the consumer who engaged with the company's product and represents a problematic and complex search for meaning. Within the vast media empire of his inception it becomes possible to see the possible meanings Walt inscribed to its various products. This inscription is written on the walls of Disneyland, in the lines that make up Mickey Mouse and the stories regarding Walt's collisions with the different persons and institutions throughout his career. Within this unravelling mythologisation, it becomes evident that the so-called masterminds of corporate dynamics are as much victims of consumption as the rest of society.

The following will offer an analysis of two aspects of Walt's existence. Firstly, his relation to his company as documented by employees, and secondly the myths that remain of the man that was. The subject of this chapter shall be the myth of Walt Disney contextualised within the early cartoon shorts he and his company produced. For Walt, the Disney institution essentially became a commercial façade that allowed him to connect to the Other in the guise of a consumer. As an editor, he chose a product that he sought to consume, a capacity that defines contemporary empowered consumers whom have access to a bespoke world of accessible consumables. The fantasy he enacted can be seen as an attempt to validate an image of himself that was intimately bound to that product. This can be seen as one of the reasons he sought an audience and financial success: to have this new ideal ego validated by the mass of an adoring Other. Walt was intimately connected to his own product; in a sense he was the archetypical narcissistic consumer. He chose to create exactly what he desired, much like the contemporary consumer does today, with access to a realm of 'bespoke' commodification.

To avoid a classically psychobiographical reading, it is important to rather focus on what McAdams (1988) refers to as a *life-narrative*. Walt's life-narrative can be considered to be demonstrative of the illusive American dream, in which the individual starts with nothing and works successfully towards self-sufficiency and actualisation. The freedom to choose and realise dreams has serious consequences, however illusory this achievement might be. The contemporary consumer is free to choose what and when they want to enjoy; the subject has instant access to worlds of consumables through the internet. Disney's narrative parallels the modern consumer's plight. When the subject is given direct access and controls to their gratification, their position can be seen to evolve into compulsive consumption, another term for addiction (Peele, 1985). In this process the Other becomes an instrument to the subject's gratification, thus becoming instrumentalised in the fashion outlined in the earlier discussion of perversion. The other is thus utilised to perpetuate a fiction of simplicity where desires are capable of being sated and dreams realised.

The present discussions of Walt Disney reference several texts: *Walt Disney: Hollywood's Dark Prince* by Marc Elliot (1993), *The Animated Man* by Michael Barrier (2007), *From Walt to Woodstock* by Douglas Brode (2004), *Understanding Disney* by Janet Wasko (2001), *The Magic Kingdom* by Steven Watts (1997) and *The Disney Version* by Richard Schickel (1968).

Marc Elliot's text is an unauthorised and rather sensational biography, and makes many unsubstantiated and controversial claims regarding Walt's private life. Schickel's text is better balanced and forms the base of contemporary Disney studies. Written in 1968 it was the first critical text to examine Walt's life and the Disney Company, though Schickel did not have access to the resources that Barrier, Brode and Elliot were able to use nearly 30 years later. Wasko's book provides a brief but well-rounded overview of 'Disney studies'. This text shall be referred to in order to contextualise the claims made by other texts.

Steven Watts (1997) approaches Walt Disney from a more sympathetic perspective, emphasizing the tremendous creative output of the company. Douglas Brode (2004) goes even further and attempts to re-write academic opinion of Disney by relating Walt Disney to the radical significance of Woodstock, claiming that Disney as an institution and 1960s radicalism were ideologically in tune. This claim is backed by textual readings and an attempt to polarize pre-existing critical discourse. Although Disney films have are likewise demonstrated within this research to counter of the psychical establishment of patriarchy, Brode ignores the sub-textual duality of Disney films. In a sense what gives Disney its radically perverse value is precisely its operant disavowal; providing co-existing messages of gratification in absentia of authority and strict obedience to external patriarchal establishments such as the government or military.

Barrier's text is the most recent to be referenced and claims to be the most even-handed biography of Walt's life. Barrier begins by emphasising the polemic nature of previous biographies that have either sanctified or demonized Walt Disney, stating that Disney studies feeds off itself, and in turn the image of Walt becomes an entity in itself much like the amorphous Disney 'Thing' they purport to study (Barrier, 2007). Barrier claims that his close adherence to facts established around Walt's life provide it with credibility that other analyses lack. This is certainly the case for the more sensationalist texts such as Elliot's, however the closed circuit of 'Disney-studies' creates its own object of study in a similar manner to how Disney is constructed at the level of society and culture. It too has created a cultural artifact that is *inevitably* related to the Disney known at the level of culture. It is this 'Disney' and this 'Walt' that is the subject of this text. Hence the main biographical text referred too shall also be the oldest and most influential (that of Schickel, 1968) as this text can be seen to permeate a wider cultural knowledge surrounding Disney.

Although Schickel appears at times to be antagonistic of his subject, he shows great appreciation and sympathy for the drive with which Walt strove for personal independence in his autocratic approach to his work. Although personal freedom through autocracy may seem contradictory, it is precisely this kind of dualism that marked Walt's interactions within his company. Walt sought to have supreme creative control over all Disney productions, having the final say on any product. He even went as far as denying many of his employees credits on their films, while his name is large and bold; as Wells notes: "Walt Disney is an auteur by virtue of fundamentally denying inscription to anyone else" (Wells, 2002, p90). He maintained strict control of the studio so as to retain creative control over the finished product. His freedom was paramount while the freedom of those he dominated became secondary and superfluous to the final production. Indeed he sought the kind of authoritarian control that is prevalent in perverse organisations (Long, 2008). What becomes relevant to the present discussion is that within the organisational dynamic, Walt utilised his employees to create something that would create a further dynamic between Walt and the general public, who would consume his hand-selected product. As stated before, the pervert situates himself as object of the drive, more to the point the object of the *Other's* drive. By identifying himself with his product and company, Walt achieved an egoic, narcissistic and perverse gratification from the public's adoration.

Walt had never considered himself an artist; in fact he reportedly considered much of contemporary art to be obscene (Schickel, 1968). He perceived talent as an exploitable means of income rather than the product of inspiration or expression. He often played down any intellectual or analytical take on his work, believing it to be simple, family entertainment. When asked what part of the Disney endeavour he found most rewarding, Walt replied: "The whole damn thing. The fact that I was able to build an organisation and hold it" (Walt Disney cited in Schickel, 1968, p37). Walt was a true industrialist: the organisational dynamic provided his gratification, and the monetary success of his product provided a symbolic validation, a currency he is said to have sorely lacked in his youth. This equation of economic success with achievement is very much imprinted on the American culture of the time, indeed Walt's life is viewed by Schickel as a simple and real manifestation of the American dream. His audience viewed him as a model American, and indeed Walt perceived his audience as the image of himself multiplied by many. The present analysis will thus have as much to say about the life and times of the 20th century as it will about the man himself.

Walt Disney

Walt Disney was born in Chicago in 1901. His father Elias Disney was a strict authoritarian, who continually struggled to become financially self-sufficient; his aim in life was to own a business and control his means of income. Elias would move the family several times in an effort to start businesses in new places. Eventually the family moved to a farm near a town called Marceline in Missouri when Walt was five. Walt's most commonly recounted memories came from his time on this farm. After a few years in Marceline the family ran into difficulties with a local bank and was forced to move. Schickel (1968) suggests that this is where adult Walt's hatred of bankers began: in this first instance of his family losing ownership and control of their property. Control would become a dominant issue in Walt's later life. The farm was a formative place for Walt, although he would only spend a few years there, the experience would form the base of his personal ideals: self-sufficiency and a fantasy of an intimate connection with nature. It is interesting to note that Main Street USA, an area of the Disneyland theme park in California, is modelled on Main Street Marceline. It is the only part of the park that visitors cannot avoid passing through and serves as a gateway to all the other areas. Marceline would thus appear to be central to the Disney fantasy; the symbolic gateway into Walt's imaginary world. Marceline reportedly gained further significance for Walt after the Disney family made its next move to Kansas City.

In Kansas, Elias bought a paper route which Walt and his brother Roy were forced to work without any form of pay. It was a hard job and involved the brothers waking at dawn to deliver the papers by hand. If they missed an address or were late with their work their father would brutally punish them. Even as an adult Walt claimed he still had nightmares about being late for his paper route (Schickel, 1968). It was during this time that Walt's father started beating him, a ritual that would continue for many years. Often Elias had no cause to punish him, yet Walt accepted these beatings. In this period of extreme hardship and physical abuse, Walt's older brother Roy became an emotional support. He was nurturing and kind to his younger brother and for the rest of his days would provide a pragmatic and restraining influence in Walt's life. The beatings continued until Roy convinced Walt that he did not have to be beaten to keep his father's affections. After Walt overpowered his father during a beating, he was never abused again.

Elias wanted his son to gain trade skills and so as a teenager Walt was allowed to enrol in art classes, his first creative experience. Elias decided to move from Kansas to buy a jelly factory in Chicago; as his sons were old enough to work he decided to leave Walt and Roy in Kansas, essentially setting them free. Walt began working his first job selling food and sweets at a railway station, similar to his father who also worked for the railways as a young man. This is perhaps where Walt developed his love of trains, an obsession that would last into his later years.

At the age of sixteen Walt was seeking adventure and decided to join the army. In 1918 he lied about his age so he could enlist to fight in World War I. He was not accepted into the army but managed to go to France as a red-cross ambulance driver just after hostilities had ceased. This was where Walt got his first paid artistic work; he and a friend made a small business faking war artefacts and designing insignia for soldiers. After he returned from Europe he moved back to Kansas where he worked for a local newspaper called the *Kansas Star*. It was at the *Star* that Walt was introduced to commercial art. This experience was quite different from what he learned in art school and forced him to pragmatise work rather than perfect it. It was here where Walt learned the true marketable value of artistic practice. It was also at the Star that Walt met Ub Iwerks, a talented artist who would become an integral part of the Disney studio. The first time they met, Walt was practising his signature; a practice that would later prove significant to the Disney Company.

The newspaper imposed lay-offs and both Walt and Iwerks lost their jobs. After working several positions the pair decided to go into business for themselves. It was during this time that they became involved in animation; making short films to be shown before cinema features. Walt had to borrow a camera from the office he worked at so that he could make the short animations from home. The shorts were made for the *Newman Theatre* in Kansas and thus bore the name *Newman Theatre Laugh-O-Grams*. Walt eventually made enough money to start a small studio himself, retaining the name Laugh-O-Grams and taking on a number of unpaid apprentices. The company soon saw capital as it sold its first seven minute shorts, *Puss-In-Boots* (1922) and *Little-Red-Riding Hood* (1922). Walt signed only his name to the credits of the films, leaving out those of Iwerks and their apprentices. The films were quite simplistic and not of the standard of established animation houses of the time. With Laugh-O-Grams Walt also produced *Alice in Cartoon-land*, a combination of live-action and animation that would prove successful for Walt when he moved to Hollywood. The Alice series has probably aged the worst out of Disney's early productions. Even for its time the quality of the animation and effects were quite poor.

Alice in Cartoon-land

The *Alice* series starred child actress Virginia Davis, a doll-like child with blonde curly hair. Alice would typically get into mischief and avoid her punishment by escaping into an animated cartoon world. In *Alice Gets in Dutch* (1924), Alice becomes involved in a prank that soaks her teacher in ink. She is forced to sit in the corner of the classroom wearing a dunce's hat. She slips into a dreamland filled with animated animal characters that dance and play music with her. Her teacher begins to invade her fantasy with anthropomorphised books in tow. She and her books fire a cannon at Alice and her friends, interrupting her fun. Alice and the animals fight back and defeat the imaginary teacher but alas Alice wakes up again back in the classroom.

The majority of narratives within the *Alice* series involve the clash of the fantasist with symbols of authority. Walt often tried to portray himself as a similar sort of character in his youth. In many interviews he recounted mischievous tales of his time on the farm, although Elias' brutal control of his household would seem to put these stories in question. It is more likely that the *Alice* series was Walt's first attempt to live vicariously through his films and that he was attempting to portray a youthful rebellion he never had: his first attempt to show up his father, even if only on screen.

Laugh-O-Grams was receiving income from a New York distributor although this relationship would prove costly, as their contact was beginning to take more profits for himself while Disney was seeing less returns on each release. Laugh-O-Grams was eventually driven into bankruptcy and Walt was forced to let his staff go. He decided to sell his camera and move to the West Coast to start a business in Hollywood, the newly founded home of American cinema.

Hollywood at the time had a complex relation to American society of the time. Film-makers of the 1920s and 30s were beginning to feel pressure from governing bodies to produce cleaner moralistic films. To revitalise and essentially clean up Hollywood films for the American market, the major studios appointed William Hays to chair the Motion Picture Producers and Distributors of America, the purpose of which was to create a regulatory body within Hollywood itself that could encourage studios to self-censor to certain standards (Lewis, 2000). Hays would become the figurehead of this censorship body, which released the Motion Picture Production Code (MPPC), also referred to as the Hays code, in 1930. The code was conservative to say the least. It prohibited a broad range of supposedly immoral and transgressive acts being depicted on screen, such as depictions of interracial romance, physical passion or disregard for American nationalism.

After arriving in Hollywood, Walt was able to stay with an uncle for a fee of $5 a week. He was even allowed to set up a small animation studio in the garage. In this studio Walt put together a sample reel of his work and managed to have it shown to the owner of a chain of theatres who liked his simple gag shorts. His brother Roy was also in Hollywood at that time and provided Walt with financing for the show-reel. This marked the beginning of the brothers' business relationship, which would ensure both of their successes. In 1923 Walt also received word that Charles Mintz, an East-Coast distributor, wanted to screen a series of *Alice in Cartoon-land* episodes. With Roy, Walt set to work on the series and soon sent for Iwerks to come and join him in his new venture. The company was now called The Disney Brothers but would soon be renamed Walt Disney Studios (Wasko, 2001).

Despite the bland nature of the series, the *Alice in Cartoon-land* contract was renewed by Mintz several times. By 1925 the company was now earning a small but significant profit. With this limited success Walt and Roy were able to live a frugal existence. It was in this time that Walt met his future wife Lillian Bounds, who was originally hired as a clerk for the office. With characteristic pragmatism and a utilitarian approach to romance, Walt decided to marry Lillian when his brother was moved out of their shared apartment, as he would need someone to share the rent (Schickel, 1968).

Chapter 3

The Phallus and Disney Animation

Before beginning the analysis of these first Disney films, it is necessary to mention several points concerning fantasy and film. As stated, fantasy acts as the "*mise-en-scène* of desire" (Cowie, 1984, p159); fantasy represents a domain in which it is possible to stage solutions to desire; in which we can experience fleeting moments of *having* what we want. Film as a signifying practice has a very special connection to fantasy. The subject enjoys fictitious scenarios as they allow a space in which fantasies of gratification may be acted out and identified with. Although fantasies are themselves multiple and unique to each subject, their form and structure are similar in that they have this capacity to satisfy an audience. The nature of this satisfaction is of course dependent on the content of the film. In his discussion of the structure of perversion, Serge Andre (2006) mentions that fantasy is at its base intrinsically perverse; what is fantasised can function outside the Law and to an extent the symbolic. Films can likewise become realisations of perverse gratification as they permit the subject a partially restricted fantasy-scape with which to realise scenarios of gratification. While there are administrative bodies in the Real that curtail this enjoyment (such as the puritanical Hays office), the process of a film's production is capable of combining the fantasies and desires of writers, directors and producers, all of whom influence production. The end result is the product of desires and fantasies met with censorship and restriction. It is no surprise then that the structure of film expresses an implicit disavowal: perverse friction between law and desire, as there are so many conflicting desires already at work in its inception! It is interesting then that the end result seems to satisfy the fantasy demands of an large and generalised audience while simultaneously satisfying the desires of conflicting organisations of individuals that produced it. How then does this perverse disavowal express itself? Perhaps

39

somewhere between the overt and latent content of the film. The first part of this analysis shall begin by describing the overt content of the Disney films that contains what can hazardously be referred to as 'perverse' imagery. That is not to say perverse as some perceived form of aberrant sexuality, but rather perverse as demonstrating a hypocritical sexuality; a sexuality of disavowal. In this way it will be possible to create an understanding of the particular manner in which Disney presents the 'perverse'.

Oswald the Lucky Rabbit

By 1927, *Alice in Cartoon-land* had become stagnant and Mintz ordered his Hollywood representative George Wrinkler to persuade Disney to produce something new. They called the new project *Oswald the Lucky Rabbit*. Oswald was of a higher standard of animation than Alice and became a significant commercial success. The character of Oswald was influenced by Walt's love of Charlie Chaplin; Oswald was an incorrigible vagabond, getting into random pickles and always getting the girl. Oswald was often aggressive and sadistic. Schickel (1968) comments that this was a common theme in early cartoons, which were often defined by their de-emotionalised sadism, indeed cartoon violence is best associated with indestructible and elastic animated characters, available for infinite sanitised cruelties.

There are many curious images that abound in these early shorts. In *Great Guns* (1927), Oswald is pictured fighting in the trenches, beheading one of his enemies and then using an elephant (mascot of the Republican Party) to fire projectiles at a cat dressed as a German officer. In this particular short Oswald shares both Walt's nationalistic drive to fight and a sado-slapstick sense of humour. Villains shoot at Oswald with a large cannon, which has a long barrel that goes limp and floppy after it fires.

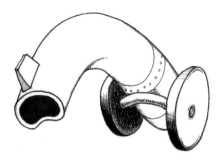

The Great gun goes limp!
(Image by Rupert Norfolk)

In *What A Knight* (1927) the villain is a great rat whose power is embodied in his giant lance, whereas Oswald defends himself with a small sword. Nevertheless Oswald triumphs and rescues the girl. The same scenario and imagery occurs in *Rival Romeos* (1928) in which Oswald putters along in a small car and beats his rival (seen smoking a long cigar and driving an elongated, phallically shaped car) to win the girl. The phallic imagery is obvious and can be read as a fantasmatic slight on the paternal metaphor, whose 'big gun' puts the child in its place. This is reminiscent of the fantasies of Little Hans whose castration anxiety manifested as a phobia of a large horse biting off his penis (Freud, 1909). In a dream Hans fantasised a crumpled giraffe: a symbol of the father's aggrandized potency being reduced to a crippled semblance. Lacan (1957b) argues that Hans' anxieties and subsequent phobias were a direct result of his derision of the paternal, that his anxieties were related to guilt and desire. It is this derision which underlies the narratives of these Disney shorts; they provide a safe rendering of the slight on the paternal, one that is fun and free of consequence.

The aggrandized phallic opponent
(Image by Rupert Norfolk)

Schickel's discussions of Walt's relation to his medium are quite provocative. He suggests implicitly and explicitly in his analysis, that animation was itself a psychologically perfect medium for Walt to work with, it provided him with absolute control over the world he created, down to the finest detail. It would be exciting to think then that we are offered a path into Walt's innermost world through these films, but of course that would be to far-fetched a claim to make. But the Walt that is ever under discussion in 'Disney studies' is himself a product. It is this Walt that was able to instil elements of his fantasy life into the cartoon world, bringing something of his private space into reality and selling it to whomever would watch and enjoy it, thus providing this Walt with validation. This is very much the position of Walt's psycho-biographers, and indeed it makes intuitive sense. Walt had reportedly struggled through a complex adolescence that was riddled with ambiguity and inconsistent emotional feedback from his father. It is possible that cartoons became an outlet that allowed him the space to enact the fantasy of defeating his brutal father, and in turn provided an object he could identify with. Indeed, more recent critics have also suggested that Disney cartoon shorts were an attempt by Walt to recapture his own lost childhood that was fraught with trauma and ambiguity (see Berland, 1982). In *What a Knight* (1927) Oswald's donkey is crossing a pond when his tail is torn off by a crocodile; the scene focuses completely on the act of the tail being severed.

The threat of castration
(Image by Paul Byrne)

The donkey then grows his tail back in defiance of the hungry crocodile. It is possible to relate this image to the Oedipal child for whom the father is an intruder. A father whose attempt at castration is foiled within the cartoon. Thus the Law that threatens castration loses its seriousness. It allows the viewer the safety to imagine-away the threat of castration. The father (as phallic rival) becomes non-threatening as he looses his potency. Perhaps this was another reason why our mythical Walt kept making cartoons; to repeat the fantasy of rebuked castration. Selling the cartoon would then have become a priority as it provided a means for Disney to validate this fantasy.

In many ways Oswald was quite similar to Alice: both are child-like in character. His opponents are always pictured ordering him about or bullying him, much like the image Walt reportedly had of his father.

Mickey Mouse and Donald Duck, the Ego Ideal and the Id

In 1928 Walt went on a business trip to New York to discuss his distribution contract's renewal. Mintz, who was now associated with Universal, told Walt that his Hollywood contact George Wrinkler had been systematically signing new contracts with Disney's key employees and that the copyright for Oswald now belonged to Universal. Mintz was pushing for a renewed contract, one that would dramatically cut Disney's profits. Walt told Mintz the employees were no real loss as they were disloyal in the first place, and that the studio would produce a better product than Oswald. This would be one of many documented events that can be seen to shape two of Disney's most obvious organisational characteristics. First, it would give Walt further reason to retain total control of the studio's productions. Even cartoons as early as Oswald and Alice were clearly personal for Walt. He despised losing control of the series; it was of paramount importance that his name would be attached to the product. Secondly it reinforced his suspicions of his workers, whom he viewed as his second family. His employees would never be able to live up to his expectations. Employees, unlike family, are paid to take part in an organisation, a reality our Walt often disregarded.

Walt's response to the Mintz dilemma was the creation of Mickey Mouse. Although there are several accounts of Mickey's creation it is generally thought that Walt created the famous mouse with the help of Ub Iwerks, as Iwerks was by far the superior artist (Wasko, 2001). The original incarnation of Mickey Mouse bore a strong resemblance to Oswald. Elliot (1993) claims that the semblance was intended as a jibe at Mintz, adjusting the image they had lost to him so as to keep control of the Disney product. With the capital from Oswald, the Disney Brothers could start production on Mickey Mouse without additional financial backing, although it would be a high-risk venture for the small company. Despite Iwerks' part in Mickey's creation, Walt took credit for Mickey publicly. As with Oswald, Walt developed strong projections and identifications with the character. Indeed, Mickey did have Walt's reported humourlessness and farm-boy enthusiasm.

In this light Mickey can be understood as a representative of the ego ideal. The ego ideal is simply the image that the subject's ego aspires to, an idealised image of the self (Lacan, 1954b, p133). It is an image that is difficult for the subject to live with. Identification will inevitably cause disappointment as the subject can never realise this ideal; it is always a concept in the abstract, beyond reach.

Mickey Mouse took quite a functional appearance. He was composed of several circles and a pear shape. This made him easier to animate as he would hold a similar shape from different angles. Like Oswald he was an anthropomorphised animal, taking the appearance of a cartoon human with a mouse's head and tail. The image of Mickey itself was designed to suit three criteria:

- Production reproducibility

- Audience appeal/attraction

- Simplicity

These three creative axes can be shown to provide the blue-print for nearly all Disney endeavours, and in a sense serve as a formula for how most large companies choose their products. Walt's own conscious and unconscious contributions were of course significant aspects of the productions, a human element that would be completely lost when Walt died.

The image of the mouse resonated with American society, which was starting to feel the effects of the Great Depression. Mickey soon became a symbol of the under-dog. At the very bottom of the domestic food-chain, Mickey represented the anxieties of working-class Americans being driven to financial ruin by powers far exceeding them. The mouse was the rascal trying to scrape up enough resources to survive harassment from the fat-cat and other familiar adversaries. The Depression era would become the golden age of Disney studios. It was pre-war, pre-union and largely pre-conflict within the organisation. This would change with the war-time funding problems and the 1941 animators' strike. This period would shape the base of 'traditional' Disney values that would colour the succeeding Disney productions.

Plane Crazy (1928) was the first Mickey Mouse short to be made by the studio. It was a silent film, shot in black and white, as was the second Mickey short, *Gallopin' Gaucho* (1928), made the same year. While the films were in production a significant event occurred in Hollywood; Warner Brothers released the *Jazz Singer* (1927), the first feature-length film to be made with sound. Within the year sound had revolutionised the film industry and Disney sought to stay as far ahead of the competition as possible. Walt decided to scrap what they had already filmed of the third Mickey short and re-shoot the whole film with sound, at a great expense to the studio.

Steamboat Willy

Steamboat Willy (1928) would be the first animated short to use sound. It utilised the 'Powers Cinephon' technology, a cheaper alternative to what other studios were using. *Steamboat* was first screened at the Colony Theatre in New York and received a significant amount of positive press. Walt decided to handle distribution himself, as he was still apprehensive of giving up that control after his dealings with Mintz. This was difficult for a small studio, and involved approaching cinema managers individually, but in this fashion Walt was able to ensure that he was not being taken advantage of.

The short was a triumph of technical achievement in its day. What differentiated *Steamboat* from other early sound films was that sound was used interactively with other elements of the film's form, to the point that the film's narrative and visual elements became dependent upon and related to the use of sound in the film. Mickey is introduced to the viewer at the wheel of a steamboat, tapping his foot to the rhythm of the music. The music itself begins as non-diegetic and becomes fully diegetic through the course of the short. He is foisted off his post by his boss: a large imposing cat. The cat is a typical villain in Disney films: grouchy, controlling and a bully. Mickey thwarts the cat's attempts to force him to work and makes his escape into mischievous adventures on the boat. His love interest Minnie Mouse comes aboard and joins him in his frolicking. The rest of the story provides a build-up to an exciting end, in which a musical number climaxes with Mickey playing various animals like instruments, providing solos to the tune. In all of the films that would follow, sound would not be used simply as a gimmick but as an integral part of the film's diegesis. The difference is immediately obvious when comparing *Steamboat Willy* to *Gallopin' Gaucho* and *Plane Crazy*. Sound was added after the earlier films were made, and as a result neither had the narrative drive that the intensifying music and rhythm created.

It is interesting to note that in the first vocal track for *Steamboat Willy* (1928) Walt used his own voice for Mickey, but the initial result was quite poor. It was only when he redid the take with a high androgynous falsetto that Mickey's character was complete (Mollenhoff, 1940). In his appearance it is unclear whether Mickey is a man, woman or a child; his voice is a shrill and high.

Music would become an integral part of the majority of pre-war Disney films. Mickey would improvise using various instruments and create tunes that would relate to the story, as in *The Opry House* (1928), where he and an

45

orchestra play to a large audience, or *Wild Waves* (1930), where he improvises a song to cheer up Minnie, who at the end exclaims, "My hero!" and kisses him.

Disney shorts were implicitly enjoyable for a young audience. Mollenhoff (1940) attributed the appeal of musical cartoons to their reliance on rhythm and repetition, this he suggested was particularly engaging for children. following Freud's discussions of early psychical development, Mollenhoff notes the capacity of rhythm and repetitious action to hold attention and calm anxiety. Indeed children from a very young age are able to recognise patterns in beat and tempo. Freud proposed that the joy that children derive from rhythm begins in rhythmic thumb-sucking (Freud, 1905a, p99). Rhythmic processes hold the child's complete attention and later form an important part of sexual enjoyment.

Freud notes in *Jokes and their Relation to the Unconscious* (1905b, p174) that children particularly derive pleasure from rhythmic nonsense. This is most evident when a child is learning language, they will make nonsensical sounds to a rhythm in an attempt to mimic adult communication. This however becomes forbidden as the child is forced into a relation to language governed by rules and Law.

Disney's focus on rhythm and 'nonsense' provides a symbolic safe-ground for children to enjoy beyond language; an enjoyment free of Law and *sense*, both of which carry a paternal character. The child is permitted a space in which they can silently watch and enjoy something which harkens back to an early and simplified state of enjoyment, which is in a sense transgressive to the paternal order; as bringer of a more 'adult' knowledge, and regressive as it refers to the pre-Oedipal. Freud also describes how the same appeal of nonsense is held for adults who can, on occasion, let down their guard and enjoy the ridiculous (Freud, 1905b). Some contexts permit this, for example: when adults enjoyed Disney as a technological marvel or as artistic object, the status as a 'curiosity' or spectacle provide a safe and indeed regressive context: an excuse to enjoy the cartoons freely. Thus context can have the capacity to disguise or explain away perceived transgression.

The early films present Mickey as quite libidinally driven: he aggressively pursues Minnie through the different stories, defeating various rivals for her attention and continually grabbing and kissing her. His initially precocious character changes in dramatically in later films, which see Mickey become quite a different character; in *The Karnival Kid* (1929) Mickey defeats his rival as per usual, in the process he wins Minnie's affections, but once he has the girl he does not seem to know what to do with her: he shyly and awkwardly blushes while she embraces and kisses him. He is seen here to be markedly less rambunctious than he had only a year previously. At this point he becomes a more pure and reserved character, and although he frequently saves Minnie from various perils, his reward seems to take the form of her sexual precocity and activity. In the early period of primordial Mickey, there was a place for a lusty Mickey Mouse, but as the series progressed the love between the protagonists would be replaced with familial and platonic relations. Years later Walt would tell an interviewer that Mickey and Minnie's relationship was purely platonic, further playing down any overt sexuality in Disney films (Schickel, 1968). This kind of relation was perhaps better suited to the fantasies of someone as controlling as Walt Disney was reported to be: these scenarios were simple and easily digestible for a more conservative audience. Walt never appreciated complexity; he liked his fantasies to be clean-cut and free from even the slightest hint of what he would consider to be smut.

Mollenhoff (1940) comments that the key to gratification within Mickey shorts was that "the day dream is playfully substituted by a series of pictures in which smallness is victorious throughout" (Mollenhoff, 1940, p20). Mickey's early character was often put into situations in which he attacks figures of authority and escapes into a fantastic adventure, this being the reoccurring theme in these early Disney shorts from *Alice* onwards. The 'fantastic' is precisely the place where anything can and will happen. It is the essential childhood fantasy: it allows the viewer to be placed in a realm where anything is possible. It provides the illusive suggestion that fantasies can be materialised in the Disney realm. Reality becomes unified with fantasy in a dreamlike cartoon-scape; a utopian *mise-en-scène* that provides both support for the ego and satisfaction for the id (Mollenhoff, 1940). Our mythic Walt was an authoritarian director of these fantasies; as a young adult he was reported to be a conservative and prudish man, not given to free and easy fun. Perhaps this is another reason why the sexually innocuous environment of the cartoon held such appeal for young Walt Disney.

To strengthen the company's growth, Walt and Roy sought other avenues with which their company could diversify and find returns. In 1930 when on a business trip to New York, Walt was approached by a man who offered $300 to have the image of Mickey Mouse on school tablets. This was their first foray into merchandising, a move that would save the company during many times of box office disappointment and economic turmoil. As with all other Disney enterprises, the choice of which merchandise to permit licensing to was strictly controlled. Walt was adamant about Mickey's likeness only appearing on goods of the highest possible quality. Early Disney merchandise included everything from diamond bracelets to radiation caps and medicine. Generally Walt aimed to avoid any products that could carry negative connotations for children, a strategy that persists in Disney to this day (for an excellent rendering of Disney merchandising practice see Bryman, 2004).

By the late 1930s his interest in shorts had become secondary to his complete focus on the studio's feature-length animations, all of which were love stories featuring fairy-tale romances or the protagonist's struggling to remain the eternal child. It is this re-investment in larger scale animation that evidences the beginnings of Walt and the Disney audience's addiction to the world of a specific kind of fantasmatic love: love without the added complication of symbolic predication and the other's desire. This is a perverse facsimile of love (or perhaps it's penultimate expression); one that has its roots in early childhood, and becomes dependant on a disavowal of paternal and symbolic functions (Andre, 2006). The Disney world is thus the world of the child's fantasies and wishes: "to satisfy his desire is still the supreme law. Acting follows seeing without the interposition of thinking" (Mollenhoff, 1940, p25). What is presented in the action-without-thought is not desire but rather the expression of un-socialised demand, which is perhaps closer to the illusory qualities of romantic love. So perhaps unbridled demand best expresses the perverse structure motivating the Disney fantasy. Curiously enough, the unsocialised expression of this perverse demand would become the defining characteristic of Disney's 2nd iconic character: 'the duck'.

The Duck

The mouse was initially a crafty and flirtatious character but eventually becomes an innocuous hero, devoid of obvious desire and aggression. Mickey no longer found himself in surreal and absurd situations. By the 1930s the 'fantastic' elements within the films had to be contained within a character's dreams, such as in *The Mad Doctor* (1933) and *Mickey's Garden* (1935), or in the relaying of stories, such as in *Gulliver Mickey* (1934). This new, simple and pristine image of Mickey was becoming difficult for Walt to sell to a fickle audience, as he had become far too limited and was starting to require supporting characters to make the shorts more dynamic and gratifying. Hollywood was indeed getting tired of Disney's leading man, a fact that our

Walt took quite personally; Mickey had already become intimately intertwined with his own ego ideal.

To diversify its storylines the studio introduced a host of secondary characters. Mickey's dog Pluto began appearing in the early 1930s. He took the part of Mickey's simpleton mascot, getting into the trouble that Mickey was clever enough to avoid. Goofy made his first appearance in *Mickey's Review* (1932) as Mickey's clumsy, befuddled but somewhat intelligent sidekick. Although both Pluto and Goofy were entertaining characters in their own right, though they did not provide the depth that the Mickey shorts were lacking. This led to the focus on another peripheral character, Donald Duck, who would prove to be the most popular of the new characters.

Donald Duck first appears in *The Wise Little Hen* (1934), one of Disney's *Silly Symphonies* series of shorts. Donald and his accomplice (a greedy pig) are trying to avoid helping an old hen that has hired them to do her farm work by faking stomach aches. In the end the hen gives them a bottle of castor oil instead of sharing her hard-earned meal. Donald eventually found his way into Mickey shorts and appeared in *Orphan's Benefit* (1934) as an act supporting Mickey. Donald throws a tantrum on stage and Mickey becomes the voice of restraint and authority, even castigating him: "Donald! Behave yourself!" The orphans harass Donald throughout the show, providing the comic relief for Mickey's apt but dull stage performance. Donald provided the comic relief that the new Mickey no longer could. Mickey's character had become relatively confined. While he was the family-friendly hero this also meant that he had to be both invulnerable and unwaveringly honest in order to live up to audience expectations, which paradoxically made him a less dynamic and engaging character. By the 1930s Mickey was consistently being presented as a more conservative authority figure, the opposite of his vagabond roots. In *Gulliver Mickey* (1934) Mickey takes a paternal role, telling children stories of his adventures, much like in *Mickey's Orphans* (1931) where he and Minnie become surrogate parents to a litter of rambunctious kittens.

Donald on the other hand is the eternal impulsive child. His motives are always selfish: he is greedy, angry and demanding, much like the early Mickey. Although as a character he is far more extreme than the early Mickey, he flies into a fury when things go wrong and is constantly testing the patience of the other characters. In the full colour Mickey short *The Band Concert* (1935), Mickey is conducting a small orchestra and Donald perpetually attempts to intrude, and his musical improvisations provides the lead melodies to the tune. The duck attempts to force his way into the music with his flute, while Mickey repeatedly tries to remove him and his flute without success. Mickey acts like the scolding father, taking away and breaking Donald's transgressive instrument. The flute is another phallic symbol, one that is small and at risk from authority. Mickey is attempting to castrate the Duck but Donald keeps fighting back against the father's rebuke, relying on a never-ending supply of backup flutes. The short ends with Donald playing in defiance to the whole band's protests.

Elliot (1993) provocatively suggests that Donald provided the emotive breakthrough for the less public side of Walt Disney. He is referring to the side that his employees were privy to: his temper tantrums and rages, his unrelenting demands and unpredictability, as documented by numerous biographers (Barrier, 2007, Schickel, 1968). In a sense Mickey had become an extension of Walt Disney's externalised Hollywood ego ideal, a public and established simulacra and the idealised façade created for and reinforced by the endless adoration of his audience. The audience was key to solidifying the Disney image.

The look of the Other is essential to the consolidation of the ego. It provides the illusion of the subject occupying a stable position and staves off the primordial sense of fragmentation the subject experiences in relation to their own body. The look of the Other, as embodied by an audience, served the purpose of securing this image of Walt as a publicly adored persona, synonymous with the success of Mickey and Donald. This is perhaps why the image of Walt became so firmly attached to Mickey Mouse. Mickey became the hub for the look of the Other as audience. Walt's theorized identification with Mickey's popularity thus provides an avenue with which to unite an ego with its ideal, a dynamic in which the Walt Disney company becomes instrumental.

It is enticing to consider a remark made by Sachs (1933) which describes the animistic use of anthropomorphised demigods in the pre-industrialised world. Ancient peoples used half-animal, half-human deities to serve as ego simulacra in a strikingly similar form to these early Disney characters. Perhaps dressing the idealised humanoids as half-animals detracts from the initial uncanniness of a perfect simulacrum and allows their form to be enjoyed more freely on a fantasy stage. It is the simulacrum of humanity that makes the image enjoyable, while the rendering of the animistic calms the anxieties associated with the ideal ego. As Cowie (1984) notes, a fiction will fail if it seems too far-fetched (such as an ideal), or if the characters seem completely inhuman (such as a pure animal).

The appearance of the characters hints at their different functions within the Disney genre. Mickey's eyes are small and dark and his face becomes less expressive in the later cartoons. His face provides a hiding place for his lack of character, making him appear dead and expressionless. Donald however comes dressed in a little sailor suit, the uniform of humiliation among the children of the time. His face is expressive and he is perpetually fraught with emotion. The uniform itself can be seen as a container for Donald's seemingly unrestricted behaviour; Yvonne Tasker (1993) describes the uniform's capacity to stabilise a body image by referencing patriarchically sanctioned images of power. This stabilisation within film has the capacity to release anxiety. Thus the uniformed body is a stable body via its relation to paternity. In this way Donald's uniform contains the libidinal charge caged within it. It is curious then that this uniform has no pants, leaving Donald's non-existent genitals exposed. It is thus an incomplete and contradictory cover, just as he is a bipolar and explosive character. He becomes the symbol not only for the tragically ridiculous – the boy submitted to the uniform of paternity – but for unbridled desire and escaping the confines of Law.

Miriam Hansen (1993) collates the arguments of Adorno and Benjamin to produce two theoretical positions on Disney's place in popular culture. This is done to situate the positions of both writers with regards to where they saw Disney, and in particular Mickey Mouse, within the greater American industrialised hegemony. Benjamin perceived a subversive quality that animation, and particularly Mickey Mouse, offers in relation to the industrialisation of the West. However, Benjamin would eventually become disenchanted with Mickey's subversive potential as he became progressively domesticated and moved from the position of the incorrigible vagabond or eccentric (as in Chaplin) to a more vacuous heroic role, and thus subservient to the dominant ideological position of Hollywood (Whitley, 2008). Esther Leslie (2002) later picks up this appraisal of early Disney animation in her text *Hollywood Flatlands*. Here Leslie describes in detail Benjamin's excitement and the structural radicalism of the early Disney shorts. Disney's move towards realism would rob the form of this potential, abandoning the 'flatlands' of two dimensional animation, in a sense moving from traditional animated films to something more hyper-real and formally deceptive. This move towards hyper-real fidelity can be seen to be economically motivated and in turn perpetuates dominant ideological values by enchanting the viewer in an illusory and escapist state. Benjamin and in turn Leslie see a utopian potential in the early anarchical Mickey Mouse. He is the agent of destructive transformation, the little-man standing up against authority. Sadly it is this aspect of the films that would become so inalterably transformed in the transition to what we understand as the contemporary Disney.

Adorno (1944) on the other hand was avidly opposed to Benjamin's initial position. He saw the inherent sado-masochism of Disney characters as a cathartic vent for the masses to release their frustrations. Both Adorno and Benjamin perceived the potential for a psychical release, though they differed on its hegemonic purpose. Adorno discusses Donald Duck in *The Culture Industry*, noting that the duck is continually punished and castigated in service of the viewer's gratification. He suggests that this enjoyment is through a simultaneous identification with Donald's helplessness and a subsequent schadenfreude (enjoyment of another's suffering) for the brutalisation of this projected weakness. This weakness Adorno sees as the proletarian subjection to powers outside of their control. Donald is the impulsive child who asks for his *needs* to be satisfied. This is perhaps why he becomes used to greater effect later in the war-time period, as he offers the audience an object of disdain for their own unheeded demands during a time of war and rationing.

Berland (1982) describes Donald as the id incarnate, the id being the unconscious un-socialised drive to gratification and destruction. Mickey Mouse acts as the embodiment of the ego ideal and in later shorts represents an agent of the super-ego: the symbolic introjection of Law. Mickey's relation to Donald is one of moral superiority, he is the voice of common sense when relating to that which is impulsive and destructive. Mickey as related to the *viewer* may be better described as an ideal ego, the illusion of unity the subject strives for in its investment in the ego (Lacan, 1954b). Mickey becomes the psychical figurehead of the unity that the ego models itself on. This is further evident in Walt's discussions of his characters. He typically referred to Mickey by his first name but Donald was always *the duck* (Schickel, 1968). Mickey can be discussed as a named other, whereas Donald becomes an 'it'.

It is thus possible to surmise that Walt strove to invest in an ego ideal through his identification with Mickey, perhaps because his own traumatic childhood left his ego fraught with instability. The viewer as unit of the audience takes Mickey as an ideal ego, enjoying the implicit solidity of his form. This gratification forms a dynamic relation between Walt as mythological auteur of Mickey (who derives gratification through identification with Mickey as object of the other's drive) and his audience (who derive gratification from the image and actions of Mickey). Donald on the other hand offers a cathartic valve to transgressive and indeed regressive enjoyment, a core constituent of the Disney form.

Analysis

Thus a dynamic has been established between Walt, his company, his product and the audience as accomplice. Within this dynamic Disney films can be seen to produce a perverse dynamic, hidden behind a front of slapstick humour and innocuous fun. The uncanny closeness to perversion is hidden behind the image's relative triviality. One of the characteristics thus far mentioned in relation to Disney films is the consistent appearance of phallic imagery, even at this early stage of the genre. It can be argued that the presentation of the phallic image is perverse in its disguised representation: the phallus as both present and absent; it is hidden but operant at the level of disavowal. All of the male Disney characters lack any obvious genitals, but that is not to say they are femininised. All physical cues that suggest sexual differences are absent; as Berland (1982) notes Mickey is essentially a hermaphrodite. The audience is given few definitive symbolic markers that suggest boy or girl; Mickey wears shorts, while Minnie tends to wear dresses. In the early Mickey series, the male characters tend to take an aggressive, active, masculine role, whereas the heroine tends to be passive. This is typical for the gender roles assigned within classic Hollywood narratives. This later alters to enable a masculine passivity that is supported by female activity within a near-maternalised relation: the boy is good and receives affection for his actions.

In her oft cited paper on *Visual Pleasures*, Laura Mulvey (1975) comments that for the viewer to enter into a gratifying relation within the cinematic apparatus of mainstream film, their look must conform to the male gaze, a gaze which is structurally dependent on a masculinised protagonist as agent of an active look, and feminised characters as passive objects to be looked at and enjoyed. What radically alters within the progression of Mickey shorts is that this gender binary becomes reversed. The later Mickey becomes a less potent character, object of both the viewer's gratification and that of the similarly objectified female within the diegetic space. This left Donald Duck to take the archetypically male behaviours, which makes it even more apparent that the phallus is absent in the Disney male lead. Donald (the archetypical male) and his exposed bottom half are a pertinent reminder of the lack of genitality. While Mickey is passive and successful within the

53

narratives, Donald is active in a trivial fashion and consistently unsuccessful. Thus the male (the phallic and active) role becomes trivialised within Disney shorts. Despite Disney's attempts to create a sex-free but sexualised world, the phallus makes other symbolic appearances in the films: the giant gun in Oswald that shoots its load and becomes limp, the long car that symbolises Mickey's opponent's attractive potency for Minnie, or Donald's little defiant flute, the cause of Mickey's consternation.

The plight of the pervert mirrors this presentation of the de-sexualised phallic object, as the phallus is also the token of sexual difference. For the pervert the problem of sexual difference is directly related to their difficult relation to the Oedipus complex. The Oedipal child is confronted with the Other's lack, as signified by the Other's desire (Lacan, 1958). The child is forced by the imposition of desire to re-evaluate their status as the phallus of the Other, the cause and focus of their desire. The child is forced to make entry into an understanding that although it cannot *be* the phallus for the mother, it can at least *have* the phallus: the capacity to give the mother what she lacks (Dor, 1999). Her lack of a penis becomes synonymous with the child's realisation that its mother lacks and therefore desires. Thus the child successfully makes its way from the imaginary register prior to the Oedipus complex to the early stages of genitally oriented sexual development.

The subversive phalluses in Disney provide the viewer with a product that does not challenge the perverse dilemma but rather enhances it. This could provide an enticing insight into why so many cultural theorists define Disney by its 'unchallenging' nature. The perverse is always enjoyable; the audience is drawn to Disney's implicit sexual appeal but can enjoy the denial of genitality embodied within the cartoon characters. The subversive relation to the phallus within Disney is simply an expression of the cartoon's unavoidable sexuality. The fact that they are hidden in sexual neutrality expresses a perverse denial. Berland (1982) comments that the cartoon figure's genital neutrality cannot rouse envy or jealousy. Jealousy and envy are expressions of an extraneous desire to the central figure of the cartoon and thus demonised within the diegetic space. This leads to the question of what cartoon characters truly represent within the Disney genre.

Though they are certainly not people, they have human characteristics that are veiled behind anthropomorphism.

Leonard Malten comments in his introduction to *Disney Treasure: The Chronological Duck* (2005) that as Mickey became more popular his charac-ter became more confined to being a hero and thus a simpler, morally black and white figure. When the Disney conventions became solidified the different characteristics of the more complex primordial Mickey had to be split into different characters. By dividing one multi-layered character into several 'pure' characters there is a compartmentalisation of mental characteristics. This compartmentalisation allows stories to progress using different characters to express different antagonistic emotions that in reality are present within a single viewer. This allows for a complete reduction of ambiguity and the complexity of human emotion. Donald is the aggressive demanding child, Pluto is impulsive and un-socialised, Goofy is smart but awkward and Mickey is invulnerable, vacuous and cold. Why would the hero have these qualities?

The hero is designed in this way because he or she provides a solidity and certainty that the other characters lack. If the other characters were to be amalgamated they might construct a single plausible semblance of a human being: ambiguity, contradictions and all. But Mickey is the only character that provides a superhuman illusion of solidity, a solidity that can fight off the anxiety roused by the other characters partial nature. Mickey is a homunculus; a simplified and caricatured representation of an aspect of mental topography, specifically the fetishistic receptacle of the viewer's gaze and desire. This is the conceptual homunculus that forms the core of the Disney entity manufactured in Part One, and is the subject of the next chapter which shall conclude by tying these two constructions together.

Chapter 4

The Conceptual Homunculus

The term homunculus has its origins in medieval alchemy, but as a concept it can be traced to antiquity. Paracelsus used the term to describe an alchemically created artificial man. When this man (grown in a test tube) develops into an adult, he has the capacity to reach either positive or negative extremes. He can be either a giant or a pygmy, a great or monstrous man (Campbell, 2010). The homunculus is also the most basic unit of man in preformationist thought (which supposed that the sperm cell itself contains a tiny man, who in turn contains a tinier man and so on into an infinity of smallness). This infinity that is structurally expressed in the homunculus is the expanse of the primordial abyss: the state of pre-subjectivity in which the child exists with the archaic mother.

The production of the homunculus was considered significant as it was done without the female organs; and represented an object of a purely masculine nature (Campbell, 2010). This distillation of masculinity seems to reaffirm a culturally constructed male centrality. The homunculus of Paracelsus is therefore a distillation of the male gaze; an absolute and pure object that satisfies a male egoic idealisation. The Jewish Golem is another apparition of the homunculoid form, though instead of being formed from a single sperm cell, it is birthed by virgin soil. Like the homunculus described in Goethe's *Faust* (1832), the Golem is servant to man's will. Both involve a simultaneous servitude to masculine designs and result in death and destruction (Campbell, 2010, p13). This duality of function is key to the homunculus' status as a fetish object in service of the gaze.

Within the present discussion, the homunculus is used to describe the prototypic cartoon body contructed to suit a regressive, pre-gendered gaze. It is the locus of the cartoon form, the cartoon essence that Scott McCloud describes as: "an empty shell that we inhabit which enables us to travel in another realm" (McCloud, 1993, p36). The cartoon body is fundamentally a caricature: a simplification and exaggeration of human facets. Too much awareness of the messenger obscures the message, thus the cartoon image must be refined to more basic emotional characteristics (which are perhaps better described as *caricaturistics*).

Freud (1923) references the homunculus as representative of the ego; it is an abstraction of the psychical perception of the body and self. Mickey Mouse is an archetypical example of an empty and exaggerated semblance of an ego without the subject attached. An amputation of an ego as mask: deprived of soul with small black eyes. It gives a solid un-emotive façade, a pure ego. As stated in the previous chapter this purer ego can reference both the ideal ego and the ego ideal. The ideal ego represents an image of unity of self that the subject struggles with. This is the image the subject is confronted with in mis-recognising the image of its body in the mirror, a significant psychical event that occurs in Lacan's mirror stage (Lacan, 1954b).

The mirror stage represents a phase of psychical development in which the child achieves an image of the self that constitutes the ego. This ego is dependent on the look of the other, the eyes of whom act as a mirror; the look of the other has the capacity to consolidate the subject's fragmented sense of self. When the subject gazes at an object, they find that the object already gazes back at them; this look from the object occupies the same purpose as the other, whose look aids the subject's egoic consolidation (Lacan, 1954b). As an image of solidity the other provides the subject with an illusory unity of being, likewise the homunculus provides the viewer a solidity of identification that the ego is doomed to never achieve. Thus in gazing at the homunculus as object, the subject is gratified by their own beautification. Symmetry and solidity suggests a whole, similarly the homunculus aids in the disavowal of the subject's fragmented sense of self that exists before the institution of the ego.

The homunculus' absolute and idealised image functions as a kind of fetish, providing the ability to cover up lack with the most simple and vacuous of forms, caricatured to the appeal of a mass audience as an ideal of both image and solidity. The purpose of the fetish is to allow its user to cover up the threat of castration and the reality of the castrated mother (see Freud, 1927). By providing a fantasy that is genital-free, Disney provides a fetishised safe house from sexual difference, one which protects the viewer from anxiety. Thus the homunculus can be seen to occupy a fetishistic role.

Fetishism

Parveen Adams (1996) describes fetishism as the root of perversion. Fetishism itself involves the disavowal of the mother's lack of the phallus (mirrored by her very real lack of the male organ itself). It is thus the precondition upon which perversion is based. Cryptically, Lacan refers to fetishism as the "perversion of perversions" ("la perversion des perversions, celle qui s'appelle le fétichisme" – Lacan, 1957d, p194), suggesting that the fetish supports, institutes and enables the disavowal of the pervert.

Roger Dadoun (1989) suggests that the fetish is composed of many parts, among which:

- The archaic mother and the phallus of the mother
- The sexualised phallic object
- The missing phallus
- The fear and anxiety of castration
- Defence mechanisms

Some of these aspects have already been addressed (the missing/de-sexualised phallus and the defence against lack); the rest will be addressed during the course of Part Two and related to the structure of Disney itself.

The fetish is, along with these facets, a means of denying sexual difference (i.e. the difference between mother and father is the phallus, that which gives both the male and female subject power or lack-of in the eyes of paternal authority). It is a material element that consecrates the perverse disavowal yet it is also a memorial to castration – a token of protection and triumph over the father. The fetishist displaces this maternal phallus onto another part of the body or an object; it is thus a referent totem of the pre-Oedipal mother (the primordial/archaic mother). It is a totem that carries reference to the abyss of the primordial child/Other relation (the domain of jouissance), yet simultaneously protects against it. The process of fetishism is one of displacement, not of replacement, it is the fetish that the fetishist desires, not a substitute for the mother but rather an object of distraction (Adams, 1996).

The disavowal of the mother's lack is in turn a disavowal of the father. He is abolished from the symbolic; the fetish thus also has the capacity to ward against his intrusion (as defence mechanism). This disavowal represents a partial removal of the paternal function, which maintains the subject's distance to jouissance and the anxiety it represents. The symbolic father has the function of removing the child from the possibility of incestuous union with the mother; his role is thus protective as he prevents the child from falling into psychosis (Lacan, 1966), the death of subjectivity that is implicit in the fusion with the archaic mother. The archaic mother is threatening; she is the mother of the primordial abyss, the mother that absorbs the child into a state of fusion which is essentially subjective obliteration and marks the fall into psychosis (foreclosure of the paternal function).

As Dadoun (1989) suggests, there is a positive side of fetish: protection against the archaic mother by proxy of being a referent of the paternal (the fetish is *phallic*), as fear of the archaic is essentially fear of slipping into psychosis. The archaic is the referent of the terror of fusion and formlessness. Dadoun uses the example of the viewer's fear of the vampire; fear of oral absorption through the contagious devouring bite.

In Dadoun's analysis of the character of Count Dracula, he situates the vampire itself as the phallus. Dracula, he posits, represents the substitute for the maternal phallus: he is a fetishistic form that disavows lack and castration. He represents a move from having/not-having the phallus to *being* the phallus (the primordial, pre-gendered position of the child). This is indicative of an identification with the archaic mother. She does not have the phallus yet is phallic; a totality in herself that threatens the child as phallus with absorption. Yet the subject requires the fetish to protect against the anxiety of this absorption, which essentially threatens the loss of subjectivity and psychotic collapse. As a stand-in for the phallus, the fetish also acts as a totem of the paternal, as the phallus is essentially the father's endowment. As such, it likewise acts as a safeguard against an encompassing maternal figure. Indeed, *Dracula* (1931) ends with the 'true' phallus (i.e. the stake and scientist) triumphing over a fake one (Dracula, feminised and maternal by virtue of his immobility and capacity to be penetrated). Thus fetish referents of the paternal represent the positive capacity of the fetish, and referents of the primordial mother, those that are absorbing and devouring, are negativised.

The homunculus is fetishistic in that it enables the subject to escape the anxiety of fusion and the interdiction of the father. Its purpose within film is to create an idealised focal point. The homunculus is a negative fetish in that it enables the subject a regressive return to the primordial. As shall be demonstrated in Part Two, the apparatus that the viewer secures itself in relating to the screen homunculus is implicitly regressive. The regressive nature of Disney narratives shall be briefly introduced in the following section on Disney's *Silly Symphonies* series of shorts, through discussions of anal eroticism and regression.

Anality and Rivalry in the *Silly Symphonies* series

Although Mickey represents the core values of the homunculus, the position of this concept within Disney shorts was consistent throughout the studio's output, the conventions of which were established early in the studio's conception. The character and story conventions of the *Mickey & Co.* series were relatively fixed by the 1930s.

Disney's other series, *Silly Symphonies*, provided the ground for more cinematic experimentation. Silly Symphonies were an unrelated series of shorts that featured single use characters put to music. The first of these films was *Skeleton Dance*, made in 1929. *Skeleton Dance* was a ghoulish Halloween story in which skeletons rise from their graves and dance to a musical score. It was more artistically challenging than Mickey Mouse shorts and received critical acclaim. It was similar to *Steamboat Willy* in that the animation was dependent on the music, which would build within the film into a rhythmic climax. The *Silly Symphonies* series were generally based around visual interpretations of music or visual and musical interpretations of popular stories. It was a series of imaginative and entertaining shorts that allowed the animators and story-men to explore a vast array of ideas. Despite the freedom of stories and content, the films were still connected by qualities that demarcated them as Disney films.

The Disney studio kept at the forefront of Hollywood through its appreciation of technological advances. These advances often kept Disney films ahead of rival studios. As soon as more cost effective colour film became available Disney invested in the process. Once again Walt halted production of a half-finished project called *Flowers and Trees* (1931) and had it re-shot with the new process. *Flowers and Trees* received high acclaim, becoming the first animated subject to win an Oscar in 1931. This short featured a romance between two anthropomorphic trees, the hero and his love interest. While the hero is trying to earn the female tree's love an evil tree approaches and intrudes on their romance.

The hero fights off the villain, in revenge the evil tree sets a fire that threatens to engulf the whole forest. The forest animals band together and manage to put out the fire, but not before the evil tree dies in the flames. It is a classic Disney story, and as shall be demonstrated in Disney's feature-length films, it follows a narrative format that would be often repeated in Disney films,

61

A Conflict of Trees
(Image by Rupert Norfolk)

albeit with minor variations. This was also one of the first appearances of an altogether evil adversary in Disney films. The bad tree is jagged and ugly; his eyes are large and green. He is barren of foliage and has grey skin; the image of sickliness. He is jealous of the good tree and seeks to steal his love away from him.

Jealousy is a recurring characteristic of Disney's villains. If the homuncule main protagonist is representative of an idealised ego simulacrum, then the villain presents the viewer with an extraneous desire. This desire is a foreign element, an intruder that seeks to occupy the same position as the homunculus. This functions in the film's idealisation of the hero because it acknowledges that the position of the idealised ego is so ideal that even the villain wishes to attain it. Thus the rival as intruder is a malevolent force, but not one that is powerful enough to truly threaten the homunculus. Making the rival envious of the hero further validates the hero's status as an ideal. There is no real damage or threat that the malevolent force can do to this hero. Thus if the intruder represents the paternal function as intruder, then his/her jealousy validates the ideal's position as object of the Other's drive.

Among the more popular episodes of the *Silly Symphonies* series was Disney's interpretation of *The Three Little Pigs* (1933). This short gave the studio its first hit musical number: *Who's Afraid of the Big Bad Wolf?* The film was a commercial success, the story resonated with Depression era Americans who similarly were losing their homes to forces beyond their measure. It was a film for the 'little guy' pitted against seemingly unmanageable odds and surviving through moral conservatism.

The oldest and wisest pig is presented as the model conservative, building his house wisely and living frugally. The wolf is a forceful and malicious character, who attempts to get at the pigs by dressing up as a Jewish man who tries to sell them trinkets. This was an obvious anti-Semitic jab that would have been popular in 1930's America. The wolf is similar to the evil tree in his appearance, as a dark jagged malevolent force, but the wolf is a villain by nature not a rival, as he merely wants to eat the pigs.

The first two pigs are attired similarly to Donald Duck. Neither wears pants, one sprites about playing a flute while the other is dressed in a sailor outfit. The older pig is dressed respectably in overalls. He is the conservative worker, the pillar of common sense. The younger pigs are naked apart from their upper half, leaving their buttocks exposed. Their frolicking ends when the wolf enters the scene and chases them to their houses. He is an unstoppable force and blows down the first two houses, but finds that he cannot penetrate the house built by the older pig. In this story the two pleasure-driven pigs are subordinate to the prudish reserved pig: whose values and actions define him as the hero. This is quite a similar dynamic to the Mickey and Donald cartoons that would show these different extremes working in tandem but with one subservient to the other: Donald's impulsive enjoyment contrasted to Mickey's prudish good values. In *The Three Little Pigs* and other *Silly Symphonies* shorts, an aspect of Disney becomes evident that has been much discussed by several authors: that of regression and anal eroticism.

In *The Water Babies* (1935) the opening shot reveals small nymph babies emerging from water lilies and frolicking in the water. The babies are presented as little caricatures, with rosy red cheeks and pink skin. Though they are entirely naked they have no genitals. The buttocks are an object of recurring focus within the film. Flowers smack a baby on the buttocks to wake it up and the babies slap each other's buttocks in jest. Schickel (1968) takes note that Walt Disney seemed to have a particular interest in the posterior. Walt would frequently work the buttocks into many of his gags and would request the buttocks to be present in character artwork so as to make the animations 'cute'. Brody (1976) and Berger (1991) argue that the theme of anality within Disney's work is related to Walt's fixation on the anal stage of libidinal development. Their argument is that Walt's lack of interest in adult sexuality (his puritan character and reported disinterest in the opposite sex) demonstrated a discomfort with the genital. He thus resorted to an anal fixation to stave off his sexual anxiety. Brody lists Walt's anal personality traits: his obsessional personality and entrepreneurial zest for money. He suggests that Walt was deeply uncomfortable with the realities of the world: sex, dirtiness and a lack of absolute control. Walt attempted to create an idealistic world of simplicity, a cleaner world free of the complications of sex and dirt.

While these analyses are provocative to say the least, they fall into the trappings of psychobiography. Firstly, the authorial capacity of Walt Disney is hard to substantiate, and second, analysis based on biographical information relies far too heavily on speculation and inference. While the concept of fixation on prior stages of sexual development offers its own interpretations of the content of Disney films, it is perhaps more fruitful to emphasise that this content is *regressive for the viewer, rather then for our mythical auteur.*

This regressive characteristic of Disney narratives provides the last piece necessary to complete the analogical homunculus underlying the structure of this chapter and illustrating 'Disney' as an object of study. Chapter one provided a theoretical framework with which to situate a dynamic process between the subject and the socio-cultural institution of Disney. Chapter two proceeded to add a pseudo-historical, mythobiographical analysis, which was followed by textual analyses of cartoon shorts in chapter three, chapter four produced the homunculus as concept. These elements together form the analogical homunculus: a simplified and illustrative model of Disney as an object of study. It is thus possible to continue this research in Parts Two and Three, which are intimately dependent on this early conception of Disney, which will be consolidated and elaborated in subsequent discussions over the course of this text.

To construct the analogical homunculus as a whole, it can be surmised that a series of theoretical identifications between the mythic figure of Walt Disney and the Disney company led to a construction of 'Disney' as a socio-cultural institution. This institution would take its organisational structure and characteristics based on mass culture identifying the company with the man. The animated film and character of Mickey Mouse act as a psychical currency to provide validation of the existence of Disney, via a circuit between Walt, the company, the mouse and the viewer. This dynamic operates in a structure that has been outlined theoretically in chapter one. The summation of these parts represents a simplified illustration, an analogical homunculus that can be referred to as Disney.

The following chapters shall utilise the model that has thus far been developed to discuss at length the feature-length films that comprise Disney's classic era of film-making. It is possible to see these films in a progression towards a very particular regressive mode of story-telling – one that will be demonstrated to return the viewer to a primordial sexual relation, which can be described as regressive and perverse.

Part Two:
The Regressive
Apparatus

P art Two is composed of a series of detailed textual analyses that are situated in their industrial context and discussed psychoanalytically. The points gathered from these analyses will be synthesised into an aesthetic and narrative product of the Disney entity, as constructed in Part One. This analysis shall extensively describe the scenes, images and narrative of the films of this period. This level of detail and attention is necessary as these films represent the core of Disney's media output. The filmic style implicit in these films is the essence of what would become known as 'Disney' in popular culture. Although Disney Studios would be best known for these feature-length animations, it was the shorts they had been making for 10 years before that formed the base of the classic Disney iconography. These films laid the groundwork for Disney's genre and narrative conventions, and these conventions would remain consistent over the company's evolution with only minor alterations. The emphasis on moralistic, clean and family-friendly entertainment would never change. Even in later years when the company branched out into different media ventures, the label 'Disney' would be kept separate from new formats and story types. It would become a family-safe stamp that the company could attach to its product (Giroux, 2000). The following discussion of Disney's first feature-length animations will form the 'classic' Disney period that spans from 1937 to the start of World War II. This discussion will begin by once again locating Disney films within their social and organisational context. These analyses will expose narrative and visual trends that will culminate in a psychoanalytic under-standing of the Disney form. The following chapters shall continue discussions of the homunculus and further discuss Disney character tropes.

A conception of the cartoon body will be introduced as a result of the discussions of Disney formal qualities that become conventionalised within this period. Part Two shall thus be structured by discussions of the different Disney narratives that can be shown to experiment with the cartoon form, in scenarios that seek to maximise viewer gratification within a transgressive space that is manipulated in such a way as to emphasise mass appeal.

Chapter 5

Disney Character Tropes

In 1930 Disney came into conflict with Pat Powers, the man who had sold Disney their sound system and had distributed their shorts. Walt had travelled to New York to ask Powers for money owed to the studio. Instead, Powers disclosed his plan to steal Iwerks from the studio in an attempt to blackmail Disney into signing another more restrictive contract. The venture ultimately failed and Disney terminated its contract with Powers. Thus the studio lost Iwerks, who went on to start his own animation studio. Iwerks may have been the superior artist but his cartoons failed to be as popular without Walt's story-editing abilities. Walt eventually rehired Iwerks but never forgave him the betrayal. Disney was now in need of a new distributor and began working with Harry Cohn from Columbia Pictures. Cohn provided a great deal of capital for the productions, which had since doubled in cost to produce. Cohn also allowed Disney to retain absolute control over his product. Despite its success Disney was still struggling to maintain financial solvency. This and other factors led Walt to his first emotional breakdown in 1931. On the advice of his doctor, Walt and his wife took a short holiday. On his arrival back to work he took up horse-riding as a vent for his stress. Walt signed his next distribution contract with United Artists, a deal that provided a great deal of financial security for the company that had struggled for so long (Schickel, 1968, Wasko, 2001).

In this period Walt became increasingly obsessed with his work and his hobbies. At home he was quite different from the emotively engaged studio head and was reportedly detached and uninvolved in his family life. In work he was a far more potent paternal figure, but his highly patriarchal and often inappropriate relation to his staff caused a great deal of strife. While he insisted that his staff refer to him familiarly as 'Walt', he made it very clear he was the father of the Disney family. The studio environment was fraught with stress and Walt's frequent emotional outbursts. Kevin Shortsleeve (2001) describes the Disney studio as a place dominated by *Waltitarianism*, which he describes as an Orwellian awareness of being watched and fear of reprisal. Walt's presence was often perceived as an intrusive force, judging and spying on employees. He was renowned for flying into unprovoked rages and firing staff with little or no warning. His attitude to his employees was a mixture of favouritism and totalitarianism. He often paid personnel vastly different wages to staff working similar jobs, this was based on personal preference rather than responsibility or how long they had worked for the company. These behaviours were strikingly similar to the contradictory and abusive relationship Walt had with his father (Schickel, 1968). Unfortunately his employees did not react kindly to this involvement with his fantasy life. This would climax in the 1940s when his staff went on strike, an event that he took as another very personal betrayal.

In 1932 the Disney studio added a new story department, in which storylines for cartoon shorts could be put together and edited separately from the animation department. One of the inventions of Disney's new story room was the story-board: a comic-style telling of the film which allows the film-maker to arrange camera angles, shot composition and story at the same time. This and other innovations would enable the production of Disney's first feature-length animation which would become their most challenging work.

Mass Appeal and Regression

By 1935 Walt Disney had received international acclaim, and was presented with a gold medal by the League of Nations for his work on cartoon shorts. By 1935 Disney had studios in both London and Paris so as to aid distribution. By 1937 Disney films were dubbed into Spanish, French and German, while Disney storybooks were translated into over 27 world languages. Mickey was becoming so popular in the 1930s that President Roosevelt proudly exhibited Mickey shorts to foreign dignitaries; in fact George V admitted to only wanting to see Mickey Mouse films.

Mickey received mixed reactions across Europe and Russia, where he was considered by the Soviet government to be an example of capitalist meekness (Schickel, 1969). Despite Soviet reservations regarding Disney and Walt's own anti-communist sentiments, he met Serge Eisenstein on several occasions. These meetings and Disney feature-length films inspired Eisenstein to write a series of papers that attempted to explaining Disney's appeal. Eisenstein (1941–1946) posited the basis of Disney's appeal as the answer to the fundamental problems of film-making. He describes appeal in visual arts as a delicate balancing between sensuality and logic. The contrived and the conceptual will not emotionally register with a viewer unless it also appeals to primordial aspects of the psyche. Thus art must play on a regressive quality to the gratification it offers its viewer. He conceptualises Disney as a "return to a world of complete freedom" (Eisenstein, 1941–1946, p3). This is a regression to a golden-age of childhood, comparable to the infantilism of Charlie Chaplin. He also discusses Disney as a liberation for the slave-like oppression of Depression era America, and compares it with the utopia offered by Socialism. He seems to argue that both utopian socialism and Disney promise a reprieve through child-like freedom. This echoed Benjamin's position, and contrasted sharply with the reactions to Mickey from the political right. Nazi propaganda equated Mickey with jazz and black Americans, suggesting he was a pest. This was countered by those in the German left, who wore Mickey Mouse pins to jokingly mirror the swastika pins worn by party-members (Leslie, 2002).

Eisenstein was also curious about the role of animism in Disney, as the regression of man into beast seems to mirror the return to a child-like state (Eisenstein, 1941–1946). The 'animistic' forms the roots of the sensuous; in regressing to primitivism the viewer regresses to simplified gratification. Though these words are not Eisenstein's, the psychoanalytic inference is clear. Indeed, Eisenstein goes so far as to call the animistic, sensuous state "pre-metaphoric" (Eisenstein, 1941- 1946, p49). This can be understood as structurally synonymous with regression to the pre-Oedipal and pre-linguistic state of sexual development; flight from the symbolic order, regulated by Law.

Regression in the work of Lacan, and indeed Freud, is not a temporal concept but rather topographical. It does not refer to a literal return to a child-like state but rather a structural return to previous organisations of sexual development. It is a process that denigrates the symbolic and emphasises the imaginary (Lacan, 1957c), a return to an order that emphasises demands over desire (Lacan, 1958b). Thus demand becomes particularly significant in regression, or more precisely what is demanded (although it should be mentioned that although the object of gratification changes, the demand is always for love). The concept of regression can be used to understand audience gratification, but first there is a need to address the cinematic apparatus.

A Disney Apparatus

Although Disney films of the classic period may appear varied in terms of story and theme there are many stylistic elements that tie the films together. It shall be argued that these stylistic elements combined with narrative trends to form the substance of Disney as a genre. The use of 'genre' is meant to delimit the possibilities of the films' diegetic content, to build audience expectations (Bordwell, Staiger and Thompson, 1988). But genre conventions also serve as the apparatus of the auteur, who seeks to rework his ideas in order to make them more accessible for public consumption (Cowie, 1984). The development of such rigid genre conventions within Disney would work to the company's benefit; it would label the studio as reliable, safe for families and young children, thus allowing its product to appeal to broad audiences around the world.

An analysis of the Disney genre necessitates a discussion of the similarities in the films' narrative and formal elements. What is present and has been omitted from the original texts these films were based on is likewise significant in an analysis of the Disney cartoon feature. The altered narratives reproduced in these films illustrate the perverse undercurrent in Disney, where the subject is able to enjoy certain co-existing contradictions and gratify in a fantasmatic state in the absence of authority or reprisal. While this may sound radical or revolutionary it is in fact the opposite. The perverse is the essence of hypocrisy; enjoyment based on an anti-law that structurally debilitates the freedom of the other in the social realm. It shall be argued that this regressive element within the cinematic apparatus is what makes the Disney genre so gratifying for the mass audience; thus it is important here to discuss the role of fantasy in filmic gratification.

Cowie (1984) notes that fantasy is at its base a space in which the subject imagines the process of having what they do not have, thus attaining what they desire. Fantasy is enjoyable as it allows for scenarios in which solutions are offered to lack. Within film, as in life, the role of fantasy can be considered to be a more literal *mise-en-scène* of desire: the staging of unsatisfied demand. As there is no absolute access to the objects of desire, fantasy provides a platform for identification with scenarios in which the subject attains an imaginary construction of what is desired. Both the scenario and the imagined object are constructed within dreams and fantasy. As Metz (1977) describes in his discussions of the cinematic apparatus, film provides an arranged setting with which to stage and resolve desire. Thus the viewer adapts themselves to the story they are presented with as it offers gratification.

Pleasure is found in viewing because the narrative plays out in a way that creates the illusion of satisfying desire. In her text *Fantasia* (1984), Cowie analyses several films in which she describes how fantasy can be manipulated to direct the gratification of the viewer. This process can easily be understood in Disney films, particularly the manner in which Disney relays its stories and character interactions. Disney represents a particularly regressive form of the cinematic apparatus.

The first of the films Cowie discusses is *Now Voyager* (1942), which depicts a woman torn between guilt and desire. She has to make her choice between obligation and love. In the end she chooses obligation but with a tiny opening for love made possible through signification. The film climaxes with the main character sacrificing the possibility of romantic love in favour of a compromised love. She is not able to have the man she loves but instead she is able to look after his daughter, who represents a token of his affection (Cowie, 1984). The viewer's demand for resolution is given the token of the daughter and the maternal role of the lead, thus confirming her as a phallic mother; she is satisfied with having the child as phallus. Cowie's argument is that the film's narrative is perverse, due to the scenario it offers of the mother having the child and becoming a phallic mother. Thus the child is a fetishistic replacement for the phallus and resolves the lack perceived in the mother. The film's solution is not ideal, yet it is gratifying to the viewer as it enables a solution to the narrative via a substitution for romantic love in the form of the daughter.

Next Cowie discusses *A Reckless Moment* (1949), a tragedy that features the love between a reforming criminal and the women he tries to blackmail. The film ends with the criminal giving his life so that his love may go free. While he is dying she gives him her love and coddles him, taking on a maternal role, after which he dies. The Other, represented here by the woman who becomes maternal, obliterates the lead character as a subject, absorbing him through maternal affections, ending in his death. Here is an incomplete resolution, one that leaves the viewer with a melancholic vision of desire: that to achieve the object that causes desire is to cease to be a subject. This narrative plays on a perverse need for conflict resolution; in the end it frustrates the viewer, but by the same measure exposes the viewer to an unsettling aspect of desire. In both films desire is staged in such a way so as to keep the viewer engaged, but both end by reflecting the subject's own desire, which is by its nature incomplete. Both films are characterised by a lack, yet *Now Voyager* offers a more complete and satisfactory end to the narrative, which Cowie argues is perverse and in turn more intrinsically enjoyable.

Both of the films Cowie discusses are different to Disney's which consistently end with the main character existing in a state of unity with the Other. That is to say that structurally Disney films end with the mother having the phallus: the Other complete with the subject. There are no substitutions for love in Disney films. In Disney lack is always treated as an ugly outsider, and radically foreclosed in the course of the narrative. This can be demonstrated in the repeating characters seen in Disney films, and how these characters interact within Disney narrative conventions.

Snow White

Disney has often been criticised for simplifying its narratives into obvious binary oppositions of moral black and white, or good and bad characters. With a more in-depth analytic reading of the films it becomes evident that the character differentiation is more complex than simply good and bad. The Mickey series separated character traits into several characters, the same can be said for features, although the differentiation is more subtle. Janet Wasko (2001) describes the repeating character classes in Disney films, as suggested by an article in a 1998 issue of *Entertainment Weekly*. The article posits six character roles, based on the backlog of Disney features. These are described as the following:

- The *Hero/Heroine*: embodiment of American sex appeal.

- The *Love Interest*: the object of the Villain's lust, the other half of the Hero and often first appears as the Hero's opponent.

- The *Sidekick*: acts as a younger sibling of the Hero and provides comic relief.

- The *Mentor*: who is forced by fate to aid the Hero.

- The *Villain*: who desires omnipotence and is typically pictured as snobbish. May also die by falling.

- The *Henchman*: ineffectually supports the Villain and bears partial responsibility for their downfall.
(Wasko, 2001)

Although the tone of the descriptions is satirical the observations are apt. Wasko also notes that Disney narrative structure follows classic Hollywood conventions. The Hero is set a task, he or she overcomes obstacles and meets the love interest on their way to a happy ending. The typical Disney story utilises fairy-tales as source material but then forces the original folk story to conform to these mainstream story-telling conventions. Most of the fairy-tales Disney films were based on did not conform to Hollywood's narrow conception of narrative and were originally far darker stories and rarely linear. In Carlo Collodi's *Pinocchio* (1882) Pinocchio runs amok through his father's life and even tries to kill the talking cricket that would later be known as Jiminy in the Disney feature. Maria Warner (1995) comments that Disney had a tendency to remove many features of the fairy-tale and emphasise elements that would polarise the narratives into good and bad positions, in which the good would inevitably prevail. The Disney translation of these stories was obsessed with producing softer digestible narratives for children, even though the original folk tales were written specifically for children.

While Disney films were often scary, these moments were carefully contextualised so as to minimise the anxiety of the audience. Thus what differentiated the child for whom the folk story is written from the child targeted by Disney is a matter of adult perceptions of childhood. Disney films are more concerned with addressing the child as the innocent, whereas the seemingly 'nonsensical' narrative of the folk-tale can be seen to address the child on their own terms (Bettelheim, 1976).

Changes in translation from folk-tale to film are inevitable. Film is an altogether different medium to folk-tales and Collodi's *Pinocchio* lacked the linear narrative and intuitive cause and effect dynamic that mainstream audiences of the 1930s required. It is the ideological differences between film and folk-tale that present the qualities that can uniquely be called Disney. While Disney features were full of elements that were considered nearly too scary for young audiences, the darker aggressive elements of the original stories were omitted. It is these elements that Bruno Bettelheim (1976) considered to be most important for children, as they present a safe context within which to stage aggressivity and anxiety, thus facilitating early development.

The Grimm brothers' telling of *Snow White* (Grimm & Grimm, 1857) is similarly a much darker story. Originally the evil Queen eats a boar's lungs and heart believing them to be Snow White's. The story ends with the villainess being forced to dance on hot coals until she dies. In his analysis of *Snow White*, Bettelheim suggests that the fairy-tale is a fable of the problematic path the child faces in the Oedipus complex. For Bettelheim the story describes Snow White's passage through the Oedipal dilemma, she accepts that she cannot remain joined to the Other and moves into a world of more complex relations; "We are all expelled eventually from the original paradise of infancy, where all our wishes seemed to be fulfilled without any effort on our part" (Bettelheim, 1976, p214). He suggests that the time Snow White spends with the dwarves marks an archaic period of unity that she must leave behind. In challenging the evil Queen, Snow White ascends to the world of responsibility.

The fundamental message of the Grimms' fairy-tale is radically divergent from Disney's telling of the story. What first becomes obvious when viewing the Disneyified version of *Snow White* is how far it differs from its original folk roots. From the moment the credits begin in *Snow White and the Seven Dwarfs* (1937) it is apparent that the viewer is entering a Walt Disney film. His name is large and dwarfs all other names listed on screen. The opening scene is a live-action shot of a story book with the title *Snow White & the Seven Dwarfs*. The book opens and the viewer is sucked into the animated world. The live-action shot acts as a bridge between reality and the Disney-scape of the film. Nearly all of the Disney animated features of the classic period through to the 1960s begin in this manner. The live-action sequence acts as a bridge between reality and the animated, this style of introduction would form one of the most oft repeated Disney conventions.

The film opens to the face of an attractive but malevolent Queen, who asks her magic mirror, "Who is the fairest one of all?" The mirror replies that it is the young princess Snow White, a reply that sends the Queen into a jealous rage. This introduces a malevolent force of the film: the evil character who is shown to be vain, adult in appearance and jealous of the lead character's role. There are very few negative depictions of biological mothers in Disney films. It is nearly always the non-biologically related guardian that mistreats the hero or heroine. The Queen is Snow White's stepmother, and is represented as a malevolent force: the embodiment of vanity and envy (Davis, 2006).

Snow White is the heroine of the film, and makes her appearance dressed in rags, happily humming to herself. She sings to the birds, "Make a wish into the wishing well, that's all you have to do". The song is about her melancholic pining for love; it expresses a nostalgic longing for unity which perhaps parallels the viewer's own nostalgia for connection with the Other. She does not have to wait long for her wish to come true, as the handsome Prince sneaks into the castle to hear her sing. As she looks into the mirrored refection of the wishing well the prince peeks his head over; suddenly appearing beside her.

Mirrored meeting; Snow White and the Prince
(Image by Paul Byrne)

He starts singing his own song, the crux of which is that he has but one love and by a striking coincidence it is her! This must surely be true love, how else would he know if they have only just met? Love at first sight would at least imply lust, but lust is altogether absent in Disney films. It is perhaps more accurate to suggest that this is the epitome of what can be referred to as 'fairy-tale love', or perhaps a uniquely 'Disney love': an attractive but artificial idealisation of the sexual relation. For Lacan (1964a), love is always imaginary – an exchange at the level of the ego that involves the love of the other, solidifying and cathecting the ego of the subject. Love is the illusory fantasy of fusion with the Other. Love is thus narcissistic, and concerns a drive to realise the ego: the ego libido.

Love is opposed to desire, yet similar in its structure. Desire is a symbolic process that seeks part objects within the confines of the pleasure principle (and the symbolic order). Love seeks a fusion that exists beyond the limits of social reality, and has the capacity to obliterate desire, since love is based on a fantasy of oneness with the Other: a utopian refiguration of the primordial connection between mother and child in which desire and subjectivity do not yet exist. Through love the subject attempts to abolish the difference that creates and perpetuates desire (Lacan, 1973).

Thus love seeks to drive the subject to jouissance, which is not pleasurable but rather painful, marking death to subjectivity. Thus for Lacan, love seeks subjective death. What Disney produces is a Disneyified love, one in which the primordial unity is glamorised, safe and gratifying. A sexual utopia of "totalitarian dependency" (Lacan, 1938, p23).

The Queen watches the proceedings through her window with an expression of jealous rage. She plots to have Snow White murdered and in the next scene speaks to the Huntsman. The Huntsman is an atypical character within the classic Disney period. He is the only figure to be endowed with moral ambiguity. The Huntsman is one of the more realistically represented Disney humans as he is divided between emotion and obligation, a choice he cannot easily make. He is presented with his head bowed forward, black hair and a beard, with a permanent grimace on his face. He appears as an agent of the Queen's malignant evil. Yet when she instructs him to bring Snow White into the woods and kill her, he reacts with a start: "But Majesty!" The Queen cuts him off, telling him it is his life or Snow White's. He accepts his instructions to bring the Queen back Snow White's heart as proof he has killed her. In the original story the Huntsman takes on a paternal role. He is a strong character that contrasts Snow White's weak father (absent in the Disney feature) and her jealous step-mother (Bettelheim, 1976). Despite this he remains perhaps the only adult masculine character of this period who is not altogether malevolent.

On bringing Snow White to a remote meadow, the Huntsman finds that he cannot kill her. With his voice shaking he tells her: "I can't do it!" He then explains to Snow White that the Queen has gone mad with jealousy and that she must run and hide far away. The human quality of the Huntsman is contrasted against the two-dimensional qualities of Snow White. Her reactions seem dampened and caricatured. She is still kind and vapid even when terrified. This lack of emotional depth makes her character seem less real, a caricature of implicit goodliness. When the Huntsman is contrasted against the extremes of the Queen and Snow White, he appears a less solid character. His ambiguous humanity cannot stand up against the black and white polarities of the heroine and the villainess. His potency is removed by contrast to the other characters as he remains the only character who is not idealised within the Disney space. Davis (2006) remarks that the drive for realism in human characters was intended to make the audience take them more seriously, though when examining the huntsman compared to the Queen and Snow White, this appears not to be the case. Schickel (1968) notes that when the studio started to push for more realistic-looking characters the end result appeared to be more subtly false. This move towards realism did not include emotional realism but was far more concerned with appearance, what Warner (1995) references as a division and separation of characters into positive and negative extremes.

The studio used live-action shots of an actress which they then animated. The result is a hyper-realised image of a girl-shaped entity with pink skin and large eyes. The contrast between realism and the artificiality of her character becomes all the more evident when she is put in an antagonistic situation, where strong emotions, such as fear or anger, would seem to be the natural reaction. Her two-dimensional reactions to every situation expose her as an image of goodliness, with little depth of character. In fact Snow White is considered by some to be one of the least active and dynamic of Disney's classic era characters (Davis, 2006). This perhaps makes her the true prototype of Disney heroes and heroines.

After Snow White flees the Huntsman's warning she runs through the forest and is confronted at every turn by trees and animals, which appear to her as frightening apparitions of monsters and demons. Under the stress of her flight from harm she collapses in tears; she is quickly surrounded by woodland creatures that approach and warm to her. She abruptly changes from panic to ambivalence: "Don't run away, I won't hurt you," she says calmly to the animals, and asks the little birds what they do when things goes wrong. Apparently they sing. She starts singing with the birds and all traumas are forgotten. It is quite a dramatic change of pace in the film's progression: the animals are used to calm the anxiety that moments of horror had briefly created.

This image of a bestial messiah or beast-master is a recurring theme in Disney films. This image echoes Sachs' (1933) description of the Ptolemaic conception of man as the centre of all nature. In this scenario the subject becomes a natural ideal, adored by the bestial mass which confirms his or her egocentric idealisation. This scene confirms Snow White as a similar idealisation, an ego ideal to be adored. This adoration of others in the diegetic space can be referred to as an a*doring mass*.

The animals take Snow White to a small house. As she enters she remarks, "Seven untidy little children must live here…maybe they have no mother!" This sets up the maternal role that she will take on for the dwarves who live there. Meanwhile, the dwarves are away, working in a mine. Diamonds are everywhere, as are other valuable gems, just waiting to be plucked. The seven dwarves appear as seven paupers living in squalor. Yet they work all day mining precious gems and then hoarding them together in a safe. They consume raw wealth which they do not even need to exchange for goods and services: the consumption by itself seems to satisfy their lives' demands. They are beings of pure consumption and demand, charmingly gorging themselves on the raw objects of commodity.

Come 5pm, they start a different song: "Hi ho, hi ho, its home from work we go". Meanwhile, Snow White has fallen asleep on a few of their beds tucked together, emphasising her size compared to the dwarves. The dwarves arrive home and think someone has burgled their house, a monster or ghost. They sneak up to her bed and cast threatening shadows across her body with their weapons raised, much as the Huntsman did. This is the second scene in which we see the threat of violence encroaching on Snow White, the surrogate of the viewer's ideal ego. The solidity offered by her homuncule image is momentarily threatened with destructive fragmentation: being attacked. The threat of violence has an interesting effect within the filmic space. The encroaching shadow of the dwarves' weapons and the Huntsman's dagger threatens the solidity of the homunculus. This provokes anxiety, as it threatens a phallic attack on the solidity and invulnerability of this idealised form; penetrating an already phallicised and fetishistic form. The encroachment of castration anxiety, threatened by a phallically empowered, dark mass in a very controlled and pristine space, keeps the viewer captivated. The viewer is engaged by the need to maintain this solid and whole form, the threat to this image instigates a lack in a form that should remain seamless. As discussed later, this threat of disrupting the homuncule solidity plays on an unquiet pleasure in violence inherent in the subject's relation to an ideal.

When the dwarves pull back the covers they are in awe of her beauty. Snow White is not at all perturbed by waking up surrounded by little men and proceeds to woo them with her cooking. Like a mother, she checks their hands to see if they have washed and refuses to let them eat until they do what she has commanded. It is a surreal reversal, with the child-like Snow White taking a maternal position. It is not unlike watching a young child mothering her dolls.

There are seven dwarves, all of whom are named by their temperament: Sleepy, Dopey, Grumpy, Bashful, Sneezy, Happy and Doc. Although Doc is not a description of temperament, the name implies authority: Doc is the leader of the group. This is in keeping with what we have already discussed in terms of the compartmentalisation of character traits. Bettelheim (1976) comments that in giving the dwarves different personalities Disney robs them of their unconscious value. In Bettelheim's analysis of the original fairy-tale, the dwarves represent a pre-individualised state of being, i.e. the connection with the Other, that Snow White must transcend. He argues that the dwarves as a unit in themselves represent an early phallic state of being. The troop of dwarves are all 'pure' characters, in that their characteristics have been so delimited that they are completely predictable. This contrasts to the Huntsman who holds sufficient ambiguity of character to produce genuine anxiety. We know that the dwarves will not attack Snow White on purpose; this is less clear for the Huntsman. The dwarves are such innocuous characters in their singularity it becomes abundantly clear that they are merely an extension of Snow White herself. She is depicted as implicitly connected with the dwarves who together form the binary opposition to the Queen.

Although the dwarves' admiration of Snow White is based on her beauty there is no sense that she represents their love interest, but rather an object of adoration and worship. Dopey is perhaps the rawest character of the dwarves. He is depicted as an impulsive child, being the only dwarf who lacks a beard and does not speak. His lack of speech puts him in the role of a creature of pure *demand*. He perpetually harasses Snow White for kisses, seeking bodily gratification. Demand is presented as innocent and innocuous; Dopey initiates a relation for the viewer in Snow White's initial misrecognition of the dwarves as children. They are non-genital and sexually impotent; in this light un-socialised demand for affection and gratification appears to the viewer as being acceptable.

Contrasting with the unitary nature of Snow White and her dwarves, the Queen now stands alone and holds in her hands a box. She shows it to the mirror and asks it again, "Who is the fairest one of all". Despite the fact that the heart in the box is unseen, the image still disturbs. It is an element of gore that is present by suggestion but absent from the frame.

When the mirror informs the Queen that Snow White is still alive, she plots to kill her once and for all. She creates a spell that will transform her own appearance and in an intensely psychedelic sequence she completes her transformation. She is now an ugly woman, with even greener eyes and a large crooked nose. All malevolent characters in the Disney classic period have green eyes, perhaps to suggest envy; they are all green-eyed monsters, jealous of the homunculus, just like the evil tree in *Flowers and Trees* (1931), the first green-eyed Disney monster. Jealousy is a useful trope in constructing evil characters as its purpose is two-fold. First, it positions the jealous character as a rival and opponent to the hero/heroine. Second, it reaffirms the importance and idealisation of the hero/heroine. The main character is so good that even the bad character envies them. Thus the motivation of jealousy does not denigrate the image of the hero.

The Queen creates a second potion that poisons an apple. Consuming the poison will send Snow White into a sleeping death. The victim of the sleeping death can only be revived by love's first kiss, but the Queen hopes Snow White will be buried alive. Back at the little house Snow White is sending the dwarves off to work, kissing them as they leave. Dopey wants a kiss on the lips and keeps coming back for

Hidden dismemberment and the evil queen
(Image by Rupert Norfolk)

more; again he is an image of sexual precociousness and demand. We even see Grumpy pruning himself for her to kiss. He grumpily storms away but still manages to look heart-warmed – not even he can resist her charms. Snow White is alone when the disguised Queen comes to the house. She corners Snow White and makes her eat the poisoned apple. Although we do not see Snow White 'die', we do see her hand going limp and dropping the apple. As the Queen leaves the house she is chased by the dwarves. She tries to set a boulder loose to crush her pursuers but a lightning strike interdicts, knocking her off a conveniently placed cliff, falling to her death. Vultures descend from their perch as grim symbols of mortality and decay. In this scene the potent ugliness of the Queen's extraneous desire is neatly removed from the diegetic space, though her momentary presence has now created a tangible threat to the heroine, who lies in a state of waking death.

In the last scene the dwarves surround Snow White's bed sobbing; the animals watch motionless as part of the scenery. The dwarves place her in a glass coffin and keep a vigil. The Prince enters the scene; he leans down to kiss Snow White's inanimate form and she magically awakens. Nothing else is said as Snow White and the Prince ride off into the sunset. The film cuts to a shot of the live-action story book which reads, "and they lived happily ever after". Thus all ends are tied up and the story finishes neatly...

Disney Character Tropes

In an interview about the characters in his films, Walt Disney stated that, "We don't want them to be just shadows, for merely as moving figures they would provide no emotional response from the public. Nor do we want them to parallel or assume the aspects of human beings or human actions. We invest them with life by endowing them with human weaknesses which we exaggerate in a humorous way. Rather than a caricature of individuals, our work is a caricature of life" (cited in Schickel, 1968, p174). It is a curious statement considering the lack of parody or satire involved in the Disney caricature. If the films caricature singular aspects of human beings, what is it that makes Disney so emotionally engaging and enjoyable for the viewer? It is rather the interactions of these different characters (or caricatures) that give the films their emotional appeal.

Rather than discussing the characters in terms of who they are in the plot, i.e. their diegetic roles, it is more fruitful to discuss them as character tropes, that act as psychical representatives within the *mise-en-scène* of desire. Berland (1982) suggests that the Disney characters embody universal aspects of the human personality, the thus viewer projects and identifies with the characters within the narrative and the narrative influences the relation between these projections. The content and these pre-existing psychical elements combine within the process of viewer identification, an identification that is "multiple and fractured, a sense of seeing the constituent parts of the spectator's own psyche paraded before her or him" (Ellis, 1982, p43). Likewise Warner (1995) criticises the assumption of psychoanalytic interpretations of fairy-tales that the reader identifies with the main protagonist, whereas identification is typically fractured and transitional between characters. John Ellis (1982) describes two kinds of identification that operate within the cinematic apparatus: the first of these is an identification that concerns itself with the subject's fantasies and places the subject in fantasmatic scenarios. The other form of identification is predicated on narcissism. This narcissistic identification involves an image that the subject takes as an extension of the ego. This ego is validated and perceived by an other, an other that is internal to the film's diegetic world. This image reflects on the aspirations and the ideals that the viewer takes as reflections of the self. The forms on screen thus have an intrinsic aesthetic appeal based on this appearance and character. While they might seem to be representative of fragmented aspects of the psyche, they are totalities in themselves. The cartoon itself functions as an idealised specular image for the subject, of which the ideal ego of the homunculus is but one part. This fragmentary idealisation can be found in images of the hero, heroine, villain, accomplices, etc., and can oscillate between active and passive positions within the film. Thus the spectator does not simply identify with the protagonist, but rather with multiple images on the screen, their imagined presence and their complex interactions supply the fantasmatic gratification that operates in tandem.

The description of the characters offered up here shall refer to the viewer's projections and identifications within the film. Where the present discussion on Disney diverges sharply from what Ellis discusses in terms of other mainstream films, is that Ellis points to the regulation of gender roles as being central to the enjoyment of film. He suggests that transgression of the binaries between male and female is essential to the spectator's negotiation of the text. Where Disney in the classic era differs in terms of gender identification, is that the image and state depicted are in many ways pre-gendered and regressive. The images of these early features are only complicated by such questions as phallic femininity or impotent masculinity; rather the child as phallus of the Other is central to Disney narrative progression. The play between the characters as elements of narcissistic identifications enacts a perverse fantasy that is structured by the centrality of the main character and their construction as the phallus of a primordial mother.

The primordial in Lacan is essentially the field of *Das Ding* (the Thing). *Das Ding* is a point of contact with the Real, it is a thing that remains outside of signification (Lacan, 1959). As language puts the Real out of contact for the subject, *Das Ding* is also representative of the object of desire, as the Real becomes the domain which illusively offers the subject fusion with the Other. The Thing is representative of the field of the Other before language is actualised within the Oedipus Complex, by the interruption of the symbolic father, thus forbidding the affective fusion with the Other. This forbiddence subverts the Thing into part-objects. In this function it becomes transparent synonymous with the *Objet Petit a*, which Lacan would later position as the cause of desire.

In *The Ethics of Psychoanalysis* (1959), Lacan describes a "prehistoric" and "unforgettable" (Lacan, 1959, p67) Other that represents the entirety of what *Das Ding* refers to. The pleasure principle is erected as a boundary to the jouissance implicit in contact with the Real, and thus by the same measure it forces the subject to maintain distance from the Thing. This absolute and encompassing mother becomes synonymous with the term *Nebenmensch* in Lacan (1959). Elvio Fachinelli (1997) describes the Thing as an absolute; the original Nebenmensch (the other person/the neighbour) that the subject seeks to return to. The expression of this is the sense of nostalgia that Lacan refers to in *Family Complexes* (1938). The primordial mother Fachinelli characterises is a central void and it is the attempt to cover the void that produces desire.

Returning to the discussion of Snow White, it is thus possible to categorise the character tropes the viewer is presented with in Disney features and conceptualise how these characters operate in terms of viewer regression and the primordial. These tropes can be described as the following:

- The *Homunculus* is the central character of the Disney film. This character tends to be the least developed and simplest, yet represents both the ideal ego and ego ideal. As a fetish object it is a stand-in for the phallus: "as a total object it is not supplied with libidinal energy of a living, creative sort, but with emptiness, irreality, non-being." (Dadoun, 1989, p43) The homunculus tends to display very little emotion; it is an empty shell that appears solid from the outside. If its contents were full of something (for example, conflicting emotions) the illusion of solidity would be challenged as its partiality would undermine its status as the stand-in for the *phallus*. The homunculus acts as a fetish for the viewer; it is thus a substitute for having the phallus (in that it creates the illusion of the possibility of *being* the phallus for the Other). It covers ambiguity by appearing as something true and certain. Were Snow White a figure in the Real, she would act as a perverse accomplice to the fetishist; her passivity would allow the pervert to impose their fantasy into a sexual dynamic. She is not Real as such, she is a two-dimensional soulless thing. She can be better described as the pervert's fetish, as that which staves off anxiety and enables gratification. Mickey Mouse is emblematic of the first Disney homunculus and as we shall see the role is oft repeated throughout Disney's features and shorts. The homunculus' desire dictates the world of the film; although this desire is challenged, it will always win over all extraneous desires presented.

  Mulvey (1975) comments that for cinema to be satisfying it must allow for an identification mediated by the male gaze. This becomes dependent on the fascination of misrecognition with an image that becomes crucial during the mirror stage. This misrecognition creates a tension between viewer and the image. The image has the outer appearance of an ideal ego but is internalised as an ego ideal: the internal ideal the subject aspires to (Lacan, 1954b). Thus the image itself is disquieting as it offers two unreachable ideals, the solidity of being and an idealised ego.

- The *Malevolence* tends to be irreducible to a single character but is rather a theme that ties different characters together. The Queen is the main symbol of malevolence in *Snow White* yet her agents appear in the guise of the Huntsman (if only momentarily) and the frightening trees. The malevolent characters are distinct from other characters in that their desire does not coincide with that of the homunculus. They are the expression of an extraneous desire to that of the main character. The malevolence is always depicted as an intruder or competitor, that imposes their ugliness onto the pristine and simple Disney world. The intruder is always necessary in Disney films as it creates a sense of drama and action, whether it be the old tree in *Flowers and Trees* (1932), the hunters in *Bambi* (1942), or the lengthy list of evil stepmothers. In his discussion of Lacan's paper *The Freudian Thing* (Lacan, 1955), Jacques-Alain Miller (2011) describes Lacan's figuring of Diana in Ovid's *Metamorphosis* as a malevolent entity. Diana refuses marriage: she wishes to maintain the Other in a state of otherness and therefore separation. It is for this reason that Lacan positions her in the place of Truth, as the truth is other to the subject's experience. It is perhaps this truth that positions her in a state of malevolence, as she embodies the subject's separation from the Other. The same can be said for the apparitions of extraneous desire in Disney, as they seek to keep the child-like homunculus separate from the Other.

- The *Demanding* character as a trope is not always immediately obvious in Disney films, yet regularly occurs. The demanding characters tend to be depicted as cute and innocent. The demand is always for over-indulged gratification, a cartoon depiction of jouissance. The innocent depiction of the character tends to soften their image as precocious and transgressive. They appear in the Disney film as the eternal child who does not need to vocalise what they demand. Demand is a common term in Lacan but it does not hold the imperative connotations of the English. Lacan situates demand between need and desire: it is the vocalisation of need, emblematic in the child's cries that enunciate its need for sustenance from the mother. As the child equates the reply to this demand with love, what is ultimately demanded is love itself: the end to subjective separation (Lacan, 1958b). The creatures of demand in Disney are raw demand embodied and sanitised for the viewer. They are usually outside and opposed to the register of desire; they are the crying child without the unpleasant noise. Dopey is the first apparition of the demanding that has been examined but perhaps the best example is the Disneyified image of Bacchus in *Fantasia* (1940). Bacchus appears as a short fat smiling man, gorging himself happily on gratification. This idealised image of gratification is a currency within the Disney realm. This gratification is a false depiction of the actuality of jouissance, which is diametrically opposed to pleasure and is painful (Lacan, 1966). As such the demanding character is central to the sexual propaganda inherent in the Disney form. The purpose of the demanding character within this space is to make the viewer comfortable with the unrelenting consumption of fantasy gratification. It makes the image of he-who-enjoys-too-much satisfying and sanitised, and open to viewer identification. The demanding creates a Disneyified image of what lies beyond the pleasure principle.

- The *Adoring Mass* is the malleable omnipresence that responds to the desire of the homunculus. The adoring mass is usually made up of animals that coddle and dote upon the lead character. They show no extraneous desire to that of the main character. They are not so much other characters as 'others', they are an extension of one. This is much like the collective of the animals in *Snow White* that praise her with messianic reverence. There are similar scenes in *Bambi*, in which all the animals eulogize the new-born faun as the Young Prince, or Pinocchio's family and fairy godmother, who love and praise him no matter what he does. The Adoring Mass takes on connotations of maternity: it is the phallic or primordial mother, un-sepa-rated from the child and outside the regulation of paternity. It presents the comfortable but perverse image that despite the trials and tribulations the homunculus goes through, it shall arrive back in the loving care of the adoring and absorbing Other.

- The *Desired* is the love interest. They are the sought-after piece of the puzzle that completes the narrative. There is never any lust or unrequited love in Disney films; the Desired is merely collected as the logical conclusion to the film. The Desired never desires what does not coincide with the primary desire of the homunculus. They often appear for the first time in a mirror, as in the case of *Snow White* and *Bambi*. In both cases the image of the desired appears as if by magic beside the main character. It creates a moment where the viewer is led to believe that a fantasy has come into reality and it has, at least at the level of the film's diegesis. This image in the mirror also bears significance in the creation of an ideal ego: the image of unity that the subject hopes to achieve in viewing its own image in Lacan's mirror stage (Lacan, 1954b). The couple in the mirror form a complete image, in which the subject's on-screen stand-in achieves unity with the Other.

To summarise the plot of *Snow White* with the terminology outlined above, it can be said that it is the homunculus that affords the viewer space within which to project themselves into the story. The homunculus is gratifying in itself due to its fetishistic nature; as a fetish it carries the illusory capacity to close this gap and annex lack. Its intrinsic appeal is validated and cathected by the adoring mass of the cartoon world: both the animals and dwarves. The cute unbridled demand of Dopey provides comic relief but also the value-check that transgressive indulgence will not be chastised. Despite the homunculus' privileged nature it is still an image that creates tension between subject and ideal. As will be discussed in the section on *Bambi*, the homuncule body is manipulated to play on and release this tension. The sex of the homuncule body is in many ways irrelevant as the position this body represents in terms of regression is similarly without gender.

The malevolent force of the story is the evil jealous Queen. Her desire is to be more beautiful than the main character. Her desire thus provides conflict; she becomes an opponent within the filmic space. By the same token, her envy validates the aesthetic value of the homunculus as ideal. She is the intruder into the main character's relation to her maternal adoring mass. The Huntsman threatens Snow White and thus threatens the viewer with castration, but is swayed by the homunculoid image and cannot kill her, once again validating her appeal. Likewise the desired Prince cannot but love her, even though he knows nothing about her! He is simply an extension of the film's singular desire and purpose, proof that the homunculus' every wish will come true. The Prince, dwarves and adoring animals all form the omnipresent Other of the film from which Snow White is ultimately inseparable, although the malevolent forces attempt to separate her from the film's space, i.e. in attempting her fake death. The film ends when malevolence is expelled from the diegetic space and the Other is joined with the homunculus, thus covering up lack and the threat of castration before setting an image of wholeness and completion.

What is ultimately outlined here is a scenario structured by disavowal. There is an image presented of a child connected to the Other who can overcome the interference that threatens to separate that connection. The symbolic father (who represents the Law and threat of castration) is present at the start of the film: he appears in the guise of a malevolent intruder. This malevolence tries to separate the child by institution of its will and fails. The malevolence exposes a lack by threatening castration but fails to institute this lack and separation by imposition of Law, as the symbolic father is depicted as an extraneous and malevolent presence. In this scenario the Law of the father is ridiculed and satirised in favour of a law of jouissance: the law that drives the subject to an image of unity and subjective obliteration that is implicit in fantasmatic illusions of love.

The story complies to mainstream cultural expectations but this is done in such a simplified fashion as to engage an audience beyond the symbolic stricture of the paternal order, at the level of a fantasy of primordial fusion.

This kind of story-telling appeals to the simplest forms of enjoyment that are perverse in nature and reliant on an idealised conception of jouissance. Bettelheim (1976) comments that pre-Oedipal stages of development are rarely dealt with in fairy-tales. Disney fairy-tales could be considered unique in that regard as they focus on a scenario of connection to the Other that is specifically pre-Oedipal. They do not try to resolve the Oedipus complex in a functional capacity, but rather paint an appealing and nostalgic picture of a primordial relation to maternity. Mulvey (1975) discusses nostalgia as having little to do with desire for a historic past, but rather it is always for a state of prior narcissism. This nostalgic narcissism is a form of resistance to social responsibilities. Mulvey uses the example of Hollywood Westerns to emphasise the dynamic between nostalgic narcissism and the law implicit in the symbolic. This tension is represented by the threat to the hero posed by social integration and marriage to a woman, both of which consign the state of secondary narcissism to the past and establish the protagonist as castrated subject. It is this dynamic that the homunculus successfully transcends during the course of the Disney film: for Snow White her imagined marriage to the Prince is symbolically invalidated by the hollow nature of his appearance as an extension of her desire. He is merely an object and tool for the gratification of the un-castrated child.

Chapter 6

The Industrial Process and the Father

A Lexicon of Regression

*S*now *White and the Seven Dwarfs* was a costly venture for Walt's company. Initially the proposed cost of production had been $150,000, but by the time work had finished it had cost Disney $1.5 million and was threatening to bankrupt the studio. From the time of its release it became immediately obvious that the feature-length cartoon was going to be a success. *Snow White* grossed $8.5 million and delivered Disney an Academy Award in 1939. With the production of cartoon shorts Disney began to cover its costs. The introduction of a successful feature-length animated film started to make sizeable profits and the studio was able to move to a new location in Burbank, California. The new location was a sterile industrial environment, which reportedly altered the company's earlier 'company as family' dynamic. Animators were in a separate building to story-men, editors and painters. This separation was made to streamline the production process, but invariably led to the production house becoming a more factory-like environment. This new production setting created an efficient animation machine, not just in terms of streamlining production, but for streamlining the creation of mass consumable fantasy. With the new bureaucratic organisation in place Walt was able to manage the complex process of animation production in a more precise fashion. He was able to make editorial decisions that would be carried out by the relevant people without the negotiation that a smaller scale work-place had involved (Short-sleeve, 2001).

As the studio grew and the process of making the cartoons became progressively industrialised, the Disney animators developed their own lexicon to describe and guide their work. This lexicon allowed the animators to communicate the principles of animation aesthetics: the dimensions in which the image could be manipulated. These principles were collected and put together as teaching aids for new animators. They are concisely described and listed in Thomas and Johnston's text *Disney Animation: The Illusion of Life* (1984), and are as follows:

1. Squash and Stretch

2. Anticipation

3. Staging

4. Straight Ahead Action and Pose to Pose

5. Follow Through and Overlapping Action

6. Slow In and Slow Out

7. Arcs

8. Secondary Action

9. Timing

10. Exaggeration

11. Solid Drawing

12. Appeal

Squash and Stretch refers to the ability of animators to make an object seem flesh and blood rather than solid and motionless. When an organic object moves, parts of it stretch and squash, such as the muscles in the arm. When the arm is extended, one muscle contracts and squashes, the other stretches. Early animations such as Oswald or the 1920s Mickey Mouse, showed very little mobility in movement, and appeared rigid and wooden. Later cartoons would show the entire character's body moving with an action. The end result is much more mobile; the character appears to be soft, pliable and elastic. With the awareness of this principle came a competition among animators to create progressively more mobile characters. The end result is the unreal cartoon figure being made up of something reminiscent of the human body but super-human in respect to its elasticity. Each character in Disney would have calculated amounts of stretch and squash, such as those that bore closer resemblance to human beings (Snow White and the Huntsman) and others that were characteristically rigid, such as the wooden Pinocchio. In general this principle taught animators that these exaggerations could provoke *stronger reactions* from the viewer. It is this aspect that can be shown to underlie most of these principles.

Anticipation is likewise another tactic involved in over-emphasising aspects of the image. This process relies on providing a graphic cue with which to anticipate a following action. Thus a cartoon character will visually make an intention obvious before carrying through to an action. This takes pressure away from the viewer to make an inference between one scene and another. Montage is almost entirely absent in Disney films, rather the studio's animation favours the more invisible style of editing which these anticipation shots lend themselves to. This minimises the cognitive work needed on the part of the viewer. This process is what Disney animators refer to as *Staging*: making ideas as obvious as possible for the viewer. This is evident in the vast majority of Disney animations, whether in the over-use of signifying props or the caricaturing of various characters, emotions and actions. As Thomas and Johnston say, "There is no attempt at realism, but considerable carica-ture of the attitudes" (Thomas and Johnston, 1984, p16). Caricature is essentially a process that streamlines emotional responses and forces a regression in the viewer to simpler emotional reactions. Scott McCloud (1993) describes the cartoon character as an "amplification through simpli-fication" (McCloud, 1993, p30); a focus on particular details to emphasise and amplify their meaning. This is the essence of the universality of the cartoon image: in its essential caricature it is both regressive and mass-ap-pealing. McCloud uses the example of the simplification of the human face: by distilling the face into key features it is possible to create the effect of an emotional heuristic. Thus a more simple cartoon form is capable of produc-ing a clearer and stronger emotional response.

While some of the other elements cited in Thomas and Johnston are important to the process of animation itself, they do not necessitate a mention here. The universal quality of all these constructive elements is an emphasis on maximising "clarity, appeal and communication" (Thomas and Johnston, 1984, p25). These are again the main constituents of the Disney phenomenon: creating a strong, simple and comprehensible message to excite and entice a mass audience. This is clearest in the principles of *Exaggeration* and *Appeal*. The idea of 'exaggeration' in Disney animation came from a misunderstanding arising from Walt's call for more 'realism' from his artists. What the artists discovered is that the 'realism' Walt was seeking was nothing of the kind but in fact a particular form of emotional caricature; what Thompson and Johnston (1984) refer to as a *caricature of realism* as opposed to a caricature of reality. The difference is subtle but important: a caricature of reality exaggerates the thing in the Real, whereas the caricature of realism exaggerates the process of representation itself. Thus the latter provides an emotionally and ideologically loaded image one step removed from the Real. Appeal is likewise an attempt to capture the viewer's emotional engagement. Disney animators are taught that no matter what character they draw, whether it is intended to be beautiful, ugly, evil or foreboding, it has to have appeal. Nothing can be truly 'ugly' or unpleasant, each image must be laden with qualities that will captivate the desire of the viewer.

In his discussion of the psychological appeal of art, Ramachandran (2008) discusses the impact of abstract caricatured forms as a biological predisposition in both humans and other animals. He cites experiments by Tinbergen (1954) which involved feeding herring gull chicks with progressively abstracted images of their mother. At first the birds react strongly to a wooden stick with a red dot (mimicking the beak of their mother), though not as strongly as to their own mother's beak. When they are presented with another stick with an abstracted and exaggerated image of the mother's beak, the chicks respond more strongly than to that of their own mother. This feature of cognition is described as *peak shift* as it shifts the peak excitation from the natural mother to the caricature. Ramachandran also notes that caricatures of politicians are often recognised better than photographs of the same person. This quality of the abstract suggests that simplified forms have greater and more profound impact to the viewer. The movement towards the abstract in cartoons is a process that emotionally cathects each character for the viewer; it is also what motivates the animator to take the steps in connecting the images of the cartoon to the unconsciously cathected tropes previously discussed. All of these different elements further illustrate the processes that create what is intrinsically and uniquely Disney. From quite early on in the studio's life, these elements construct a palette of regressively responsive elements. The film-makers thus make a conscious effort at reducing the symbolic processes the viewer must engage with in terms of the narrative, instead emphasising the simple and regressive elements of the *mise-en-scène*. The processes used in the encoding of the film are themselves laden with the same message that permeates all levels of the Disney form: something must be sexually over-simplified to appeal to an infantilised family audience. The tendency towards regression is implicitly transgressive as it represents an escape from and slight on the Laws that govern mediation with the other. The regressive quality of Disney films is apparent in its negotiation of paternity and representation of the father (or fathers). This is perhaps most evident in Disney's next feature: the 1940 adaptation of Carlo Collodi's *Pinocchio* (1882), considered to be the studio's most consistently acclaimed yet terrifying film.

Absent Fathers: Disney and the Real Boy

The original Pinocchio (1882) was written by Carlo Lorenzini under the pen-name Carlo Collodi. The tone of the story is one of disinterest in the miraculous: the surreal happenings within the narrative are construed as unsurprising by the characters within. In the course of the story, Pinocchio runs amok through various adventures, each one ghastly in its own right. He acts in a selfish and impulsive fashion, his misfortunes increase with every chapter until finally he learns the error of his ways and repents to his father. The story's focus is on the collision between the child and the Law as embodied by the father's will.

Pinocchio is born from a talking piece of wood. The wood is fashioned into a puppet by the carpenter Geppetto, who becomes his surrogate father. When Geppetto first attempts to institute the Law, Pinocchio rebels and leaves his father. In the story there are different apparitions of the Law, each of which comes into conflict with Pinocchio's nature. One of the first instances of this is when Pinocchio meets the talking cricket, called Jiminy Cricket in the Disney version. He appears early in the story and says to Pinocchio, "Woe to those boys who revolt against their parents... They will never do any good in this world. And sooner or later they will repent bitterly" (Collodi, 1882, p.21), after which the defiant Pinocchio crushes the cricket, killing him. The different apparitions of the Law represent a super-egoic agency for the reader. As the story progresses the conflict between Pinocchio and the Law becomes ever more severe until Pinocchio finally starts to heed paternal advice, as a result of the guilt he feels for his transgressions and the isolation that results from his choices.

For the majority of the story, Pinocchio seeks "To eat, drink, sleep, and amuse myself, and to lead a vagabond life from morning to night" (Collodi, 1882, p21). With Pinocchio's increasing follies, he begins to learn the error of his ways. The more he acts impulsively and selfishly the more he comes to pain and disappointment. The cricket later appears as a ghostly apparition of guilt, pointing out to Pinocchio that his warning was true. With the pains of his misfortunes also comes the isolation and loneliness of being left outside the social order. In an attempt to assuage his guilt, Pinocchio returns to his father to seek forgiveness, but finds him in a boat, being swept out to sea. It is the guilt from losing his father that pushes Pinocchio to become a good boy. He is helped in this journey by a blue-haired shape-shifting fairy, who represents a maternal force within the story. As his penultimate act of maturity Pinocchio saves his father from the belly of a giant shark. Thus the father is once again erected within the space of the story and Pinocchio is rewarded by being transformed into a real boy. Pinocchio had no direct desire to be a real boy, rather he wanted to be a man one day, to enjoy the adult world. It is the blue fairy who tells him that he must first be a real (i.e. good) boy before he can become a man, this instigating his move beyond the primordial relation to gratification.

The Disney version of Pinocchio may seem to follow a similar narrative path, but the tone and content are radically different. Watts (1997) argues that *Pinocchio* was written with the populist slant that defined many early Disney shorts and features; it is essentially a story of meek and humble beginnings as the staging place for the miraculous. West (2008) sees *Pinocchio* as a tension between Freud's (1920) reality principle and pleasure principle. While the pleasure principle has already been established in Lacanian terms, the reality principle is simply the realisation of limits to pleasure; the child learns that enjoyment is not limitless and they must conform to society's rules. Thus society's rules become internalised to place limits on gratification (what Lacan refers to as the Law that mediates the socio-symbolic realm). West notes that within the translation of *Pinocchio* from Collodi's story to Disney's film, there is a repositioning of the super-egoic agency. In Disney it is embodied in Jiminy Cricket. Collodi, however, positions this agency within Pinocchio. While the puppet receives moralistic advice from a host of supportive characters on his travels, it is his collected knowledge that starts to form this paternal agency *internally*.

The Disney version carries two important themes that are absent in the original: a disavowal of the father in favour of an infantilisation of the subject, and the preservation of the child-image of the homunculus. The film opens with a song, the lyrics to which are: "When you wish upon a star, makes no difference who you are, anything your heart desires will come to you ..." (*Pinocchio*, 1940). This line exemplifies the Disney ideal of consumption and wish fulfilment: that wanting instigates having, and that possession and achievement are rights of the viewer. Once again the film opens to a book, in front of which the viewer is introduced to Jiminy Cricket. It is he from whom the song originates, acting as a gate-keeper to the Disney fairy-tale.

Introduction to the Story Book
(Image by Rupert Norfolk)

"I'll bet you folks don't believe that..." says the cricket, "Let me tell ye what made me change my mind..." He thus introduces the viewer to the story. The book opens and the viewer is brought into the cartoon world, through multi-plane layers.

The multi-plane camera was yet another innovation of the Disney studio. The camera photographed animation cells in layers placed at different levels. These different layers could be moved at different speeds, thus producing an effect similar to three-dimensionality. It is possible to produce an effect of the camera passing different layers that expand and pass out of focus (De Roos, 1994). Multi-plane shots were extremely expensive and time-consuming for the studio. As such, they were used strategically as a transition between the outside world and the inner diegetic sanctum of the filmic space. In *Pinocchio* these images draw the viewer into a night-time townscape.

The camera proceeds through the town until it appears to have landed on the ground and then starts hopping towards the warm light of a house. The frame is a first-person-perspective from Jiminy's point of view. The viewer thus goes through steps: firstly introduced to the story, talked to directly by the story teller, secondly brought into the story, through the shifting of *mise-en-scène* (from live-action to multi-plane animated to 2D animated), and thirdly positioned directly from the point of view of the narrator. The viewer is brought into Jiminy's line of sight and literally his frame of mind. Jiminy thus positions himself in a super-egoic position for the viewer: an integral aspect of how the viewer engages within the space of *Pinocchio*. The super-ego is the internalisation and interpretation of Law within the subject's psyche (Freud, 1923). In terms of film and the viewer's engagement, the filmic super-ego regulates the diegetic law of the film.

The early scenes in Pinocchio take place inside Geppeto's house and workshop. It is a maternal space and is presented as warm and creative; the walls hold toys and cuckoo clocks. It represents the kernel of the fantasy that the film is trying to create: a space where the Other resides, the archetypical womb which contains the pre-formed, pre-symbolic child. The workshop is the space of the Primordial Mother; a space that permits the child to escape from the paternal symbolic (Kaplan, 1990). Among the items in the room is an unfinished puppet, fully constructed and painted except for a mouth. This immediately becomes the focus of Jiminy and in turn the viewer. Geppetto enters into the workshop humming a song, followed by his cat Felix. He sets to work finishing the puppet, painting its mouth and giving it the name Pinocchio. Geppetto provides a symbolic function, giving the name to the focus of the gaze; we are oriented in the direction of the thing that he has produced and named. Geppetto is at first established as a symbolic father, the father who must separate mother and child and institute language (Lacan, 1957a). In the same moment that Geppetto names the marionette, he paints a mouth and therefore the potential for speech. The symbolic father holds the paternal function of instituting signification and with it desire, which must proceed outside the mother/child union. But to accomplish this, the paternal function must also impose the Law (Lacan, 1966).

In Birger's (1984) discussion of the unpublished notes of Géza Róheim, he describes a splitting of the paternal-function in *Pinocchio* (1942). Róheim suggests that Geppetto is positioned as an absolute, positive character while the negative aspects of the paternal are projected onto the threatening figures of Stromboli, the Coachman and Monstro the Whale. Pinocchio's negotiation of these poles represents the id achieving the restraint of the super-ego, embodied in the voice of Jiminy Cricket. While the concept of splitting of the paternal function is utilised here, the focus shall be on what functions are attributed to which father. The maternalisation of Geppetto is likewise of great import in Disney's radical rewriting of the original fairy-tale.

Geppetto plays with the lifeless Pinocchio, pulling his strings and making him dance. Even at this early juncture, before Pinocchio's first transformation, we see that he is literally tied to Geppetto. Geppetto also appears as a clingy and maternal entity that tries to reunite with Pinocchio throughout the story. In the course of the narrative his function transforms from that of a paternal (provider of name and speech) to a maternal figure. Although his actions of naming and providing speech may represent the paternal function, these acts are depicted as a passive and creative function. Geppetto is impotent with regards to the institution of the Law. He is the creator who maternally loves Pinocchio unconditionally, yet he is also phallic in his connection to the order of names and his tools with which he constructs and connects himself to the puppet. In fact, it is Geppetto in the Disney version that wishes for Pinocchio to become a real boy. The maternal capacity of Geppetto creates the position of the most literal homunculus: Pinocchio, the little man who is constructed for the purpose of the viewers' gratification being erected in the cartoon world. The other maternal entity that makes its appearance is the Blue Fairy. The fairy is reminiscent of the form of Snow White. She is a real photographed woman, drawn over and hyper-realised, lending her a more human and sensuous form that is also implicitly uncanny.

Freud (1919) conceptualises the uncanny as a reference to a recurrence of the repressed in aesthetics. It is a class of frightening thing which is not something alien or foreign, but rather something too familiar. It is a thing that is too much present when it should be absent. The ideal place for this disturbing thing is buried in the unconscious, repressed and absent from sight and thought. Thus for Freud the uncanny is something which the subject wishes to be hidden, that has been made visible. Uncanny is also something in the present day that can be seen to reference earlier organisations of psychical structure.

The uncanny can be seen in the pretence to the real in fiction. The author creates a disavowal of reality and promises an opening which conflates fantasy and reality. This allows for the illusion of access to the fantasmatic figurations of the Other, a reference to earlier organisations of sexual development, that which will later be discussed as the *archaic*. This archaic is implicitly anxiety-provoking as it references subjective obliteration through loss of boundary (Dadoun, 1989). This fear of obliteration is the core of the uncanny as an aesthetic choice which positions a Thing where it should not be. In the case of Snow White and the Blue Fairy, it is the animated skin and two-dimensionality that appears inconsistent with the human form that they attempt to simulate. It is this aspect of their form that references the possibility of a loss of boundary between reality and the imaginary, a process that shall later be discussed in terms of the hyper-real.

The Blue Fairy is an uncanny character within *Pinocchio;* the reality of her form sits uncomfortably within the film's diegesis. She is an omnipotent force, who appears at three points during the story, each time to grant a wish.

The first wish granted is Geppetto's desire to have Pinocchio come alive, the second to free Pinocchio from the monstrous Stromboli, and the third when she grants Pinocchio and Geppetto's wish that he become a real boy. Thus her role is at its base to return the child to the Other and in the process grant the child its wishes in order to overcome obstructions to its gratification.

When Pinocchio comes alive the Blue Fairy gives Jiminy the job of being his conscience. To Pinocchio she merely lays out the ground rules: that he must prove himself brave, honest and unselfish in order to become a real boy, and thus grant Geppetto's wish. Thus the desire of the child and the mother are essentially transparent, allowing Pinocchio to remain the phallus for the Other: the point of focus of the adoring mass. This juxtaposition of paternity and maternity represents an antagonism of the symbolic father, the father who enters the Oedipal trajectory to interrupt the union of mother and child. Rather than portraying a mother and father, Disney omits the father by replacing him with the image of a phallic mother, or the primordial mother, the mother who exists before the Oedipal interruption of the father (Dadoun, 1989). The primordial mother is the negative mother, who mirrors the desire of the child, as opposed to what is considered the positive mother who is supports the child's individuation (Kaplan, 1990).

Disney essentially glamorises the negative mother. Geppetto is all-forgiving and understanding; he never chastises Pinocchio, even after he wrongs his father and disobeys his commands through the course of the story. This difference between the maternalised father as primordial mother and a paternal father is one of the essential differences between the Disney film and Collodi's book. Collodi's Geppetto is an aggressive and assertive father, who is able to institute the Law by imparting to Pinocchio what is right and wrong. When Pinocchio steers the wrong course, he loses his father. In disappointing his father and losing him to the monstrous shark, Collodi's Pinocchio comes to understand the error of his ways; he has to learn this lesson as a precondition for becoming a real boy. This is different to Disney's Pinocchio, who is from the start an intrinsically good child. So good that he actually has no desire or will of his own. He simply becomes a vessel for a maternal law, externalised in the form of Jiminy who represents what Zizek (1991) terms the maternal super-ego, and a desire, externalised in the form of Geppetto (Card, 1995). Thus from the outset we are never in any doubt that Pinocchio desires to be a real boy, that everything he (and in turn the viewer) wishes, will come true. Essentially the viewer has already been convinced of a happy ending. Once Pinocchio has come alive the maternal

An awkward moment
(Image by Paul Byrne)

space of the workshop is complete. After an initial shock Geppetto embraces Pinocchio as part of the family. The child is with the Other as an adoring mass. Although Geppetto tries to instil in Pinocchio the law he is too meek and kindly to present any real vision of authority. Jiminy is likewise ineffectual, which is only further emphasised by his tiny stature.

Malevolence and the Castrating Fathers

Pinocchio as a character is perhaps best defined by his impotency while venturing outside the maternal embrace of Geppetto into the 'sleazy' outside world. After he joins a puppet theatre there is a disturbing scene in which Pinocchio awkwardly tries to dance with the little female puppets, all of whom are devoid of life and animated only by their strings. He becomes confused and tangled up in the marionettes. He is depicted, as with most Disney male leads, as awkward, shy and passive. Pinocchio's awkwardness likewise becomes a problem in the scene immediately after Stromboli's threat, in which he is trapped in a cage and pleads with the Blue Fairy to set him free. When the Blue Fairy asks Pinocchio what happened he lies, and with each lie his nose grows longer. The growth of his nose carries obvious phallic connotations and causes him a great deal of embarrassment (Card, 1995).

This equation of lying (i.e. being a bad boy) and the phallic is another slight on the drive to maturity. Being a 'grown-up' (i.e. acting fully feminine or

99

masculine) is often equated with dishonesty in Disney, such as the lying Coachman and Honest John. The Blue Fairy uses her magic to do away with Pinocchio's nose and sets him back on the right path. However this does not represent castration as the Blue Fairy is yet another representation of the phallic mother who is not castrating but rather absorbing. The removal of the phallic token is a reward for the child from the mother. The Blue Fairy removes this token and grants Pinocchio the freedom with which to return to the maternal space of Geppetto's workshop; to no longer have the phallus but rather to be the phallus for the primordial mother.

On the first day of Pinocchio's life he is accosted on his way to school by the cunning fox Honest John and the dopey cat named Gideon. The pair are the first representatives of the malevolent forces at work in the film, and perhaps the least threatening. Honest John is depicted as frivolous and camp, a down-and-out actor looking to take advantage of the innocent Pinocchio. This again mirrors the conservative, working man's ethic of the Disney ideology. Honest John and Gideon trick Pinocchio into following them to join the theatre where they sell him to the evil puppeteer Stromboli. In Collodi's text Pinocchio goes to the theatre of his own accord, selling a school primer (for which his father had traded his own jacket) in order to gain admittance. It is at the theatre where Collodi's Pinocchio makes friends with Mannequin and Punchinello. Thus we see again a divergence between the lead character in the fairy-tale and the Disney homunculus. Both maintain a position of focus for the viewer or reader, yet one is robbed of its essential substance: its aggressive, self-serving and most importantly *childish* values.

Another divergence between fairy-tale and Disney film is the treatment of Stromboli. As mentioned before, Collodi's Pinocchio joins the theatre of his own accord, whereas Disney's Pinocchio is stolen away by the monstrous gypsy Stromboli. Marc Elliot (1993) suggests that Stromboli represents an evil father, the binary opposite to Geppetto. While this much is obvious it is perhaps more accurate to put Stromboli in an altogether different position to Geppetto. He is better understood as the imaginary father (the imago that exists prior to the symbolic father) who is represented as an intruder, interrupting the primordial and incestuous child-Other world (Lacan, 1957b). Stromboli carries more masculinised traits than Geppetto: his voice is booming and gruff, he is dark, hairy and has a great beard. When he is scolding Pinocchio for asking to leave the theatre he hurls an axe, which up until this point he had been brushing against a particularly phallicised finger.

The axe hits a discarded marionette, cutting its chest in two. Images of cutting wood recur in *Pinocchio* and wood is an apt metaphor for the substance of the homuncule body. This is an overt and aggressively made threat of castration from an image of intimidating potency.

The next aggressive and castrating father is the Coachman, who steals Pinocchio away to 'Pleasure Island' with the help of Honest John and Gideon. On Pleasure Island Pinoc-

Threats of Castration …
(Image by Paul Byrne)

chio and his friend, the ruffian Lampwick, enjoy a particular kind of fun. They wander the bars and streets with the other children, playing billiards, smoking, drinking and committing acts of vandalism. They are basically indulging in adult or adolescent kinds of fun, not normally something to associate with being a rebellious child. In the original text the island is called 'Play-land', it is a place where children enjoy games and going on rides. Play-land is the children's paradise because "There's no school ... no masters" (Collodi, 1882, p189). It is a more innocent sort of fun that is devoid of adult influence. The absence of the Law of the father, embodied in school and a master, is essentially what is problematic with Play-land: it is the Law of the father that forces Pinocchio to leave this child-like place. In Disney's Pleasure Island the Law of the father is present, although gloomy in its apparition. The Coachman puts a stop to the children's enjoyment, turning them into donkeys and sending them to work. They are piled into cages by ominous, hairy monsters in his service.

This scene of children turning into donkeys supposedly had its origins in a reoccurring nightmare of Walt's, the theme of which was nearly always some form of punishment (Schickel 1968). The scene does have an aggressive intensity that had not been seen before in Disney, yet the Coachman does the reverse of castration: he casts a spell that makes the children hairy, connoting the growth to a masculine adulthood, and they are forced to work. One of the children cries out, "I want to go home to my mama!" but the Coachman denies the child's return to the mother. Underlying *Pinocchio* is

Messengers of the Castrating Father
(Image by Rupert Norfolk)

an ideological statement on male adulthood and development. To mature is to become gruff, hairy, sleazy and immoral, whereas to stay the child is the idealised happy space of Disney, in which the child is inherently good, moral and deserving. Pinocchio does not survive his brush with adult pleasures unscathed and gains the long hairy ears and tail that greatly distress him. Again like the nose, the elongation of bodily features carries a phallic exaggeration of the homuncule image. The last part of the film can be viewed as a drive to a penultimate solution to these unsettling brushes with gendering.

After Pinocchio returns home from Pleasure Island, he finds an empty house. His father has gone looking for him and in the process has been swallowed by Monstro, a giant whale. When Pinocchio is searching for Monstro under the sea, the name of the whale sends all other fish away in fear. Róheim describes Monstro as the cannibalistic father (Birger, 1984), who overwhelms and absorbs the child (a description that overlaps with the position of the primordial mother) it is perhaps more significant to emphasise the threat of the name he carries. His name carries a foreboding weight, it is the Name of the Father – the signification of the paternal function (Lacan, 1955–1956). The father has directly stolen the mother away from the child, actualising the Oedipal dilemma by swallowing up the primordial mother and denying the child access. Monstro is the climax of malevolence: giant, dark and green-eyed. He thunders angrily through the water and dwarfs all other creatures. He is an overpowering force levelled against the child. In escaping the whale with his father, Pinocchio is left unconscious and inanimate in a puddle. Geppetto returns him home and the maternal space is completed once more, bar that the child has been deprived of its animation and bears the marks of phallic change (the ears and tail). Geppetto cries motherly tears and the Blue Fairy's voice intrudes into the filmic space. The voice recites the conditions of Pinocchio becoming a real boy and he is turned into a perfect child (i.e. a real boy).

Thus his brush with phallic development is warded off and he is granted the gift that closes the narrative: becoming once and for all a pre-gendered child. This aim mirrors that of the Disney viewer's engagement within its regressive apparatus: to become a child once more.

Disney's regressive pre-oedipal utopia is very different from what is seen in Collodi's original text. Collodi's Pinocchio is continually disappointing Geppetto, until all of his follies are paid for by the father, who is swept out to sea and swallowed by a giant shark, a metaphor for Pinocchio's destructive behaviours. The guilt of putting his father through this ordeal finally motivates Pinocchio to take responsibility for his actions. He must take responsibility and thus move in the direction of maturation. The first step of this is to become a boy. Collodi's narrative is fundamentally different in both its tone and structure. The action that brings the book to an end is not becoming a boy, it is becoming a boy with a view to becoming a man. Although a pre-Oedipal regression is completed by the end of the Disney version, this previously enclosed state has been severely threatened during the course of the film. Pinocchio is a perfect expression of the homunculus, the vessel of the viewer's desire to be infantalised in a fantasmatic scenario. Like a child, and in true homuncule fashion, Pinocchio is steered by the drives of other psychical elements: the super-egoic Jiminy cricket, the maternal desire of Geppetto, the aggressive symbolic fathers of Stromboli/the Coachman and the malevolent forces of Honest John, Gideon and the evil black shapes of the Coachman's helpers.

Pinocchio presents an appealing fantasy, a simplified and regressive path to gratification. Pinocchio is free of decision, responsibility and choice. He is merely guided by the waves and the winds. He is never forced to confront his father and accept lack in the form of separation from the Other. During the story he is confronted by separation, but it is only a matter of time before this gap is covered again, until he is returned to an idealised vision of a maternal and womb-like space in Geppetto's home. This space of the safe unified womb is the domain of the primordial mother (Creed, 1993). Instead of the puppet the viewer repositions themselves as a real boy, joined to the Other happily ever after, without the pain and trauma of lasting or scarring loss implicit in the paternal symbolic, the progenitor of desire (Lacan, 1955–1956).

Threat to the Homuncule Body

The momentary invasions of this state of incestuous unity are striking. These are the moments when the solidity and sanctity of the homunculus are challenged: when Geppeto's gun goes off, when Pinocchio's finger catches fire, when he grows the appendages of a donkey, and finally when he drowns. The last three of these images are direct assaults on the body of the homunculus: they represent threats to the fetishistic vessel of the viewer's gaze, the sacred artefact of the cartoon body.

The first moment of threat is perhaps the most interesting. In the scene in which Pinocchio first makes himself known to his adoptive father, Geppetto accidentally fires his gun believing Pinocchio to be a burglar. The blast of the gun puts a hole through a wooden shelf and sets off many of the clocks in the workshop. In this sudden moment of violence there is a quick succession of mechanical clocks each depicting different scenes. The first shows a little man attempting to chop off a turkey's extended neck. The next shows a man firing a pop-gun at a bird in a tree and the last shows a mother spanking a child.

The first image bears a threat of castration: the axe reoccurs throughout Pinocchio as an object that (obviously) chops wood, the substance of Pinocchio's body. It bears the threat, not only of that which can castrate the child, but the viewer's connection to the Other via the homunculus within the space of the film. The next image is a symbol for impotency: the gun fires a cork that bounces back, trivialising the gun itself; the hunter is in effect 'firing blanks'. The last image is one of maternal chastisement, although it should be noted that the mother is pictured as stocky and large, masculinised even. These are three images which reference the ineffectuality of the child's position, which is absent from the overt content of the film. These snaps are tiny vents to the transgressive nature of the subject's precarious engagement with the filmic space, and thus find a way back into the film's diegesis.

Within *Snow White* and *Pinocchio* there is a move towards a more aggressively regressive narrative. This is to say that both films are essentially regressive in their content but *Pinocchio* pushes what is at stake for the viewer even higher. Thus the threat becomes greater to the viewer's gratification as the malevolence becomes more threatening. The maternal space which contains the homunculus is constituted of the adoring mass and the desired, all of which are crystallised in Geppeto's warm maternal workshop. It is the place where the Other and child (screen image/viewer) are one. The threat is represented by the jealous rivals who manipulate and take advantage of the homunculus, separating it from the Other and threatening the sanctity of the homuncle image itself. The body of the homunculus, like the ego's connection to the image on screen, is fragile and tenuous. The more this body's structure is depicted as fragile (i.e. being made of wood) the greater the anxiety when a threat is levelled against its form; the fire and the axe are directly antagonistic to the homuncle body and thus to the viewer's vicarious relation to the Other through this surrogate body. They are grim reminders of castration: castration of the viewer's relation to the homunculus, the first point of connection between the viewer's desire before entering the baited space of the Disney narrative in search of the glamorous primordial Other.

This analysis of *Pinocchio* has introduced the body of the homunculus as the gratifying locus of the viewer's intra-diegetic look. This engagement regulates the viewer within a primordial maternalised space which is threatened externally by the paternal. This paternity is indicative of the symbolic father and as such threatens castration and therefore the child's connection to the primordial mother (Kaplan, 1990). What makes *Pinocchio* more frightening and engaging for the viewer is the threat posed to the homuncle body, the body that represents an ideal ego and ego ideal in its pure, unitary and regressive nature.

Although *Pinocchio* is considered by some to be Disney's masterpiece (Schickel, 1968), it was heavily criticised by the popular press of the time for being too frightening for children. Despite this it became immensely popular and is still considered the apex of the classic Disney era. The next feature, Disney's *Fantasia* (1940), elaborates and sexualises the cartoon body to an extent not previously attempted in Disney features and shorts, and would define the presentation of the cartoon form for decades to come. It does this through mediating paternity and the primordial; by flirting with transgression.

Chapter 7

Fantasia and Eroticism

T his chapter discusses the transgressive quality of Disney imagery as an erotic form. *Fantasia* (1940) is perhaps the most appropriate film to discuss in this context as it is the most reliant on raw imagery and the least reliant on linear narrative within the classic Disney era. Describing *Fantasia* as a classic Disney feature is problematic as it does not follow many of the typical Disney narrative conventions. It is composed of a series of classical music pieces set against animation. There are eight segments, which vary thematically in style and narrative. Each segment is separated by a return to a live-action interlude that introduces the next piece. The live-action segment is of the Philadelphia Symphony Orchestra which was used in the recordings and was conducted by Leopold Stokowski. Providing a commentary and introduction to each piece was classical music critic Deems Taylor, whose role was to introduce an unfamiliar audience to classical music. While the first segment takes the form of abstract colours and images that represent the sounds of the orchestra, the segments that follow have vague mini-narratives. Most feature creatures from myth and legend, others claim to capture the images that might pass through the viewer's mind while listening to an orchestra. The focus for the most part is on these images and the commentary claims to guide the viewer/listener in such a way that will allow them to appreciate classical music. The inference being that the mass-audience requires an authority to teach them how to enjoy high-brow pleasures. This melding of high and low creative traditions (classical music and Hollywood animation) represents an attempt to bring divergent aspects of society together in gratification.

The animation itself begins with a portentous image of the conductor silhouetted against a red screen. He is alone except for shadows of the orchestra, and presents an overbearing image of authority. Stokowski remains faceless for the duration of the film, while Taylor's voice becomes disembodied; we do not see his face after his initial introduction to the film. Essentially Taylor and Stokowski's forms are merged, producing one entity: the paternal agency. The purpose of this agency, as shall be demonstrated further, is to guide the viewer by taking the position of the paternal super-ego, contrary to the *maternal super-ego* so emphasised in Disney narrative-based features. This concept shall be established later; for now it is sufficient to say that the purpose of the paternal super-ego within Disney films is to impose a consciously contrived ideological vision, which is in its nature utopian.

Fantasia's Utopia

Utopia refers to an idealisation, one with its basis in fiction and fantasy. In *Utopia* (1516) Thomas More emphasises the rule of nonsense over the island he calls *Utopia*. He produces the island as an absurdist image of functionality, while illustrating it as essentially a non-entity. His naming of people and places of Utopia is implicit ironic; Hythlodaeus (Nonsenso in Turner's (1965) translation) represents the narrative's mouthpiece. More uses his imagined Utopia as a vessel of secret desires hidden behind a satirical tone that mocked the European society of the time (Turner, 1965). Utopia is essentially a place in which *need* is vanquished. Poverty ceases to exist, plenty invalidates theft and life is organised so as to foreclose complexity. Despite the idealisation of the structure of Utopia, More is keen to highlight that this is not a pleasant place to live. For More, idealisation is done at the expense of smaller pleasures: the people of Utopia must live in a restricted environment in which gratification is limited. Thus *Utopia* is both an idealisation and a warning: that the ideal is itself treacherous, that libidinal investment in an absolutist image complicates gratification.

Fantasia is the only film structured and motivated by adhering to a paternal super-egoic construction of a Disney utopia in the early Disney features (though the utopian vision of child as phallus is consistent throughout). This formula would not be replicated until *The Reluctant Dragon* in 1942, which was made strategically to alter perceptions of the studio's response to the Disney strike action. The utopian vision espoused in *Fantasia* is that of fusion between high and low culture (Watts, 1997). This vision would become actualised in the 1950s, when America's middle class assimilation of the working and upper classes would create a new leisure class, a wide consumer base that Disney and other commercial entities could market to. For now, it is only necessary to view *Fantasia* as a failed attempt to create consumer consensus, as it essentially failed to capture either audience. Steven Watts (1997) retrospectively describes *Fantasia* as a partial success, in that it "walked an aesthetic tightwire between modernism and sentimental realism" (Watts, 1997, p115). The success of Disney's typical naturalism fused with modernist abstraction is debatable. In terms of audience response, *Fantasia* was slated by classical music appreciators for its heavy-handed approach, poor musical choices and mediocre renditions, as well as by a mainstream film audience who found it to be patronising and pretentious. What is curious in Disney's attempted synthesis of high and low aesthetics is the manner in which it moves to an overt sexualisation of imagery. Disney strategically utilises erotic imagery to purvey and package ideological intentions. Eroticism is employed in this case, as Eric Smoodin (1994) suggests, because sex sells. This is exemplified in the opening section of the film, in which Taylor guides the viewer into a fantasmatic staging of music, guided by erotic imagery.

The music in the next segment of *Fantasia* is the Toccata and Fugue by Bach which, we are informed by Taylor, represent music without a definite story, but rather that conveys certain moods. He then informs the viewer that they will be shown what one could imagine seeing when listening to this music. This curious statement along with the presentation of Taylor/Stokowski as master puts the viewer at a disadvantage of knowledge. Within this dynamic the viewer is guided into abstract images of clouds and colours that start to represent the bows of the orchestra. As the segment progresses these shapes become increasingly detached from the images of the actual orchestra. The quality of animation is not consistent through-out *Fantasia* and indeed this first segment is marred by clumsy attempts to depict sound as images. The first half of the segment ends as it begins, with the image of the conductor silhouetted, but now lit from below to emphasise his power.

The next half features glowing fairies playing amongst flowers and spiderwebs at night. The fairies are nude and their bodies are skinny and adolescent. This scene is followed by a procession of dancing mushrooms, which take the form of caricatures of oriental dancers. Next the flowers start to move in sync with the music and finally we are left in a dark underwater scene. From the dark we begin to see a display of exotic Arabian fish, a display that is garish in its clumsy veiled eroticism.

There are many moments in *Fantasia* that are provocative without being directly sexualised. In this scene sexuality and sensuality are refined down to shapes and movements. While they have little resemblance to actual human

109

Flirtatious fish
(Image by Rupert Norfolk)

shapes, the curvature of the fishes' tails refers to the curves of the female form. They have large eyes and lips, as well as long fluttering eyelashes to emphasise their gendering. While they have a few obviously gendered features they manage to convey an overt sensuality. The performance of this dance by fish was a response to a letter of caution from the Hayes office on seeing the manuscript for *Fantasia* which originally sought to use oriental dancers (Cohen, 1997). Indeed several other points were also flagged as potentially problematic, as will be discussed later on.

The movements of the fish were based on a live-action dancer who modelled for the studio, further adding to a hyper-real sexuality disguised in the image of a fish swimming (Schickel, 1968). While they bare resemblance to Cleo, Geppetto's pet fish in *Pinocchio,* the shapes they make are far more conventionally sensual. Their faces themselves are condensed caricatures of femininity, pouting red lips, long eyelashes and eye-shadow. Within the fish sequence there is a great deal more abstract imagery. There are moments where the tails of the fish morph into abstract but suggestive shapes, the most obvious of these being totemic images of the clitoris. The forked ends of the fishes' tails bear the same shape as the painted W symbol on the nape of Geisha, a symbol for the labia.

The image of the fish contrasts against the seemingly innocuous naked fairies. Perhaps it is because the fairies are naked that their sensuality is played down. Their figures are skinny and thin with few accentuated curves. Were it not for their breasts and dotted nipples they would be completely androgynous. The fish however are just a series of animated curves. Eisenstein (1941–1946) discusses the plasticity of cartoon characters as being gratifying in itself, the sensuousness of this quality he also relates to the curvature of some characters. The fish/dancers' faces are exaggeratedly feminine, with oversized pouting red lips, half closed eyes and long fluttery eyelashes. They form emotional caricatures, as discussed by McCloud (1993), simplifications of the human face into simplified constituent signifiers of sensuality. Their tails are perhaps their most suggestive visual element; the swaying of the curved shapes is further sensualised by the soft lines of the drawing and the sultry gaze of the fish. What is presented here are two different approaches to packaging sensuality so as to bypass the censorship of the Hayes office and by proxy its repressive paternal agency. As shown in discussions of *Snow White* and *Pinocchio,* Disney presented two narratives that are ultimately transgressive in terms of paternity, as they emphasise the appeal of the negative mother who mirrors the desire of the child (Kaplan, 1990). The manner in which Disney makes these transgressive narratives permissible to a mainstream audience is by claiming to contextualise them within a 'sex free' medium. By radically opposing its films to the more innocently raunchy cartoons of the Fleischer brothers, Disney was able to transmit films of baser perverse appeal within a family-safe package. *Fantasia* follows a similar practice in these first two segments, by introducing imagery that was transgressive to the paternal institutions of Hollywood and the Hayes office, internalised by the similarly utopian drive of the paternal super-ego.

Disney had to contextualise the imagery in such a way as to make it permissible for a conservative family audience. Thus the erotic Arabian dance is safely contained in the bodies of cartoon fish and the nudity and breasts of the fairies are made safe by their infantile appearance and magical setting. The fourth part of the film is a rendition of Beethoven's *Pastoral Symphony* and is set to a mythological scene at the foot of Mount Olympus. This meandering visual narrative presents yet another scenario of viewer gratification, this time presenting a simple if not uneventful narrative. It contains themes similar to previous Disney shorts and films, yet like other sequences in *Fantasia* it contains more overt sexualised imagery.

Pastoral Symphony

The focus of this segment is on bodily indulgence: it depicts a care-free paradise of blossoming sexuality. This space resembles a Garden of Eden, populated by mythical creatures. The sequence starts with young fauns and unicorns at play. The scene is followed by families of winged horses which

111

offer the viewer little else than a postcard image of the Disney family unit, with the distant father, caring mother and attached children. The familial procession ends as a flower touches water and flows down a stream to gushing waterfalls: an image of blossoming sexuality. Next is a very different scene, which seems far less family-oriented than any Disney material to this point. There are a group of nude female centaurs bathing under the waterfall being tended to by cupids. One of the female centaurs emerges from the water and shakes herself dry. Her appearance is that of a white American adolescent; she is close in her curvature to Snow White and the Blue Fairy. She appears modelled on a live-action girl but is subtly exaggerated in her curves and far more animated. This was another part of the film that elicited concern from the Hayes office, who stressed that the animators must refrain presenting the centaurs breast in too "realistic" a fashion (Cohen, 1997, p33).

Although from her hips down she has a horse's body, her buttocks are exaggeratedly human-like; it is a strangely hyper-real quality in a creature that is essentially half animal. While she and the other centaurs are naked they have no nipples. While this has been done to limit the overt sexuality of the female centaurs, they still bashfully attempt to cover their breasts, further eroticising and objectifying them to service a male gaze. The culminating effect emphasises their erotic qualities, to an extent that would seem to transgress the extra-diegetic paternal authority of the Hayes code. The female centaurs watch as a group of male centaurs come their way, sounding a horn as if back from a hunt. The males are caricatures of masculinity: broad shoulders, big arms and handsome smiles. The females begin to make themselves more attractive for the males with the help of the cupids. They don hats, make-up and adorn themselves with flowers. All of the centaurs are in coloured pairs, the gold male finds the gold female, the blue male finds the blue female and so on. This colour matching further streamlines the pairing off for the viewer, simplifying the sexual dynamics between the centaur couples. There can be only one perfect partner for each of the females. What this creates is an eroticised space that is confined, simplistic and sanitised. This marked an aesthetic evolution of the Disney formula, one that would define the later Disney, from the 1950s through to modern day. The forms of Arial and the Prince in *The Little Mermaid* (1989), made nearly 50 years later, are strikingly similar to the male and female centaurs. It is provocative to consider the essay by Edward Colless (Colless, 2007) which relates the image of Arial to the sexually simplified form of Pamela

Anderson from Baywatch, which again speaks to the continuity between images of the body in animation and 'live' action.

The last to pair up are the blue centaur couple, the cupids lead them away to a secluded spot and then draw the curtains on the viewer, leaving one last cupid to fly over and peer voyeuristically through the curtains. While he watches the inferred interactions of the centaurs his buttocks moon the audience, blush, and turn into a heart. After this awkward display there is a new addition to this highly sexualised scene. Bacchus, the god of wine, harvest and indulgence, enters atop a unicorn-donkey while being fanned by a pair of African female centaurs.

The African centaurs are a vulgar caricature of racial difference. Instead of a horse's body they have a zebra's, implying that they are an altogether different species from the other centaurs. Bacchus himself is a central figure of the Disneyified fantasy, he sits on his throne, his form is squashed, fat and red cheeked. He wears a red cloak and white garments that resemble a nappy more than robes. He appears as a drunk amorous baby; he goes red in the face at the sight of the female centaurs and chases them for a kiss. He is an image of the demanding, the drive for gratification without the rigours of social interaction. He resembles Dopey: hairless and of course silent and pre-lingual. It is perhaps better to describe this segment as the *mise-en-scène* of demand: the scene that has been set for the viewer is one of bountiful gratification, indulgence and of the drive to see. This is presented in a fashion that is unrepentantly transgressive and may not have differentiated it from the more direct sexuality of the Fleischer brothers, were it not for the interruption of this scene before a climax can be reached. The mirth of the scene is interrupted by Zeus, who throws down wind, rain and lightning.

If generous curves in abstraction are able to convey sensuality, then the jagged angles of the lightning bolt most definitely represent and convey aggressivity. In his comprehensive discussion of comic art, Scott McCloud (1993) observes that sharp and angular lines convey disturbance, whereas open and curved lines convey better feelings. In terms of abstraction, curves can be seen to reference the maternal form, such as the Venus of Willendorf (Spivey, 2006). It could be that this curvy caricature of maternity is gratifying due to the relation to the Other as it appears through the maternal. Perhaps it is then possible that the jagged lines of the lightning are disruptive to this quality in aesthetics. The severe angles are also reminiscent of the shaggy, hairy monsters and the big bad wolf. The sharp angles of the fur disrupt the character composition, hence differentiating them from the smoother, curvier characters.

Zeus chases the little Bacchus with lightning bolts and wind. But the storm finally ends with the goddess Iris drawing a rainbow over the land, after which Zeus goes to sleep. Bacchus and the centaurs emerge from their hiding places to frolic once again. This Disneyification of Greek myth results in uncanny and hyper-sexualised figures. The enjoyment of these figures is had by the infants of the screen, the cupids and Bacchus, all of whom are childish representations of the viewer's desire. There is very little threat in the sequence to keep the audience engaged; Zeus is an intrusive yet not altogether malevolent figure. Before absolute climax within the scenario can be reached, the paternal agency must interdict to keep a value check on the diegetic space, thus limiting its transgressive capacity. This parable of indulgence within the paternal confines is perhaps most evident in the second segment: *The Sorcerer's Apprentice*, which features Mickey Mouse as the apprentice to a mighty but insidious sorcerer.

The Sorcerer's Apprentice

The plan to make *The Sorcerer's Apprentice* section motivated the whole of *Fantasia* itself. With Mickey's appeal to the public waning Walt had hoped to revisit him in such a way as to revitalise his appeal. For *Fantasia* he was redrawn: an animator added pupils to Mickey's eyes to make him more expressive, a crucial change to the mouse's appearance (Thomas and Johnston, 1984). The story involves a powerful sorcerer, with a long beard and a threatening frown: a malevolent image of paternity. Despite his outward appearance he is magnanimous in his treatment of Mickey. The sorcerer is obviously a potent paternal figure, his appearance is cruel and foreboding and he commands Mickey to do his chores. The symbols of the sorcerer's potency are his long hat (a symbol of phallic potency) and his book of magic (the container of his *knowledge*: that which empowers him). When the sorcerer leaves the room, Mickey puts on the hat (thus acquiring this image of phallic potency) and day-dreams of becoming a force like the sorcerer. He casts a spell that animates a broom to carry pails of water for him. His newly created helper allows him to be lazy and sleep, disregarding his duties. In his sleep he dreams of being a mighty sorcerer who can control the elements: he parts the sea like Moses and makes fireworks of the stars and comets. When he wakes up he finds that the broom has taken its orders to the extreme and the whole room is flooded. He tries to stop the broom from its obsessional task but it has become too powerful for Mickey and tramples him. Mickey attempts to destroy the broom by cutting it with an axe, but the shards of broom turn into other brooms, which carry on the first's task. Soon there is an unstoppable army of brooms that completely flood the sorcerer's domain. Mickey is unable to stop the rising water levels and the march of the brooms, until the sorcerer returns and magics away the situation. He spurns Mickey, slapping his buttocks and sending him running back to his chores.

The story of this section is simple: the potent father has the tools with which to control the child's world. The child takes the same tools and attempts to emulate the potency of the father. The child is too androgynised and weak to take the place of the father and is over-powered by the symbols of phallic potency. The father re-enters the equation to put the world, and the child, back in its place. The child attempts to gain the potency of the father by donning his phallic power and his knowledge, but the child is not able to take this place. The scenario outlined here is perhaps the most Oedipally conventional, in that it emphasises the potency and force of the father's position. It is not hard to see the broom-sticks as other phallic signifiers that overrun the child who is too young to handle the responsibilities of power. In silhouetted scenes of violence, Mickey attacks the broom with an axe but the scraps of broom come back to life multiplying their power. The attempt to disavow the power of the phallus is met with further energy attaching to its image.

While the narrative emphasises the power of the father it also emphasises the powerlessness of the child. Mickey is an even stronger caricature for child-hood with his large expressive eyes, another visual cue the artists used to reference the human child (Johnston and Thomas, 1996). In the next interlude, Mickey approaches the silhouette of Stokowski, to introduce himself to the paternal super-ego and receive applause. Like a child, he tugs at the conductor's coat tails. He and the viewer are both put in a subservient position to Stokowski who, along with Taylor, commands the diegetic space. The fact that Taylor addresses the non-diegetic world accentuates his posi-tion as guide and co-ruler of *Fantasia*.

Death of the Dinosaurs
The Sorcerer's Apprentice is followed by a section that seems out of place among the sexualised and phallic content of the other sections. This next segment interprets the story of 'primitive-life' and the birth of living organ-isms on earth. It depicts evolution progressing through space, the Big Bang, the formation of cells and the creation of sea creatures. Until "Certain fish,

115

more ambitious than the rest" (*Fantasia*, 1940) emerge from the sea to become the first land-based creatures. These eventually become dinosaurs, who are shown as foreboding, large and explosive. The sequence shows dinosaurs of all shapes and sizes, feeding on animal and plant life. The peak of the sequence comes as a tyrannosaurus rex emerges from the jungle then battles and kills a stegosaurus, a herbivorous dinosaur with a barbed tail. The scene is dramatic and tense; life eventually dies from the stegosaurus' eyes and his barbed tail falls limp. This is followed by a procession of dinosaurs marching through a dust bowl. As they march, predator and prey alike collapse from exhaustion and dehydration. It is a bleak and startling scene. As the Tyrannosaurus finally succumbs to death, the rest of the dinosaurs slowly fade away into dust. There is then a catastrophic shift in the earth's crust, giant mountains appear from nowhere and we lose track of the dinosaurs all together. We then see a view from above the earth as the sun sets on the age of the dinosaurs.

The violence of the battle between dinosaurs and the desperation of their march to oblivion stands apart from nearly all Disney animation of that time. The aggressive and sadistic nature of the imagery is once again contextualised by Taylor's exposition, outlining the naturalistic context for their extinction. The dinosaurs are left without anthropomorphisation, featureless creatures of the super-egoic capacity for violence embodied in Taylor's explanations. Thus they actualise the threatening nature of the paternal order that had been lightly suggested in *Pastoral Symphony*, realised in *The Sorcerer's Apprentice* and now epitomised in the cataclysm of the dinosaurs.

A Night on Bald Mountain

The last segment of the film can be seen to tie these different themes together while at the same time pushing the narrative further to the ends of structural transgression. This final sequence is perhaps the darkest short that Disney put together. It combines the music of *A Night on Bald Mountain* with *Ave Maria*. Bald Mountain refers to a gathering place of the Devil, whereas Ave Maria, being a religious song, promises redemption. The imagery around Bald Mountain is oppressive and dark. The Devil stands atop a mountain over a town and conjures up the spirits of the dead. Spirits and smaller demons gather around the summit, while the Devil picks them up and casts them into the fires of the mountain. He gathers flames in his hands and magics naked fire-nymphs into existence that dance pleadingly for their lives.

The movements of fire can be seen to have an erotic quality (also noted by Eisenstein, 1941–1946), and the movements and appearance of the fire-

Pleading Fire Nymphs
(Image by Rupert Norfolk)

nymphs are indeed undeniably sexual. To entertain himself, the Devil turns them into fat, animal-headed monsters and then crushes them. When he opens his hand again they are dancing fiery blue monsters. As the music becomes more intense, so does the demons' revelry. The demons dance among the fire which likewise takes the form of naked women. Winged female monsters swoop in to take the demons away. Their forms are distorted, but obviously feminine. The music reaches its peak of intensity when a pillar of fire appears to spring from the Devil's loins and the climax of the scene is over.

The viewer is left in the silence; bar chiming church bells that send the demons and Devil back to their slumber and spirits back to their rest. Down below the mountain, in the forests beyond the town, there is a procession of lights. *Ave Maria* starts to play and we once again hear the church bells chime. The procession goes over a bridge, with three spaces below it, perhaps representing a religious triptych. The sun rises and *Fantasia* has ended. With a female lead singer's voice, we are propelled down a corridor with a thin blue opening, like passing through an opening uterus the viewer is born into a multi-plane woodland scene at dawn.

What takes place narratively is quite simple: with the night comes malevolence and evil, while day and religiosity vanquish the ill of a sensuality and sexuality which is depicted as destructive and violent. In terms of the viewer's gratification within the scene, things are quite different. The Devil and his demons are the inner workings of withheld eroticism. The play on erotic imagery, on the fetishised bodies of the winged creatures and the fire-nymphs, provides a point of desire for the intra-diegetic look, which is identified with that of the Devil.

The Devil is the holder of the intra-diegetic gaze and thus the viewer's gratification. It is he that watches the festivities around him, he who controls the bodies of the naked fire nymphs. Thus the darkness of *Bald Mountain* is reflective: portrayed as malevolent in order to disguise the transgressive enjoyment of the eroticised form developed during the course of *Fantasia*.

The father's appearances throughout the course of the film pay lip service to the paternal agencies of morality and censorship, thus allowing the eroticism of the cartoon body to take place. Viewers of high and low brows are allowed to indulge in a fusional form, bearing closer resemblance to a subversively puritanical eroticism. The climax of the gaze could not be clearer than in the Devil's orgasmic eruption of flame, after which the viewer is brought to a place of calm by the religious sanctity and the connoted purity of *Ave Maria*. The Devil falls asleep and the viewer is guided into a realm of serenity. What is most interesting about this last scene is the absolute lack of the paternal agency. Having been established earlier in the film to the benefit of the Hayes office, he is nowhere to be found in this moment of orgasm in the gaze.

Schickel (1968) describes *Fantasia* as a failure, in that its attempt to bridge high and low culture it ultimately fails to engage either audience. He also claims that it represented a missed opportunity for Disney to explore the experimental content that it ventured into. While *Fantasia* maintained a low-brow appeal it certainly did not achieve status with the art and music critics of the time (Smoodin, 1994). Schickel fails to appreciate the aesthetic values that were developed in *Fantasia*. In no other Disney films had such overt sexual content been exhibited. The qualities of both *Pastoral Symphony* and *A Night on Bald Mountain* would not often be repeated in Disney films, yet there are many traces of their influence on later Disney characters and form. This particularly 'Disney' way of conveying sexuality and sensuality in a family-friendly form is perhaps just as telling of the mechanisms at work as in the more conservative imagery of the earlier films.

Eisenstein (1941–1946) comments that *Fantasia* fails when it tries to be serious and succeeds when it tries to be Disney. He describes the few moments of comedy far surpassing the serious tone the film tries to set. Sandwiched in between *Bald Mountain* and *The Pastoral Symphony* is *The Dance of the Hours*, which features various African wild-life performing whimsical and comic ballets. This segment features no obviously erotic content, and plays on slapstick humour and absurdity for its appeal. It does not convey the stirring emotional weight of the preceding and succeeding segments; in order to create its appeal it relies on a base infantile and regressive set of aesthetic values to engage the audience. There is no obvious narrative; it is simply composed of three successive sets of dancers: awkward ostriches, fat ballerina hippopotamuses and amorous male crocodiles that pursue the hippos to a comic conclusion. There is no tension except that which arises from the chase between the crocodiles and hippos.

The majority of Disney features play on the theme of maternal abandonment to create their narrative tension and appeal. Instead *Fantasia* utilises a set of very different animated imaginings that manage to develop appeal in radically different ways. The first segments through abstract sensuality; *The Sorcerer's Apprentice* is a child's conflict with phallic potency; the age of the dinosaurs represent a primitive scene of aggressive and figurative demonstrations of malevolence; *Pastoral Symphony* is a rambunctious and frivolous indulgence of the erotic; *The Dance of the Hours* is a childlike enjoyment of absurdity; and lastly there is the guilty enjoyment of transgressive sexuality in *A Night on Bald Mountain*. This movement towards a unified erotic enjoyment of audiences of high and low culture marks the beginnings of Disney's move towards a utopia of consumerist gratification. Thus the viewer is left with a set of approaches, or perhaps experiments, in audience gratification. While this did not make for mainstream success, its categorical mode of presenting these scenarios only furthered Disney's development of storytelling practices. These segments offer a painter's pallet of compelling narrative tricks, all of which can be shown to be present in the succeeding Disney feature-length animations.

The next feature-length film *Dumbo* (1941) bears little evidence of this newly developed process of Disney narrative creation. This was perhaps a result of the studio's knee-jerk reaction to the financial failure of *Fantasia*. *Dumbo* once again relies on a narrative of threat to the pre-Oedipal. The gratifying qualities of these regressive narratives shall be described in the next section, which shall be followed by the analysis of *Dumbo* and *Bambi*, the films that present the most obviously *primordial* narratives of the classic period. However, the visual and narrative principles developed within *Fantasia* shall be discussed in further detail in Part Three.

Chapter 8

Regression and Jouissance

While *Fantasia* was structured by eroticism in aid of a conscious utopia (the creation of a cross-class consumable product), the succeeding features of the pre-war era of Disney were structured by a threat levelled against the idealised image of primordial union with the figure of the mother: an *unconscious utopia*. This chapter begins its discussion of what would become Disney's most affective narrative formula by clarifying the concept of the regressive, followed by analyses of *Dumbo* (1941) and *Bambi* (1942). These discussions introduce different aspects of the regressive narrative, the concluding points of which will be amalgamated in a conclusion to Part Two of this text: a conception of the Disney form as a regressive cinematic apparatus, utopian in its presentation.

The Regressive

The facets of adulthood and compliance with paternity are considered profoundly negative in the classic Disney era. This path away from the adult in favour of un-castrated childhood represents a regressive choice in the film's narrative. Rather than orienting the narrative along the lines of the Oedipal dilemma, the viewer is brought backwards along earlier organisations of structure. This is the essence of the Disney narrative, an essence which is intrinsically transgressive in terms of patriarchy, yet seemingly too commodified and impotent to raise issue among censors or mainstream critics. It is this contradiction that exists between transgression and innocence that leads to so many of the critiques and parodies of Disney in popular culture; these critiques shall be discussed in the conclusion to this text.

Regression thus offers a solution to transgression. By avoiding issues of engaging with the paternal function altogether, the regressive homunculus enables the viewer to seek gratification in an 'innocent' space, where the question of transgression itself is split through a disavowal that allows the viewer a safe place in which to enjoy.

Some authors argue that regressive characters have the capacity to redefine sexual roles and sexed identities, and that they critique and satirise the patriarchal structures at work in mainstream media (Modleski, 1991). Tania Modleski (1991), however, is opposed to the idea of regressive sexuality being transgressive in a manner that critiques masculinity or indeed empowers femininity. Rather the regressive is anti-patriarchal but in terms of masculinity and the pre-Oedipal child: the phallic child is still the phallus for the mother. The 'regressive' in film is typically preoccupied with size and fears becoming big, both of which, according to Modleski, are particularly masculine traits. This fear of becoming big manifests in a revolt against adulthood, seeking an escape through childhood and infantilism. This seems paradoxical when considering that children frequently fantasise about becoming big (Brandes, 1993). Fear of adulthood and maturity is perhaps more representative of an adult male rather than childhood fantasy. Modleski maintains that even though patriarchy is disavowed in regression, the feminine position is still one that is disempowered in terms of the masculine position, which still seeks the mother as an object: the solution to its desire.

While Disney is exemplary in its portrayal of regressive narratives, it is not unique. Family and children's media have often come to feature this kind of narrative, where the adult/child hybrid enjoys a privileged position, being able to enjoy the frivolous world of children, combined with the very adult ability to break free of restriction and normative adulthood. Perhaps one of the most iconic contemporary examples of these transgressive adult/children is Pee Wee Herman, whose career spanned a decade until his arrest for public indecency ended his work as a children's television presenter. This point is of great importance to the presentation of transgressive content in Disney, as it expresses a fragility of the regressive aesthetic. To create an illusion of innocence and innocuousness around content that bears transgressive material, the film-makers must partake in a careful balancing act with which they construct the film's form. Much like the exposure of negative racial connotations in Disney, sexual scandal has the capacity to break the illusion of innocence in children's entertainment. This illusion is necessary to the disavowal of the Law as it removes the anxiety associated with transgression. This problem is dealt with in various ways throughout the Disney backlog of ever-changing content.

The Law and the Primordial in Regression

The Law is precariously dealt with in regressive media, and the reference to the primordial, uncastrated child is likewise difficult to maintain for a mainstream audience's pallet. Law and the father have the purpose of erecting boundaries, obstacles to the 'too much' of the child's demand. This 'too much' mirrors the abject, the ugly, the overwhelming nature of the primordial mother and her connection to the child (Creed, 1993). The understanding of 'ugliness' as a blurring of object and subject is discussed by Cousins (1994, 1995a), and is also integral to Kristeva's (1982) discussion of the abject, as the abject is figured as something neither alive or dead; a traumatic object that overpowers and escapes signification. This is the mother of the semiotic chora – the space that exists before the intervention of the symbolic. Thus the primordial is not just over-powering, it is traumatic to the subject, who fails at its representation. Thus Disney appeals to the primordial mother in visually regressive nonsense and emotional caricature; it creates a syntax of the archaic in a fashion that disguises and covers up its transgressive and traumatic nature. This is the purpose of the homuncule cartoon body as the *fetish*.

The curtailment of the demand to transgress into the primordial is of course the realm of the pleasure principle: the inhibition of 'too much' gratification. It is the directive to enjoy as little as possible and prohibits jouissance: the excess of gratification (Lacan, 1960). The subject will inevitably seek to transgress the pleasure principle, and it is through this transgression that the subject fantasises penultimate enjoyment. The paradox is that this excess of enjoyment turns to pain and yet still remains in some way satisfying for the subject. The prohibition of jouissance is inherent in language (Lacan, 1966, p696). The same process that separates the child from the mother also initiates the subject into the symbolic order, in which this prohibition is crystallised in the super-ego. Thus the transgression touched on is the essence of jouissance, just as jouissance is itself transgression. Motivation and satisfaction from the transgressive nature of Disney illustrates the Death Drive: the perpetual attempt to break through the pleasure principle to seek the end of subjectivity and self (Lacan, 1964b). It is this drive that threatens the subject with the anxiety of becoming overwhelmed by the primordial mother. There is thus a masochistic element to the viewer's gratification within the Disney regressive apparatus. Indeed masochism can be understood as an experience of the limits of the pleasure principle – an experience that is implicitly gratifying (Adams, 1996).

The following is the complex, and at times painful, scenario the viewer is left with in the unconscious utopia of connection with the maternal: the Other and subject are re-joined through a fantasised maternal bond, the father's momentary intrusion into this space reminds the viewer of the return to the castrated state they will have to make in the film's ending, thus this father is a foul intruder. Thankfully this apparition is removed from the filmic space, reinstituting a primordial connection between mother and child.

However, this connection in reality leads to the threat of subjective obliteration, as love and death are both synchronous with the end of desire that the primordial mother spells. Disney thus uses innocence and innocuousness to create an image of childhood to adult appeal – an image that is by its nature false due to its perverting of the Oedipal equation. Love seeks affective fusion, this aim being transparent with that of the death drive: the movement towards the ends of desire (Lacan, 1973). Disney covers up this disturbing space of a transgressed boundary and obliterated subjectivity by erecting a fantasy of blissful connection to the Other; a form of sexual propaganda. This is emblematic in the happy state *Bambi* creates in its adoring mass of woodland creatures and *Dumbo* with its painful moments of threatened maternal union.

Dumbo: Regressive Narratives

Dumbo (1941) was made on a much shorter time scale than other Disney classic films. It featured simpler animation and was made without much input from Walt himself, who was not present for the majority of its production. It was the end result of two contributing pressures. First the need to make a low-cost feature that would make up for the losses on *Fantasia*, and second to survive the internal strife of Disney's unionisation. *Dumbo* is very much a commercial feature, with little of the drive to make a master-piece that had motivated the other productions. It is nevertheless a solid example of the progressively distilled Disney process of dressing up the transgressive primordial space with a love story between homuncule child and archaic Other. *Dumbo* maintains the common theme of a threat of separation from the primordial maternal: the adventures through-out the course of the film represent a passage back to this idealised utopian state. Much as other films of the classic Hollywood tradition, *Dumbo* is driven by a love story with the addition of peril. By setting the subject within the position of the child, who struggles to return to a state of pre-Oedipal utopia, Disney essentially opens the dynamics of gratification to a wider audience. The regressive play of a child returning to the primordial womb represents a universal trope with the capacity to cross cultural and even gendered difference. This is particularly the case in *Dumbo* and *Bambi*, in which both main characters are anthropomorphic child-animals, both defined by their androgyny.

Disney films, and again *Dumbo* is a perfectly illustrative example, represent a transgressive portrayal of the Oedipal dilemma. The motives of the oedipal child are singularly to rejoin the mother. The only element that is altered to suit the viewer's repression of the Oedipal dilemma is the negotiation and subversion of obvious sexuality. The erotic quality of the cartoon is very much present, though lurking in disguised form. This is the most obvious of Disney's tropes that are specifically utilised to negotiate the transgressive nature of their gratification.

Ugly Children

The film begins by establishing the connection between Dumbo and his mother, Mrs Jumbo. The scenes in which they are together are happy and full to the brim of maternal comfort. This state of the adoring mass of mother and child is continually threatened during the course of the film. When Dumbo is first introduced to us, he is a source of adoration for the mother and the viewer by proxy.

Other elephants watch him dotingly until his giant ears are unveiled, and then start to ridicule him. The ridicule is aggressive and cutting; Dumbo is oblivious and his absent doe-eyed reaction only furthers the viewer's sympathy and idealisation of his position, much as Snow White's vacant reaction to violent threat does. His mother angrily shuts the door on the cruel scathing elephants. This is the first instance of the mother aggressively defending the child and thus the viewer's connection to gratification. Ridicule is the foremost expression of malevolence in *Dumbo* and acts as the opposition against Dumbo's happy union, and eventual re-union, with his mother. It is the cruel jeers of the onlooking children at the circus that send Mrs Jumbo into a rage that leads her to being taken away and imprisoned. A red haired child tugs aggressively at Dumbo, who does not realise that the attention is bad.

Again it is the homunculus' indifference that makes its image so sympathetic. Mrs Jumbo chastises the child and rampages through the tent, fighting with the circus hands who attempt to subdue her. This scene is the emotional cataclysm of the film: as Dumbo's mother rears up and fights with the shadowy men, the viewer is exposed to violence against the maternal figure

A sad and sympathetic elephant
(Image by Rupert Norfolk)

as she is whipped and chained. The violence expressed in this scene is the first moment the viewer is confronted with the fearsome aspects of the archaic mother, who is by her nature terrifying and destructive to the child in the symbolic (Kaplan, 1990), although this intrusion of the negative image of this mother is quickly foreclosed and transmuted into the longing of the child for union in the next scene.

The next shot is of a lonely carriage where the mother resides, looking sad and listless. Her carriage is signposted "danger – mad elephant". Dumbo meanwhile sits alone crying beside his mother's feeding dish, with the other elephants jeering his mother and him in the background. This scene is crucial as it provides a vent for the anxieties surrounding the union with the archaic mother, previously erected in her violent capture.

The clowns in *Dumbo* are yet another apparition of malevolence. Their movements are aggressive and blunderous, their appearance is eerie and unpleasant when contrasted with the other Disney characters. Whereas all other Disney characters in the film have large, round and expressive eyes, the clowns have smaller expressionless eyes, much like the older silent Disney cartoons. Perhaps what makes their image uncanny is the contrast with the newer, more mobile cartoon characters. They appear as familiar apparitions of an older age of animation, aggressively taunting the homunculoid main character. Their malevolence is furthered by their silhouetted discussion in a tent where they drink alcohol and discuss how to get more money out of the circus. They discuss how to further put Dumbo at risk to please the crowd, gibing that "elephants have no feelings".

The next set of jeerers comes in the form of the flock of crows that come to heckle Dumbo and the mouse, who find themselves stuck in a tree after a night of drunken hallucinations. The crows are vulgar caricatures of African Americans, dressed as vagrants, who laugh cruelly at Dumbo's misfortunes. They do however stop their jeering when they are made to feel pity for Dumbo's plight. Their pity, much as malevolent jealousy, only validates the appeal of the homuncule image.

Out of all the jeerers it is the malicious children that pre-empt the separation of Dumbo and his mother. Like the clowns and the malicious elephants they are depicted as *ugly*. Ugliness within the Disneyified lexicon of regression is an interesting feature, as it is at all times balanced with what Johnston and Thomas (1984) refer to as 'appeal'. If we examine the images of the children compared to that of other Disney children, it is possible to say that they are formed to emphasise a 'too-muchness' in their caricature. In his papers on 'The Ugly', Mark Cousins (1994, 1995a, 1995b) asks whether it is possible to create a beautiful representation of an ugly object. He suggests that the concept of the sublime is dependent on a distance maintained between subject and object. If this distance is closed then the object becomes overpowering. It becomes realised as an overwhelming Thing; a 'too much'. Another way to consider this loss of distance is that the ugly object is essentially something in the wrong place – the wrong place being anywhere too near to the subject (Cousins, 1994). This excessive proximity is caused by a breach in laws of proportionality: a disruption of form. This is seen within some caricatures that purposefully morph their form to emphasise and disrupt the viewer's reading (Cousins, 1995a). The object itself supports the subject's egoic constitution. If the object is pleasing it is because it reflects what the subject wishes to see reflected and is thus an instrument of narcissism. The difference between ugly and beautified characters is not a matter of appeal, but a matter of what is reflected to the viewer. If the jeering children are caricatured to emphasise that which is unappealing then the homunculus emphasises that which is appealing: childhood, innocence and unity. The ugly characters often offer a negation of those values deemed attractive. Instead of the small head to body ratio they appear more adult. Instead of large expressive eyes and simple forms, they are beady-eyed and bulbous, just as Quasimodo, who is defined by his overwhelming irregularity, they are 'too much' in the wrong places (Cousins, 1995b).

Much like Pinocchio and Jiminy, Dumbo has Timothy the mouse to be his voice of reason and street-wisdom. He attempts to set up Dumbo as the centre of attention for the circus, to become the centre of praise not just for

The uncanny clown
(Image by Paul Byrne)

the viewer but for the collective Other as adoring mass. Although he would seem to represent a paternalised super-ego, his role is to reunite the child with the primordial mother, facilitating the viewer's gratification. Timothy seeks to gain Dumbo the praise of the circus audience, whose appreciation gives value to Dumbo's actions and forms the adoring mass. Dumbo's first foray into this audience's gaze is a performance in which Dumbo must form the peak of an elephant pyramid. Dumbo causes the pyramid to collapse, creating a horrible and dramatic scene of collapsing pachyderms. The ensuing disaster causes the big top to collapse and the audience to flee, another image of the paternal's crumpled semblance. Dumbo has meekly failed to capture the attention of the mass. As punishment for his failure they make him a clown: touched by ugliness and malevolence.

Another significant sequence in the narrative's interaction with anxiety and gratification is when Dumbo and Timothy accidentally consume alcohol and start to hallucinate. The hallucinations involve a procession of pink elephants that morph and change shape. There is reoccurring imagery of a large elephant crushing smaller elephants, who then in turn become larger and crush the other. This again is reminiscent of Little Hans' dream of giraffes (Freud, 1909). They have black, vacant eyes and are utterly androgynous.

They appear as Dumbo does in clown make-up, an uncanny reminder of earlier animation, devoid of features. The pink elephants carry elements of both sexes: exaggeratedly effeminate curves and gestures, combined with the phallic nature of their trunks and masculine voices. They are apparitions of the primordial mother, the phallic mother who overwhelms the child (Zizek, 1991). The intensity of these hallucinations and the blackness of the background seems to reference the gulf of subjectivity that this mother resides in, as negative mother of the primordial abyss (Kaplan, 1990). While Dumbo's real mother does not hold these characteristics, she is also a referent of the primordial mother. She is the phallic mother, threatening, empowered and connected to the child. She enacts her potency when Dumbo is threatened by the jeering children, becoming an icon of power and aggression that is subdued (momentarily) by the paternal forces of the ringmaster and the ominous dark shadows of the circus hands. What differentiates her from the anxiety-provoking images of the pink elephants is her Disneyification: a redrawing based on emphasising appeal and accessibility so as to disavow her destructive capacity to the child.

Mrs Jumbo appears at first as sad, lonely and bashful. We are first introduced to her while she watches all the other animals receiving their babies but her. She longs for the day she will have her own child. The later scene in which Dumbo comes to visit her through the bars of her prison is perhaps another emotional locus of the film. She cradles his head with her trunk, while he cries after having been embarrassed and humiliated by the clowns' performance. Meanwhile a lullaby is heard with the words: "let those eyes sparkle and shine ... baby you're fine". This moment in the film is indulgently sentimental and gratuitously manipulative, it makes an obvious play to the nostalgia Lacan refers to in *Family Complexes in the Formation of the Individual* (1938), which describes the illusory nature of love and the paradoxical aims of the death drive: "In this formula, a bit philosophical in appearance, will be recognised the nostalgias of humanity; the metaphysical mirage of universal harmony; the mystical abyss of affective fusion; the social utopia of totalitarian dependency – all derived from the longings for a paradise lost before birth and from the most obscure aspirations for death." (Lacan, 1938, p23) This is indeed the affective impact of this intimately regressive moment in which the child is re-united with the denied paradise of the phallic mother. The nostalgia that the song and imagery pander to is the illusion of the paradise of overwhelming wholeness that the primordial mother represents for the Oedipal child; the unconscious utopia of archaic dependency. What is lacking in this mirage is of course the reality that unity with this mother spells subjective death rather than the idealised Disney story of the child united with the mother. Thus the child itself becomes fetishised, becoming the phallus for the primordial mother, joined to her in an archaic and pre-gendered state.

Dumbo's hidden talent is that his ears allow him to fly; his ability to turn his particularity, i.e. individuality and 'specialness', into a commercially important skill allows him to become the hero of the film. He wins back the circus in a death-defying feat of flight, and is rewarded by a coach just for him and his mother: a return to a womb-like enclosure, as well as the adoration of the other elephants and animals. *Dumbo* is narratively structured on the basis of the regressive mother and child being separated and their relationship being threatened. Although *Dumbo* was one of the least extravagant of the classic Disney features, this formula served it well and saw to its success. This theme of maternal denial would be emphasised and exploited even further in *Bambi*, which would be Disney's most emotionally climactic film of the classic period, involving a death and rebirth of the archaic mother.

Bambi: **Death of the Mother and Jouissance**

It has been commented by some that Disney can be seen as a mediation between the polemics of humanity, animism and machination (Whitley, 2008, Gilchrist & Joelson, 2007). Walter Benjamin likewise saw Disney as a restructuring of alternate visions of the body's interaction with technology and nature, a supportive prosthesis (Hansen, 1993). Calling to mind Freud's cautious remarks:

> "Man has, as it were, become a kind of prosthetic God. When he puts on all his auxiliary organs he is truly magnificent; but those organs have not grown on to him and they still give him much trouble at times … . Future ages will bring with them new and possibly unimaginably great advances in this field of civilization and will increase man's likeness to God still more. But in the interests of our present investigation, we will not forget that present-day man does not feel happy in his God-like character."
> (Freud, 1930, p29)

Within Disney, nature is put in service of a fantasmatic machination that enables a regressive egoism; it supports the image of utopian fusion with the Other that involves the child's centrality as requisite for gratification. Eisenstein describes *Bambi* (1942) as a "shift towards ecstasy – serious, eternal" (Eisenstein, 1941–1946 p63). It represents for him the ultimate animism and gratification of the early Disney films, and is thus an appropriate object to conclude the discussion of the regressive apparatus.

Bambi was one of Disney's first forays into the naturalism Walt had claimed to advocate. The original *Bambi: A Life in the Woods* was written by Felix

Salten in 1928. It is a story about the cycles of life; that animals and people alike are born, procreate, grow old and die. Salten's text succeeds in depicting a life in the woods that is devoid of the polemics of good and evil; life and death are both equally natural, as are the Oedipal dilemmas that all children must go through. The story focuses on the life of a newborn fawn called Bambi. Bambi goes through a difficult life in the woods, losing his mother to hunters, finding a new love and eventually hermiting himself away from the other deer as older bucks do. He sees the hunters first as aggressive intruders and then one day happens upon a dead man, and realises that they too are part of the cycle. The story covers many years of Bambi's hard but naturalistic life and gives a poignant account of the realities of life in the wild: that all animals must compete for food, resources and survival. In the course of the story Bambi's mother is killed by hunters, she is taken from him prematurely. He then begins his struggle into adulthood, spurred on by the old stag: his cold and removed father. The old stag embodies the Law, the natural order that states that the child and mother can no longer be together.

This Law is put into effect even before Bambi's mother dies. On an occasion in which Bambi is lost in the woods, he calls out for his mother in a panic. The Old Stag appears and scorns Bambi for being childish and tells him he must be independent to be an adult. This event shames Bambi and the guilt he feels for being childish is what pushes him to adulthood. When Bambi's mother is killed he goes on to find a mother substitute in Feline, his cousin and childhood companion. Bambi then begins to realise that to fully actualise himself as an adult he must identify with his father and go to live by himself deep in the forest, thus becoming an image of absolute individuation. The story ends with Bambi coming across a young fawn calling out for his mother; he scorns the child and walks away, realising that he himself has become an adult and bringer of the Law to his own son.

As with other stories and fairy-tales the Disney treatment produces a radically different version. The majority of the story follows the same conventions as *Pinocchio* and *Snow White*, and there are a few key areas that are significant in elaborating the essence of the Disney fantasy: the conflict to regress to pre-Oedipal sanctuary. The same scenario is played out in *Bambi* except the emotive stakes are put much higher: the world of unrepentant enjoyment is contrasted against the death of the mother and the cruelty of the intruder. It is a similar dynamic to what is seen in *Dumbo*. Both follow the same scenario that plays on castration anxiety: fear of affective separation from the mother and loss of the maternal attention found in the primordial, pre-Oedipal state. However, what is at stake in *Bambi* is far greater and the bond between mother and child is threatened more aggressively than in *Dumbo* or in other features preceding it.

As previously discussed, the tension created by the threat to the mother-child bond (by castration) is the tension that propels the viewer through the narrative. This is a particular aspect of the Disney treatment that is nearly always absent in the original written story. As stated, the original *Bambi: A Life in the Woods* is a naturalistic fable, in which threat is considered as much a part of life as 'love'. This element is completely lost within the Disney translation; both elements of threat and affection are polarised and caricatured to the point that love and warmth become nearly over-powering and threat becomes aggressive and traumatic.

As the formula dictates, *Bambi* starts with a love story. The newborn faun Bambi is introduced to us, curled up beside his mother and surrounded by the other animals in a bestial nativity scene. All the other forest animals dote on the young faun, calling him the "new prince". The forest animals are a clear extension of the mother's adoration and focus on Bambi; all the creatures are highly tactile and embrace each other in a veritable orgy of maternal affection. As the camera pulls back there is a silhouette of a great stag in the distance.

This was only the second apparition of a father figure in Disney features. In *Dumbo* a father is entirely absent, taken out of the equation by the stork bringing the baby Dumbo to his mother. In fact there are practically no male animals in *Dumbo*. The only masculine characters are the jeering crowds and clowns, the aggressive ringmaster and the meek super-egoic mouse. There is likewise a marked lack of paternal figures in *Snow White* and the backlog of Disney shorts. While Geppetto was a father in name, he was hardly a father in function. Pinocchio is no more swayed by his words than Jiminy's, yet another ineffective apparition of the paternal super-ego. As stated before, Geppetto's maternal function places him as a maternal force in relation to the wooden child he has given birth to. The Old Stag in *Bambi* appears as a paternal figure but his function is never enacted during the course of the film. The way he first appears is as a distant image, overlooking the maternal scene. He is not an animated character, indeed he is drawn onto the background. The effect is a potent and beautified image, but one that is essentially static and devoid of character: a post-card father. During the

A postcard father
(Image by Rupert Norfolk)

course of the film the father remains absent and the story followed is that of Bambi, his course through life and collisions with the Law.

Bambi remains close to his mother for the first half of the film. As a fawn he is androgynous and sexless, speaking with the same voice as the female fawn Feline, his cousin and love interest. During the first half of the film Bambi is never separated from his mother or the adoring mass of other animals. He is consistently at the centre of attention for his friends Thumper and Flower. They are the sexual accomplices of the homunculus. All three are quite androgynous.

The sex of the homuncule body is in many ways irrelevant, as the position this body represents in terms of regression is similarly without gender. Within these discussions of sexual development a concept of a pre-gendered subject becomes clear; a stage in the child's development before it recognizes itself as boy or girl, before they differentiate themselves from the Other and give up their position as phallus. In this pre-oedipal and pre-gendered state, both the male and female subject hold the Other as point of focus and Father as potential intruder. Gendering this subject serves no purpose in discussions of psychical structure, just as the homunculus is essentially genderless.

Thus the project of defining and delimiting the homunculus and its appeal

133

the subject will not enter into discussions of gendering the subject, but rather to discuss the subject in its least divisive form. The focus within Disney narratives is the regressive quality of their structure which seeks to reduce gender difference and return the adult to the pre-gendered, archaic child. This is the core of Disney's appeal and the essence of its universality. In a sense sidestepping the issues surrounding the gendering of the gaze by returning the viewer to a regressive gaze: an apparatus that returns the viewer to an illusion of affective fusion with the Other, safe of the complications of gendering. This is expressed in the immaturity and androgyny of Disney main characters, whether the viewer follows the child-like Snow White, or the androgynous Bambi.

The critical moment and indeed *trauma* of the narrative is when Bambi and his mother stray out into an open clearing, demarcated as a place of danger, and the hunters start to shoot at them. As Bambi and his mother run away the shots continue, until Bambi is running by himself and finds himself alone in the snow calling her name. The father arrives on the scene, as an animated character for the first time, and says to Bambi in a strong and stern voice: "Your mother can't be with you any more". Bambi cries a solitary tear and the Stag leads him away. Temporally the hunters and the Old Stag operate as a unit, one removing the mother, the other signifying the castration. Both these elements are interconnected but separate. The Old Stag and the Hunters are separated by name and placement and thus allow the film-maker to separate different components of paternity. We are left with a) the father as intruder, who removes the mother from the child and b) the father as bringer of the Law and symbolic function. As previously stated, the symbolic father is the position that instigates language and subjectivity to the child's position (Lacan, 1957a).

Lacan differentiates this father from the real or imaginary father. The real father can be understood as simply the person in reality who is thought to be the child's father; "the real father is nothing other than an effect of language and has no other real" (Lacan, 1970, p127). Within Disney films of the classic era there are few real fathers. Geppetto is a carpenter who makes a wooden boy and conveys a maternal function. The biological ties to fatherhood have traditionally been avoided in Disney films and shorts, indeed in the world of Mickey Mouse and Donald Duck there exists no paternity: Donald has nephews but not sons (Mattelart and Dorfman, 1991). The imaginary father is the imago of the father, the mental representation. This representation can be polarised between perceptions of the father as the demonic, malevolent intruder and the father as a religious figure. In both cases this is represented as omnipotence outside the archaic mother/child relation.

The imaginary father threatens castration whereas the symbolic father actualises this function. Within perversion there is a reduction from the symbolic to the imaginary. This mirrors the move within regression from desire to demand and ego-libido. The imaginary father (as agent of threat) exists before the Oedipus complex, as a threatening omnipotence to the archaic child/Other relation. It is this state, of perverse regression, that is so clearly illustrated in conventional Disney narrative. This Lacan illustrates in his discussion of Little Hans (Lacan, 1957b) in which the functions of symbolic and imaginary father become separated from the real father, who fails to actualise his symbolic function. Thus the child slips into a perverse relation to the father, whom the child derides. Hans becomes anxious not because (as Freud suggests) he is afraid of the father, but because he is afraid of the gulf of jouissance that awaits him in a primordial connection to the mother – a connection that threatens to overwhelm him (Lacan, 1957b, Sauvagnat, 2002). Thus while Disney effectively relays the same scenario as Little Hans fantasises, it negotiates its images to rid the archaic overwhelming mother of its anxiety, by dislocating that anxiety onto the imaginary father as intruder. This re-imagining of jouissance has so far been referred to as an erotic propaganda, but is perhaps better described as a specifically *cartoon jouissance*.

The scene that follows the Old Stag's entry into Bambi's life is some years later. A grown-up Bambi now has horns of his own and is ready to mate (or is he?). As we have not seen evidence of Bambi's chronological path to adulthood, all that the viewer is left with is a visual relation between Bambi and his father. His antlers are a symbol of his new-found phallic potency, but they are still not as large as the father's. He is thus allowed to remain a youth in the eyes of the viewer (Payne, 1995). With his new-found adolescence Bambi meets his old friends, Thumper and Flower, and the trio are given a lecture by the wise old owl about "twitterpation". Twitterpation is essentially the story of the birds and the bees, except without the fornication. The owl describes it as a process of hypnotic infatuation that the boys will not be able to escape from. The three males are horrified by what they hear, and refuse to believe that it can happen to them. What occurs immediately after this discussion is a very particular sexual scenario that enables the boys to stay children and the females to act as both aggressors and maternal seductresses.

The three boys leave the owl, confident that they will not fall victim to twitterpation. As they walk away they are one-by-one picked off by females of their species. Their female counterparts are introduced as sexually precocious, active in the seduction of the male. The female rabbit that seduces Thumper rubs herself to emphasise the softness of her body. She has long exaggerated lashes and approaches thumper as a sexually provocative adult, even humming a sleazy tune.

Thumper is awestruck and ends up lying on the ground beside her, while she strokes his ears his leg thumps repeatedly on the ground, a rhythmic signifier of his excitement. While Bambi and Flower's seduction is not quite as blatant, in both instances it is the female that takes the active role in seduction. In all three cases the symbolic markers that differentiate the girls and boys are few and far between, though Bambi's adolescent horns are the strongest indicator of his masculinity. As with Snow White and her prince there is no complication to the courtship, the desired only has eyes for the hero/heroine. There is no courtship or ambiguity in their fraternisation. The desired object sees the homunculus and is overcome by the urge to be one with them. This further emphasises the description established of the desired character, they are simply an extension of the humonculoid lead. This is a particular kind of infantilisation in which the male wishes to remain a child. The other's role as seductress/seducer allows the desired not only to relieve the subject of responsibility, but also enables a return to a phallic maternal figure for the child. The child remains passive, subject to a maternal idealised desire: that the child is centre of the Other's world.

Feline is first seen by Bambi in a reflective pool of water. The specular image of the homunculus doubles to include an image of the mother in younger accessible form. This instance occurs twice in the film, first when Bambi is a child and he mis-recognises Feline as a double of himself and second as an adolescent when she resembles his mother. In this way the child-mother bond is reattached within ten minutes of the mother's invisible death.

Bambi is challenged by another buck for Feline, whom he fights and drives off. This intruder and the hunters that follow are other extensions of the negativised imaginary father and his threatening function: the image of the father as intruder, the bearer of castration. They fail to fully separate Bambi from his new mother Feline. Indeed there is little question that Feline only desires Bambi. The other buck acts as an intruder but not a real competitor;

Reflective Love
(Image by Paul Byrne)

even when he leads Feline away she only calls Bambi's name. The other apparitions of intrusion are the hunter's dogs, who Bambi struggles against and fights. The dogs are buried under falling rocks. In their death they are removed neatly from the film's space, just as the evil Queen is removed from *Snow White* by falling into a dark abyss.

Violence and the Cartoon Body in *Bambi*

Violence and death are quite separate in the classic Disney. While some characters die the events that lead to their demise are rarely violent, with the singular exception of the battle of the dinosaurs in *Fantasia*. Death scenes are few and far between in Disney films but they do exist, and the way that death is conveyed in these scenes is quite particular. Essentially every character of a film dies a symbolic death when the film ends; the audience often feels melancholic for the loss of characters from their attention. Within Disney films, death functions in a similar way. The character is simply removed from the diegetic space, whether it be the evil Queen falling into an abyss or Bambi's mother, simply disappearing from the shot. The term death is never used within Disney films, and the realisation of death is accomplished through inference. There is only one occasion in the classic period of Disney films where a dead body is really seen.

In *Bambi*, as the hunters make their approach, three pheasants hide in the shrubs. Although they are safe in their spot, one starts to panic and flies into the air only to be shot. As the body floats back down to earth something that was animated and anthropomorphised has been robbed of its detail: its face and its eyes are now blank. The death of the pheasant marks a trauma within the filmic space. There is a reoccurring emphasis on covering up the actual fatality, this goes for both good and bad characters. Violence however is occasionally visible if only for a few seconds in relation to death. When Bambi fights and defeats the pack of hunting dogs; they are buried beneath a pile of stones. This death is violent but again, the dogs are removed from the diegetic space before they die. The tumbling stones overpower and crush them, pushing them out of the viewer's awareness. The *threat* of death and violence is perhaps more significant as it contains an important function with regard to the cartoon body. But what is the mechanism at work in the aggressivity and enjoyment of this cartoon body?

In his discussion of the appeal of the male body in cinema, Steve Neale (1993) discusses the libidinal values that functions to draw the male or masculinised viewer to the male body as object through repressive mechanisms. The male body or 'built body' (as it is often exaggerated in its form within film, such as the muscled form of Arnold Schwarzenegger) becomes erotically gratifying for a mass male audience within certain contexts. These contexts provide a cover for this perceived transgressive pleasure. It is possible to see an obvious parallel in the discourse of the cartoon body and that of the 'built body' as discussed in terms of 'musculinity' in film (Tasker, 1993).

Both the built body and that of the cartoon are objectified and eroticised by their passivity. The muscled male body of the body builder in action sequences must take moments to pose (Neale, 1993); just as the cartoon body is presented and set to idyllic backdrops and landscapes. Tasker (1993) notes that the built body is a caricatured form that disavows vulnerability. It is essentially beyond the realm of the Real body and is something imaginarily constituted under the pretence of solidity and wholeness. The built body experiences lack only as a threat, which is usually inferred through acts of penetration. This becomes evident in *Conan the Barbarian* (1982), a highly eroticised celebration of the male form. Conan, played by Arnold Schwarzenegger, is a homunculoid image of masculinity: muscled, indestructible and practically mute. The story involves Conan's passing from childhood and loss of his parents into adulthood, where he becomes a seemingly superhuman killing machine. At the peak of his invulnerability he is captured, tortured and crucified. The built body comes under threat and he must re-establish its solidity through the destruction of his paternalistic foe. As in Disney, images of paternity conjure up anxiety and the threat of castration: the evil Thulsa Doom describes to Conan that the process in which he became a man is dependent on the deaths of his parents: the unity that Thulsa Doom has destroyed at the start of the film. Conan re-establishes this unity in the guise of his own body, thus exerting a level of control that allows him to overcome the castrating father.

This internalisation of the pre-castrated connection to the mother is likewise implicit in the cartoon body. Like the built body, the cartoon is evidence of victory of mind over matter: imaginary over the symbolic/real continuum (Dyer, 1997). It represents another apparition of fantasy instructing the Real, constructing it under the direction of narcissistic infatuation and the demand for control. As such it operates within the terms of the ideal ego (Mulvey, 1975). The ideal ego has its origins in the realisation of the specular image: the imago of a completed sense of self to which the subject strives in an effort to remove the split inherent in their own subjectivity (Lacan, 1954b). This image of the ego carries none of the deficiencies of the Real. The gap between this imaginary construct and the body in the Real becomes the source of further insecurity of the subjective position. The social/symbolic order does not grant the subject the tools with which to close this divide. The subject seeks images reminiscent of the original specular identification implicit in the mirror phase: the point at which the subject constructs the ego in a process of mis-recognising an image of the self (Lacan, 1954b). Thus any interaction between the subject and an ideal will be set on insecure and tumultuous grounds.

Neale (1993) draws attention to the ideal ego as a source of castration anxiety in itself. The insurmountable nature of the ideal can only reflect the subject's own partial nature and therefore must be denigrated to relieve the viewer's castration anxiety. This however does not seem to apply to the cartoon body; perhaps because of its regressive nature it becomes less threatening. Whereas the hyper-masculine form seen in Conan represents an ideal ego that holds phallic power (having the phallus), the Disney body has a radically different relation to paternity, in that it *is* the phallus of the primordial mother.

Even through the guise of the feminised and passified male form, the subject finds vents for the anxiety instilled from (theoretically) heterosexual enjoyment of the same-sex object. This suggests that violence against the male form is directly influenced by this uncertain libido. Without direct expression, it seeks release through the violence visited upon this form. Just as in the particularly penetrative violence seen in Conan and films of its ilk, the idealised form is assaulted to give relief to the eroticised tension of enjoying the male body within a patriarchically constituted male gaze. As Willemen (1981) describes, in the pleasure of watching the (male) body, there exists an "unquiet pleasure" (Willemen, 1981, p16) in seeing it mutilated. Leon Hunt (1993) goes further to suggest that both the male and female body come under attack and assault in film, but only the female body is truly degraded by the process, whereas the male is tested but in the end becomes stronger. Thus violence and occasionally death have the capacity to transfigure male eroticism. This same process operates in Disney films, to the extent that the hero or heroine is never truly scarred or weakened by the ordeals they face, rather they become more truly adored and enjoyed. In this way the Disney homunculus is both the phallic un-scarrable object and, as Metz and Mulvey suggest, the child's position in the pre-gendered, pre-Oedipal phallic exchange. Phallically empowered by its own unrelenting solidity, the Disneyified cartoon body *is* the phallus for the mother. This is demonstrated in its relation to the adoring maternal mass and the object of its desire. But one thing is certain: the homunculus is the phallus but it does not, wants not and should not *have* the phallus. The homunculus is structurally androgynous, this is evident in the fear Pinocchio experiences when his nose grows long or when he develops hairy ears and a tail, as these symbols interrupt the viewer's transgressive enjoyment.

The final scenes in *Bambi* emphasise the cartoon body's fragile nature, in which a fire from the hunter's camp spreads to the forest. Bambi finds himself fleeing not just the gunshots from the hunter, but the fire engulfing his home. He is wounded by a bullet and nearly succumbs to the encroaching doom, but the Old Stag steps in to help him escape. Here the body of the homunculus is violated to the gratification and anxiety of the viewer, calling to mind Dadoun's description of Dracula: "all the more rigid and impressive for being fragile and threatened" (Dadoun, 1989, p41). The father and the intruder are completely separated from each other. The fire goes to further emphasise the alien and aggressive intrusion of the outsider who is now radically opposed to the real father who is essentially functionless, other than preserving the homunculus. This of course is a far different telling than Felix Salten's original text. In the book there is a tangible continuum between all elements of the forest: the father who chastises and signifies Bambi's path towards individuation, and the hunters that take away his mother. Both are depicted as unpleasant but natural elements of a cycle, thus the different fathers are unified in the same amorphous force (the Law) that moves Bambi from his childhood. Disney's *Bambi* is more concerned with the trials of both the body and the incestuous union of the archaic child/Other utopia.

After the fire, we are shown Feline curled up with child. The new bestial nativity is an exact replica of the first, except instead of a single fawn there are now two, thus doubling the potential sexual stakes of the viewer's imagined future of the narrative. Whereas the book ends with an image of an old and individuated Bambi, Disney's *Bambi* ends with first a scene of maternal adoration and then an image of paternal subjection. The film ends with yet another postcard image of the father, except this time he is joined by Bambi, who stands by his side. While the ineffectual post-card father maintains his intangible disconnected image, it is this image that Bambi and thus the viewer identify with: a superficial and functionless image of paternity.

The analysis of *Snow White*, *Pinocchio*, *Fantasia*, *Bambi* and *Dumbo* has plotted a trend in Disney narrative and form and its ability to manipulate viewer gratification. This manipulation is based on the viewer's engagement within the regressive cinematic apparatus. This apparatus achieves viewer engagement and gratification by increasing tension through attacks on the mother-child relationship from the outside, and releasing this tension via the absence of functional paternity in the archaic child/Other space. This narrative formula exemplifies the classic Disney period and represents a regressive gratification that can be said to be essentially 'Disney'. These narratives are based on the positive imagining of a primordial mother, uncastrated and unified with the child in a safe womb-like space. This space comes under threat from paternal forces which are strategically split and eventually expelled from the diegetic world. This climaxes in tying the narrative into a safe and comfortable end and producing a post-climactic catharsis in a post-Oedipal viewer. The regressive nature of this narrative formula harkens back to a pre-gendered and pre-symbolic organisation of sexuality and gratification. It is this organisation that can be said to be perverse, in that the Disney Company uses this apparatus to convince the viewer of a narcissistic connection to the Other, a connection that spells a transgressive gratification within the safe haven of mass-produced family entertainment.

Bambi was the last film to be made in Disney's classic period. Financial problems blocked the studio's work on costly and time-consuming features. Although the work on animated feature-length films restarted after the war, they would not have the aggressive potency of these early films. The trends begun in these films would dictate what could and could not be shown in the Disney genre. But crucially they demonstrate a move towards the simplification of the sexual equation towards a utopia that is central to the regressive apparatus. The progression towards sexually primordial and prototypic story-telling is integral to Disney ascendancy to a major socio-cultural institution. It is the reliance on this sexualised sentimentality that can be shown to propel the company into the Hollywood majors, and in turn to becoming a determinant in Western hegemony.

Part Three:
The Hybrid Utopia

T he following chapters shall examine the studio's move into propaganda and its place within the greater American hegemony. This period of Disney's development marked the indivisibility between the struggle for hegemony and the struggle to create a consciously contrived consumerist utopia. The following discussions shall entail an industrial analysis of Disney's place in 1940s Hollywood, and textual analyses of Disney propaganda shorts and features of this period. There shall also be a discussion of films produced as a result of the American 'good neighbour policy' and a pseudo-documentary film produced with the intention to create popular support for the Disney management during the studio strike. It shall conclude with discussions of Disney's moves into television, amusement parks and theorised planned communities in the 1950s, which established the company as a pervasive socio-cultural institution.

Chapter 9

Hegemony

T he concept of hegemony is uniquely situated to illustrate how a company such as Disney became instrumental in achieving ideological homogeneity within a nation and indeed internationally. While having supplanted American folklore in the Depression era, and risen to popularity in pre-war Western nations, Disney had not yet achieved its capacity to directly affect consumers globally. This capacity can be shown to have developed during World War II, during which Disney actively participated in achieving hegemony both for the American government and to its own ends. This argument shall be based on a discussion of propaganda films that target both home and foreign audiences, with an array of different ideological propositions spanning industry/consumer relations, pan-American unity and intra-American homogeneity.

At its base, hegemony is a process of making an ideological position seem common sense and naturalised to the mass. As a concept, it was formulated by Antonio Gramsci during his imprisonment by Mussolini. Gramsci (from his prison note books as edited by Hoare, 1971) proposed a division between what he termed a war of manoeuvres (armed revolution) and a war of position: the battle of ideas. The idea war must take place for a war of manoeuvres to be effective. Otherwise the combatant party will not have the support of the populace and will be unable to establish a new order. This struggle is essentially for a cultural leadership that Gramsci terms hegemony.

The influence of the dominant class is dependent on the ideological acceptance of the working class, who are thus active in their own submission. Hegemony is a dialectical process with the capacity to homogenise opinion between the dominant and submissive positions in society. As such it is fragile, requiring the continual domination of the ideas of a few over the totality of a population. Hegemony is dependent on systems that disseminate information and perpetuate dominant ideals. Gramsci saw folklore as such a method, in which 'common-sense' could be propagated, as they have the capacity to normalise ideological positions. With Disney supplanting American folklore in the Depression era it was granted a special place within the dialectics of American culture as the vessel of old-fashioned (i.e. conservative) values.

Mass media has become central in discussions of hegemony as it has a tremendous capacity to homogenise opinion and transplant American cultural values onto those of other nations. Adorno in *The Culture Industry: The Enlightenment of Mass Deception* (Adorno and Horkheimer, 1944) situates ideological domination within the context of industry. He suggests that the industrial process of media is itself instrumental in producing cultural norms, thus achieving hegemony for an elite who profit from the enterprise. In this time of homogenisation by a particular set of a minority's ideals (i.e. North America, Hollywood), hegemony becomes particularly relevant. Mattelart and Dorfman (1991) demonstrate in their discussion of Disney comics that the company consciously propagated North American ideals to Latin America. This became particularly relevant during the time the text was written: the last days of the socialist Allende government. Allende's government would eventually be overthrown with American support, in what would become South America's bloodiest coup, installing the Chilean dictator Augusto Pinochet in the process (Kunzle, 1991). The innocuous nature of the comics produced a North American 'common-sense' in its readership, instilling the values necessitated by the pro-American capitalist minority that opposed the democratically elected socialist government. This relationship between the studio and state was perhaps most evident during World War II. During the war, Disney and other studios were involved in the production of a homogenised consumerist society, the purpose of which was to combat the external threat of war in Europe and internal conflicts of unionisation and social polarisation (Smoodin, 1994).

Unionisation and the Disney Strike

With the success of the first Disney features, Walt had established his company as a small but successful Hollywood production house. While the company's stock had been sold off as early as 1938, Walt and Roy were still the majority stock holders and were in control of the company at all levels. But their position within the studio would be shaken in the early 1940s with the unionisation of Hollywood, a movement that Walt strongly opposed.

With the company's economic growth the studio itself was able to expand from a small organisation to an animation factory. The studio moved from Hyperion to Burbank in May 1940. The new location was a large industrial complex and this relocation would fundamentally change the company's structure both physically and mentally for Disney employees. During the 1930s many of the people that worked at the studio spoke positively of their working environment, claiming it to be a creative and, to an extent, democratic place to work (Watts, 1997). With the change in the company's size came drastic changes in the company's organisation. The different departments – inkers, story-men, animators, etc. – were separated and connected via a series of tunnels. Movement between these departments was controlled and bureaucratised; it removed the relaxed and creative atmosphere that had characterised the studio in the preceding decade (Schickel, 1968). Disney was also the first studio to departmentalise based on gender. The studio story-men and animators were exclusively male, whereas the more mechanical and menial positions, such as inking and painting the animation cels, were handled exclusively by women.

In terms of organisational dynamics the studio was beginning to resemble what has been reported of Walt's early family life: strained by conflicting messages and abuses of position. The inconsistencies in Elias Disney's treatment of Walt became reflected within Walt's relation to his employees. Wages were calculated based on personal preference and whim rather than performance or time spent with the studio (Wasko, 2001). Walt's prejudices and preferences for different employees are likewise well documented and subject to much discussion. For now it is only important to note that with few exceptions the Disney Company was mostly white, with few women in important positions (Wasko, 2001, Elliot, 1993).

Walt was notoriously negligent of his employees' achievements. Early in the studio's existence Walt's name would be solely credited on cartoon shorts and the teams of animators, inkers and story-men would go without mention. These systematic inequalities created strain and resentment between Walt and his employees, which culminated in a union action that would cause a rift between Walt and his studio and was emblematic of the greater issues affecting American culture at the time.

During the unionisation of Hollywood in the 1930s the employees of different animation houses banded together to form the Screen Cartoonists Guild (SCG). To prevent the SCG gaining a foothold at his studio, Walt attempted to set up an internal company union that he would be able to control. The company union's failure to resolve labour injustices soon rendered it redundant and the SCG filed a complaint on behalf of Disney employees with the National Labor Relations Board (NLRB) for unfair labour practices in 1941. Walt responded to the complaint by firing a group of union activists he perceived as upstarts. The union members at Disney responded with a nine week strike. The strike exposed an even more brutal side to Walt. He physically assaulted a member of the strike and hired Willie Bioff, a member of the Capone Mafia who worked for different studios in Hollywood to intimidate union activists (Schickel, 1968).

This divergence at the level of class and labour struggle was directly at odds with the perceived need of Americans of the 1940s to present a unified and yet individualist front, with which to withstand the perceived threats posed by fascist governments in Europe (Smoodin, 1994). Disney had already become a major American cultural institution and thus part of the greater American hegemony. The highly publicised union action thus represents an obvious threat to Disney's place within the hegemonising machines of mass media. The last chapter discussed the transgressive nature of Disney narratives and the steps necessary to create a dominant reading of such transgressive texts. The next section shall outline how this functions not only in the micro-relation between viewer and screen but also within the macro-relation between the society and the organisations that regulate its messages.

Films Made in Studio During the Strike

Despite the turmoil occurring at the studio, the general public still perceived Disney in a thoroughly positive light. Wasko (2001) indicates that the industrial process at Disney's Burbank studio was a source of fascination for the general public, which seemed dazzled by the idea that fantasy itself could be manufactured. Indeed, Disney can be seen as the crystallisation of Hollywood's effort to manufacture and market fantasy and dreams (Brooker, 2010). This manufacture exposed the status of the machination for what it was, disrupting the audience's suspension of disbelief. This idealised fascination with a commercial process represents a suspension of *industrial* disbelief: the willingness of consumers to disregard the implicit ideological values of the products they consume. The finished product and the physicality of the animation factory seemed far removed from each other, to the point that the finished product was to the public something more fantasy than real, and yet more accessible and implicitly enjoyable. The glamorous fantasy of individual access and the enjoyment of consumable fantasy offers a distraction from the industrial process itself, which from witness accounts was clearly less than ideal.

Disney made subtle references to the strike action in several films. Perhaps most note-worthy is a scene in *Dumbo* in which the clowns of the circus become drunk and leery. They begin to discuss their pay and talk about how to exploit Dumbo, the object of the audience's affection, for a raise in salary. They leave their tent singing, "We're gonna hit up the big boss for a raise!". By placing the restless worker in the position of malevolence Disney denigrates the wants and needs of its own unhappy employees. Whether this was consciously orchestrated in production is unclear, yet the manifestation of such an obvious slur is unmistakable. This was a far more indicative image of the studio's attitude to its employees, as opposed to the sterile image put across by *The Reluctant Dragon*.

The Reluctant Dragon (1941) was a live-action feature that incorporated segments of animation and was made during the period of the strike. It features a middle-aged man, Mr Benchley, as he is forced by his wife to bring his nephew's pitch for a film to Disney. Mr Benchley blunders through the different studio departments on his way to a meeting with Walt. In the process he goes behind the scenes and experiences the various industrial processes of the studio. The film features characters from the then unreleased *Dumbo* and *Bambi*; the appearances of these characters acted as a promotion for these upcoming presentations. Although the feature itself is dry and narratively simplified, the content is quite rich in its ability to distract and manipulate an audience. As Dadoun (1989) notes demystification holds the paradoxical capacity to contribute to the solidity of myth.

Unlike the recently released *Fantasia*, *The Reluctant Dragon* is devoid of any overt displays of 'cartoon sexuality', which is instead replaced by awkward (live-action) sexual tension between Mr Benchley and an attractive female employee of the Disney studio. It is essentially a propaganda film, in that it actively employs emotive content to shape audience opinion and ideology for its own ends. In his discussion of *Der Ewige Jude* (1940) John J. Hartman (2000) discusses several definitions of propaganda. One of these describes propaganda as a manipulative, ideologically laden means of communication, provided by an interested party. It is difficult to make the case that information or ideas can be provided by a non-interested party! So perhaps it is best to see propaganda as an explicit attempt to persuade with a view to affecting the social order for political aims. Every medium is informed and shaped by interested parties, especially so in an industrial setting. As discussed before, the motivation to sell can be seen as a latent but integral part of all industrialised media. In this way propaganda can be seen in a continuum with mainstream film. *The Reluctant Dragon* represents Disney's first effective foray into propaganda. The studio would become quite active in the production of wartime propaganda films, as will be discussed in the following sections on World War II.

The film begins with Mr Benchley arguing with his wife against the idea of approaching what he perceives to be a busy studio head running a business, and remarks: "He can't listen to every crack pot with an idea". The narrative is structured by this statement, or more precisely proving it to be erroneous. Mr Benchley arrives at the studio with a preconception close to the image that had been witnessed by the actual employees of the Disney studio. The studio itself is depicted as a college campus: young attractive people walk in between spacious buildings with books in hand. As Mr Benchley enters the lot he is approached by a young man wearing a Disney-themed semblance of a Hitler Youth uniform; it even has a Mickey Mouse armband.

The young man formally greets Mr Benchley and informs that he has been instructed to show him around and bring him to meet Walt. In parodying the company's own authoritarian nature the film emphasises its image of whimsy. The increasingly excited Mr Benchley soon loses the uniformed man in favour of an attractive woman he sees wearing a robe, walking into a room labelled 'art class'. He tries to peek in through a window at the woman whom he hopes to see posing nude for a life-drawing class. He loses his balance and falls into the middle of the room, yet the teacher does not chastise his flagrant voyeurism but rather invites him in to look. Throughout the film, authority is depicted as innocuous and even supportive of his child-ishness and sexual precocity. This is very much indicative of the tone and direction of the film's address: to speak to the viewer as a child (Smoodin, 1994). Instead of a naked woman he finds an elephant in the room, perhaps what should be an apt metaphor for his presence in the class... The invitation to look under the pretence of seeing the female form naked tantalises the viewer. Thus the incomplete climax of his voyeurism motivates a mascu-linised viewer to stay engaged. In this way the scopic frustration of the viewer both perpetuates watching and is vented through humour, in the same manner that Freud suggests the dirty joke offers sexual catharsis (Freud, 1905b). Mr Benchley is in an exaggerated state of wonder and of a precocious sexual proclivity as he navigates the studio, free of the restraint that the young man in uniform represents.

He stumbles into a sound effects room where he once again meets the attractive woman he sought to catch a glimpse of. She takes the role of his alternative guide, whose address is based on pleasure rather than authority. The longer he spends in the studio the more his humour turns to childish giddiness as he flirts with the attractive young woman and discovers the different inventions of the studio. Among these are the multi-plane camera, story board and paint shop. He becomes a viewer at the studio, stopping in the various rooms to watch the films in production. As he starts watching the cartoons he becomes fixated on the image and lost in the manufactured fantasy, despite being surrounded by the elements of the manufacturing process. In every way he is the surrogate for the viewer within a subtly sexualised space, an overt point of engagement for the gaze which finds an object in both the body of the young woman and the regressive joy of the cartoon image, all the time escaping the strictures and law imposed by the young man in uniform.

If further evidence of the text's blatant objectification of women is needed, it is easily found in the scene in which Mr Benchley enters "the rainbow room", or the paint workshop. The workshop itself is presented to the viewer as an immense multi-coloured kitchen where women are busy mixing various ingredients. Mr Benchley exclaims: "Don't tell me you cook all this your-selves!" and "That all looks very tasty" to further denigrate the women's role on studio. The next scene takes him to a factory-like floor where female workers are inking animation cells. Apart from the attractive young woman he wolfishly follows, these are the only other women on offer at the studio, except for a miniature figurine of a semi-nude cartoon character (of the zebra-centaurs from *Fantasia*) that Mr Benchley tries to steal.

Men, however, are shown exclusively in important roles: working the com-plicated machines of the photography department, directing the sound effects and music, working playfully in the story-room and finally in the kernel of the studio: Walt's screening room.

As Mr Benchley enters the screening room followed by the man in uniform, Walt looks sceptically at the young man. The patronising regard, his casual suit and relaxed composure (even going so far as to put his foot up on a chair) appear as obvious and self-conscious attempts to polarise the infamously strict and uptight studio head against the caricature of his conservatism: the young uniformed man. Taking this unconvincing guise of a casual boss Walt says to the camera operator, "You can roll whenever its ready." Again the gesture appears self-conscious and contrived.

These live-action segments underline several key elements:

1. Sexual enticement.
2. Ideological address to an infantilised viewer.
3. Polarisation of roles.

The two short animated segments featured in the film follow the second element and attempt to further infantilise the viewer. The story of *Baby Weems*, which is featured as part of the story-room segment, features a two-day-old baby that can miraculously speak. The baby becomes instantly famous and his genius propels him to stardom and achievement, yet at the same time separates him from his mother and father. Finally, after losing his ability to speak, Weems becomes a regular babbling baby reunited with his parents. *Baby Weems* utilised quite a different style of animation that was far cheaper to produce as it did not attempt to capture three-dimensional realism but rather a more cartoon-like reality that was easier to draw (Wasko, 2001). Thus this short was a perfect example of the Disney ideological product of the 1940s – sentimental (valuation of the child in the family unit), regressive (joys of childhood over the stresses of responsibility) and economical (cheap to produce). The last short (*The Reluctant Dragon*, after which the film is named) is likewise unimpressive in terms of its animation. It features a camp and artistic dragon who is afraid of fighting, and an intellectual knight who conspires with a little boy to rid the town of the dragon without actually fighting. The short features a story once again discussing alternatives to obligation (the knight slaying the dragon) in favour of a sentimental and child-friendly (regressive) solution.

The film in its entirety attempts to democratise the space of the studio lot in an obvious and self-conscious manner. What immediately sets the film apart from the preceding features is that for the first time Disney film's credits had drawn attention to the employees at the studio. The credits feature not only an extensive list of the people that worked on the film but also their personalised caricatures, again paying lip-service to an image of democracy while deriding the staff in exaggerated likenesses. It is evident from the start that this film is straining to put across a light-hearted image of the relationship between employer and employees, and it did so successfully: the film was perceived as a documentary 'behind the scenes' look at the studio (Wasko, 2001), whereas in actuality it was an overt attempt to placate and distract an audience from the human element of its industrial process. By creating an image of the veritable playground of the Disney studio and placing the lead character into the role of a child, it does just that. Not only is the viewer patronised through their identification with Mr Benchley, but we are coaxed into a pseudo-documentary space where sex and play are used strategically to sell the innocuous image of Disney. This is done to reaffirm its place in the struggle for hegemony. Indeed the blatant nature of Walt's on-screen appearance, coupled with the heavy-handed presentation and the public nature of the strike, further emphasise how easily the audience bought into an artifice of the company's public relations.

This dynamic operates at the micro level of what Baudrillard (1988) discusses in terms of hyper-reality. Baudrillard's conception of the hyper-real suggests that the social realm has become independent of the Real to the extent that it has become a space in itself, merged with the imaginary. Simulation takes precedence over reality, forming a tapestry of signifiers that obscure the Real. A simulation is essentially a copy, to "feign what one hasn't" (Baudrillard, 1988, p167). It thus serves the same purpose as fantasy for Lacan: to create the illusion of having. Central to the creation of the hyper-real are simulacra, which are signifiers produced within media that effect and ultimately shape our subjectivity.

The human being is essentially subject to the symbolic order. Thus society as the realm of the symbolic holds precedence within human consciousness. If this society is impregnated by the signifiers of corporate media, which as discussed earlier is essentially an inescapable institution, then corporate media can shape this new and negotiated reality that the subject is unable to disengage from. These imposed signifiers are Baudrillard's simulacra. Intimately related to the simulacra is the simulation: a representation that substitutes for a thing in the Real. It is important to note that while the concepts of simulation and simulacra are compatible with and of value to a Lacanian discussion, Baudrillard's conception of the Real is different to that of Lacan. For Lacan, the Real is one of the three orders: it is that which is outside subjective experience. It is an order that language tries, but ultimately fails, to fully represent (Lacan, 1954c). What Baudrillard calls 'reality' is understood in Lacanian terms as the meeting of the symbolic and the Real. The Real for Lacan is essentially outside of subjective experience, as the subject is bound by the symbolic (and thus subjectivity and language) in their experience of reality. The hyper-real is a world in which the Real has been disavowed in favour of a merging transparency between registers of the symbolic and the imaginary.

Baudrillard suggests that simulated images evolved through a succession of phases. In the first of these the image is a reflection of reality, thus an exact copy. In the second phase the image perverts reality, as in the case of caricature. This order Baudrillard refers to as the order of malefice: of malevolent artifice. The third phase masks reality entirely until reality is entirely absent. Thus the simulation acts in place of reality. This shall be shown to be intimately related to the realm of propaganda. The last of these phases is where the image no longer bears resemblance to a reality, but rather becomes a "pure simulacrum" (Baudrillard, 1988, p171).

The commodification of mass-produced copies offers a more accessible reality. If the copy is attainable and the real thing is seemingly less so, then commodified reality will take precedence for the subject, who, as mentioned earlier, has a disposition to wish to manage their own gratification. Thus the commodified simulacrum offers the subject the possibility of administration within a controlled and commodified reality. This is the case in the viewer's vicarious gratification of Mr Benchley's regressive enjoyment. The product of the film itself offers the viewer a transgressive pleasure outside of the confines of Law. The scenario offers a gratifying simulacrum, one disconnected from the 'real' Disney and more easily enjoyable. This administration is further emphasised by a super-egoic command to enjoy, which can be demonstrated to be integral to propagandist media. In the case of *The Reluctant Dragon* the command is to enjoy a pure simulacrum of Disney, a third order simulation that forecloses the reality of the industrial process.

Baudrillard states that "Disneyland is presented as imaginary in order to make us believe that the rest [of America] is real" (1988, p172). Thus we are given a facsimile of reality: a third order simulation that perpetuates an amalgamation of the symbolic and the imaginary, while lightly referencing the Real but ultimately obscuring it. Thus, this creation, which he terms the hyper-real, has the capacity to add substance to a fantasy of America, which has overtaken any possibility of a Real 'reality'.

The hyper-real represents a sexual currency which Disney and other media industries utilise in asserting hegemony, the simulacra being the most basic unit through which this exchange occurs. Signifiers are manufactured and sold with a view to asserting ideological domination. In applying this reading of hyper-reality to the example of an image of a satisfied workforce, a magical and democratic Disney is produced in pseudo-documentary form. This fantasy is reproduced as a hybrid between the symbolic and imaginary through its choice of form and narrative content. This fantasy perpetuates the image of Disney that had been popularised in previous decades, yet had been called into question during the strike. *The Reluctant Dragon* represents Disney's first awkward attempt to consciously shift American hegemony to suit it's perverse ends: supplication and idealisation of the company for the consumer and thus social homogenisation.

It can be argued that hyper-reality facilitates the call for audience homogeneity by appealing to hyper-real sexualised imagery. This can be demonstrated in the analysis of the films produced out of the 'Good Neighbour' policy, which were produced to reinforce pro-North American sentiment in Latin American countries during WWII. Disney iconography of this period continually references themes of animation interloping and interacting with live action, a trope that shall be demonstrated as an attempt at hyper-realising sexuality to produce a 'cartoon jouissance'.

Chapter 10

Disney's 'Good Neighbour'

To diffuse tensions during the nine week strike Walt Disney was advised to leave the United States on a government-funded goodwill mission to South America. The political goal of the mission was to promote North American culture and values while at the same time encouraging support for the Allies in the event that the United States would have to enter the war. This was generally referred to as the 'good neighbour policy' (Smoodin, 1994, Wasko, 2001). While travelling Walt decided to make four films, each set in Brazil, Peru, Chile and Argentina respectively. The US State Department rejected the proposal to fund all four films and instead offered funding for a single film that would incorporate elements of each nation, reasoning that a single feature that incorporated national elements of several Latin American countries would reach a broader international audience.

Saludos Amigos (1942) was the result of this mission, featuring a mixture of live-action footage of Walt's travels, fantasy settings and overt propaganda. These elements were used to sell an image of pan-American unity. The film is split into four parts, each featuring a typical Disney narrative while referencing places or images in Latin America. The goal of the film is quite simply to take Latin American iconography and present it in a friendly light within a specifically Disney context. The first segment features a small Mexican boy and his llama interacting with Donald Duck in the manner of a cultural exchange, with the boy teaching Donald his customs. The second features a baby aircraft named Pedro who must triumph over adversity to deliver a package and make his parents proud. The third segment uses Goofy to draw parallels between American cowboys and Argentine ranchers. The fourth segment sees Donald Duck learning to salsa and attempting integrate into Brazil with the help of Joe Carioca, a Brazilian parrot who acts as his guide. All these shorts are made to be as innocuous as possible; none would bear the sexual over-emphasis of *The Three Caballeros* (1945), the other feature inspired by the trip. Thus the film uses a particular type of sexuality, or the explicit lack thereof, to reinforce the image of pan-American homogeneity: the incorporation of Latin America into Disney, a North American icon.

The Three Caballeros: Hyper-real Sexuality and Cartoon Jouissance

The Three Caballeros is perhaps the most blatant manipulation of sexual hegemony that Disney had so far released. The film demonstrates the process of hyper-realising sexuality within animation had been experimented with in Disney's production of wartime propaganda in the years prior to *The Three Caballeros* 1945 release. At first glance *Caballeros* was another of Disney's 1940s compilation features, a feature-length film made up of interconnected shorts. The narrative omits the classic Disney conventions of placing a unit under threat and instead structures itself around the build-up to a dramatic climax, in much the same way as *Fantasia*. The film starts with Donald receiving a box from South America in which he finds a projector, film and several books. The film contains several mini-narratives that the viewer watches with Donald, we the audience engage with a film within a film. The impulsive duck is our emotive guide to the filmic space. Thus the viewer begins their engagement with a text based on Donald's reaction to and engagement with the stories watched with him.

The first story follows a penguin named Pedro, who hates the cold and decides to migrate north to the tropics. This is followed by a documentary-style introduction to a variety of other birds and then a short featuring a little boy who befriends a flying donkey and becomes a national celebrity. This mini-narrative is very much the typical Disney story; it features a diminutive hero battling for recognition aided by a magical intervention. The remainder of the feature sets Donald in direct contact with Latin American culture and peoples. He finishes the films on the projector and opens the first of his picture books. The first book opens into a pop out version of Baia, Brazil where Donald meets Joe Carioca, the parrot introduced in *Saludos Amigos*. Joe brings Donald on a tour of the city and introduces him to Aurora Miranda, a Brazilian singer, and the sister of Carmen Miranda (Shale, 1982). The city-scape utterly encapsulates hyper-reality: it begins as pure animation but as the viewer is introduced to the live-action actress and actors, the action takes place on a theatrical set that has been constructed and painted to appear cartoon-like and animated. Live-action images become warped into a second phase simulation, an altered and caricatured reality. Upon meeting the live-action actress, Donald becomes instantly enamoured and aggressively pursues her while she and a group of men begin a musical dance number. Donald is jealous and aggravated by the human male protagonists.

The image of Donald and Aurora is undeniably maternal. The duck is small in stature compared to the live-action people, roughly the size of a young child. Striving for Aurora's attention gives Donald the appearance of a demanding youth, fighting against the phallic potency of the flesh-and-blood adult men surrounding her. Indeed an article in *Time* magazine reviewing the film described Donald and his relation to women in the film as "pathological" (*Time* cited in Smoodin, 1994, p112), suggesting that the audience of the time found these parts of the film disconcerting to say the least. The dance with Aurora climaxes when the other dancers form a parade and march off the screen with Joe Carioca, leaving Aurora and Donald alone. Donald shyly approaches Aurora with a bouquet of flowers. She takes them and gives Donald a big kiss. Startled and overcome with this kiss, Donald's bow-tie and collar make rhythmic stiffening and curling motions, his eyes roll and he descends into a bizarre set of hallucinations. Rhythm is an important structuring principle within *Caballeros* and adds to the physicality of the sexualised filmic space. As discussed earlier, some propose that rhythm holds a masturbatory quality that calms anxiety (Mollenhoff, 1940). In this case the anxiety concerns the flirtation with boundaries. The first boundary is the subtle blurring between the animated and the live; Donald is attempting to break the boundary between the drawn and the photographic and finally he succeeds. The second transgression is that of the pleasure principle: as Donald approaches the object of his obsessive and aggressive advances he surpasses himself and the limits typically set on him. The demanding child rarely attains what it is that captivates their focus, thus Donald provides the fantasy of attainment. But instead of the jouissance that we expect from such transgressive pleasures, he is embroiled in a unique *cartoon jouissance* – a gratification that embodies the subject's fantasy of what lies beyond the pleasure principle: boundless pleasure. But rather than depicting anything as crude as a sexually sated and satisfied 'post-climax' Donald, the boundaries between narrative and image lose their cohesion and he falls into a hallucinatory state without lack or desire. The surrealistic and disturbing quality of hallucinations is beyond obvious interpretation, similar in presentation to

159

the startling, near-subliminal set of images depicting castration anxiety in *Pinocchio*.

The first hallucinatory images are of different musical instruments playing themselves. As the phallic connotations within Disney films of Donald 'playing his instrument' have already been established, it is sufficient to say that what is significant here is their autonomy. They are the self-gratifying organ, achieving its penultimate aim. The pace of the editing and the rhythm of the music intensify as Donald is swept away in excess and emotion. The live-action dancers and Aurora are transposed over the progressive psychedelia of the imagery. They dance as before until two men lock eyes and transform into animated cockerels that viciously attack each other against a red background. Their necks thrust aggressively at each other as they start to transform again into live-action people. Meanwhile, Donald, Aurora and the other men jeer and goad them on. Donald appears satisfied that violence is occurring to the threatening body of the live-action actors. Even though no blows are actually exchanged, the allusion to the ferocity of the cock-fight establishes a vehemence and brutality within the scene.

As the characters start to leave their hallucinatory state, Aurora leads a carnival procession through the streets of Baia. She gives life to different inanimate objects until the entire city is dancing in rhythm to her music. Autonomous gratification (rhythm), empowerment beyond the phallic (Donald achieving Aurora while the 'real men' are occupied) and transgression (pleasure principle/intra-reality) are combined and related to each other in a sexuated space that can best be described as hyper-real: reality is permeated with animation as a fantasy-scape that leaves a live-action 'reality' ultimately obscured. Upon leaving the book, there is a rather curious segment in which Donald describes what he thought of Baia. Although he expresses himself in a childish fashion (made all the more apparent by Joe Carioca's worldliness), he is only interested in talking about the women. As he describes the beautiful women he saw, he himself takes on curves and grows breasts. At this point Joe says, "You are the wolf, take it easy". This sexually garish display speaks further of the boundaries that have been crossed. As Donald's sexually impotent form feminises, the viewer cannot help but feel perturbed at the little duck's precocity. Although the hallucinatory scenes themselves represent a climax, the sequence pales in comparison to the final part of the film. As mentioned the narrative is structured by intensification, albeit with a few breaths between segments. Each segment becomes progressively more complex, in that each time we enter a new part of South America, additional protagonists are introduced (Shale, 1982).

Opening another present, marked "Mexico", the viewer is immediately transported into yet another psychedelic sequence. The screen is bombarded with a series of abstract colours in rhythm to Mexican music. Exploding through the colours we are introduced to the third caballero, Panchito, who arrives firing a pair of revolvers and dancing. Panchito and Joe Carioca have the effect of further trivialising Donald and his efforts. They are both phallically empowered characters, particularly when Donald is situated in their company. They are presented as more confident and less libidinally driven than Donald. Panchito's pistols and Joe's magic umbrella are the visual reminders of their phallic potency, whereas Donald's phallic nature must be actualised through the seemingly desperate action of his sexual pursuits. While both Panchito and Joe Carioca are also enamoured by the women in the film, they are not driven to sexual excess to the same extent as Donald, rather they act in restraint to Donald's sexual advances.

The final part of the film begins with various stories set in Mexico, after which the three enter into a live-action segment while flying on a magic carpet. They pass through various scenes of Mexican culture and dance until they arrive above Acapulco beach. From their safe vantage point above the beach, Panchito passes Donald a telescope and says, "Have a look at what you might call, 'the hot stuff'". We follow Donald's gaze through the telescope to see various women sunbathing in swimwear. At this point the telescope starts shaking and goes hard in Donald's hands, much to his surprise and excitement.

After Donald achieves his surprising arousal, the caballeros start fighting over the telescope until all three are joining in a shared gaze at the semi-nude women, who smile and wave at them invitingly. Upon receiving this acknow-ledgement, the three caballeros and their carpet dive aggressively at the beach frightening the women and knocking over umbrellas and tables. Upon arriving Donald aggressively flirts with the women, referring to them dero-gatively as "toots". The women blind-fold Donald and play games with him, after which Panchito and Joe pull him away from the scene until he is back in his world, struggling to return. Within this scene there is a curious duality to Panchito and Joe's role. Though they act as restraints for Donald's aggressive sexual advances, they are also the providers of the scenarios, bringing him to different places where he can find expression to his libido. The cheerful manner with which they offer up the situations and women

The excited boys
(Image by Paul Byrne)

speaks to their endorsement and encouragement of the demanding, child-like homunculus. Thus the two native caballeros take a super-egoic role, providing limits to gratification but likewise pushing Donald to enjoy.

The concept of the super-ego has its roots in Freud's *The Ego and the Id* (1923). Freud proposed the super-ego as the internalisation of the paternal agency: that which internally curtails and judges the subject. Freud also suggested that the super-ego is the image that the subject aspires to, and he uses the term interchangeably with the ego ideal. In *Family Complexes in the Formation of the Individual* (1938) Lacan situates the super-ego as separate from the ego ideal, which he suggests is the idealised position of separation from the mother that the father institutes. The ego ideal becomes a symbolic introjection of a post-Oedipal solution for the child. This Lacan opposes to the ideal ego, which is the imaginary construction of the ego as the entirety of the subject's being. The subject introjects this schema of entirety from the specular image, which they come in contact with during the mirror stage. This image, that of the ideal ego, is an illusion of solidity and unity that the subject never gains access to (Lacan, 1954b).

The ego ideal is rather a symbolic template to which the subject attempts to adhere, based on the will of the paternal agency as embodied by the super-ego. The super-ego as paternal agency is borne of a need to repress the incestuous connection to the mother and force the child to move outside the Oedipal triangle. While the super-ego refers and is related to the Law, it is rather a symbolic interpretation of the Law that is learned and introjected through the intervention of the father. Thus the super-ego does not necessarily parallel the Law of the world: the Law that prohibits transgression as expressed by the pleasure principle. The super-ego as an agency does not necessarily coincide with the Law and its implicit pleasure principle. Existing simultaneously with the super-ego's regulation of the subject is a command to enjoy a little, without going to the limits defined by transgression (Lacan, 1972). It is this command that can be seen in the super-egoic roles of Panchito and Joe.

Panchito and Joe turn the page of the book and see the face of a woman singing in a starry sky. As expected Donald is instantly enamoured and the following sequences are structured by his advances. His courting of this disembodied head is interrupted by intensely surreal hallucinations which blend the stars into flowers, until the woman's face emerges from a flower. When Donald nears the flower and is about to kiss her, he is startled by Panchito whose neck and head are erected from the flower where the face should be. This image transforms into a piñata which explodes, showering the screen with gifts. In the background three live-action women appear in their bathing suits. Next we see an ensemble of semi-nude women while Donald's head materialises and watches them intently. Now it is the women who are blindfolded, leaving Donald to watch and enjoy and the viewer to identify with and engage through the duck's unrepentant voyeurism.

Ellis (1982) suggests that the viewer's engagement with the body on screen subscribes to either voyeuristic or fetishistic looking. The hyper-real filmscape is a particularly voyeuristic space in *Caballeros*, with the body objectified but kept at a distance within the diegetic cartoon world. Voyeuristic looking is marked by distance between the seer and seen, which allows the spectator a degree of power over what is seen. This becomes necessary in negotiating the enhanced nature of the simulacrum, which is implicitly sexualised to the point of becoming overwhelming: the fetishistic qualities of an essentially uncanny image become deeply unsettling via its negotiation of proximity. Fetishistic looking stops the narrative and provides moments of pure objectification. Rather than a gap between seer and seen, the fetishistic look attempts to abolish distance between the subject and the object. Both are structured by activity and passivity, and both are attempts to assuage castration anxiety. *Caballeros* fits neatly into the structure of voyeuristic looking while making a conscious avoidance of fetishising the female form. This avoidance of fetishistic reduction perhaps serves the purpose of an already strained Hayes code, or perhaps voyeurism itself creates the safe distance necessary to the viewer's engagement with a hyper-realised space. In fact the distance that the viewer is able to maintain in relation to Donald's escapades is precisely what allowed these sequences to pass the

163

censors of the time. If the viewer was subjected to seeing the 'too much' of the fetish perhaps the element of unhindered transgressive arousal would change the perception of content from the cartoon to pseudo-pornographic.

After experiencing Donald's unrepentant voyeurism the viewer is subjected to a set of discordant images. The woman's face appears in a flower once more but now she transforms into a full live-action body with flower petals surrounding her face. Donald meanwhile has taken on the guise of a bee. The obvious inference of his excitement: that he wishes to pollinate her flower. This scene transforms into another setting, featuring the same woman who is now dressed in traditional Mexican attire. She dances with Donald while surrounded by animated phallic cacti that rhythmically thrust in time with the music. The imagery intensifies until Donald is left in a darkened space being taunted by the two other caballeros. The film finishes with an enraged Donald charging a wooden bull filled with fireworks. Upon their collision the bull explodes; a libidinal eruption after which Donald is left exhausted. Amongst the climax of explosion "fin" is left imprinted in the sky. A more literal and obvious visual orgasm could not be asked for.

The Three Caballeros received quite negative reviews, firstly for its self-conscious style of animation and secondly for its vulgarity and lack of subtlety in engaging with Latin America as subject matter (Schickel, 1968, Smoodin, 1994). As mentioned earlier, the critics reacted poorly to the cartoon animal/live woman pairing. The inference of bestiality is further emphasised by the unsettling nature of the hyper-real image, of the cartoon and human figure flirtatiously interacting. There is a curious aesthetic principle of the hyper-real and in particular the simulation's proximity to the uncanny. The closer representations come to absolute human mimesis, the more anxiously the viewer will receive their differences. This is similarly reflected in the animated interloping in live-action and *vice versa*. This space, in which representation approaches mimicry and dramatically falls in its appeal, is referred to as the uncanny valley (Mori, 1970). The valley refers to the dip evident in the graph overleaf, which depicts a 'thing's' familiarity plotted against its resemblance and reference to the human form.

In the graph, the strangeness or lack of appeal is described as 'negative familiarity'; positive familiarity obviously references appeal. It is evident from Mori's figuration that as the thing approaches human likeness there is a dramatic fall in its appeal. Familiarity is graphed with resemblance to the human form; when the image becomes more human-like it will lose a great deal of its appeal, until it becomes an exact approximation of the human form. Successful cartoon representations of human beings generally emphasise dissimilarity to avoid falling into the uncanny valley, such as *The Simpsons* with their yellowed skin and four fingers (Mangan, 2007). The conflation of animated and live-action figures achieves an equally uncanny response; something unfamiliar and alien becomes too close to human representation through Donald's placement and precocious sexual actions. The hyper-real scene becomes unpleasant when it reduces the boundaries between the subject and the phantasmagoria of sexual access within the cartoon world.

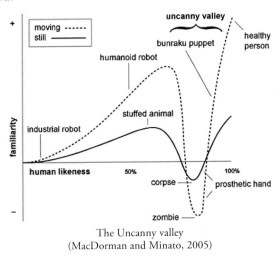

The Uncanny valley
(MacDorman and Minato, 2005)

Hyper-reality and its viewing is thus a fragile balancing of representation. The conflation of live-action and animation must be kept within the safe limits of a voyeuristic staging to maintain distance to the viewer and provide their gaze with a seemingly innocuous avenue with which to enjoy a more hidden transgressive content. However, in this regard *Caballeros* failed, as the critics of the time demonstrate. Smoodin (1994) argues that the advertising which went with the feature may have contributed to its poor reception, as it further emphasised the 'mixing' of animated animals and live women. The presentation of women in the advertising crossed boundaries maintained by the voyeurism operant within the film. Providing highly aesthetic images of the women within the add posters fetishistically attempts to engage the male gaze.

Communist witch-hunts and red fear

While Walt Disney was travelling through South America in aid of the good

165

neighbour policy Roy was able to settle with the strikers, conceding to the majority of their demands. At the time it had been the longest-running labour dispute in Hollywood. After the strike, Walt became progressively embittered towards his employees and began to lose interest in the Disney production process. The environment of the studio would never recover its pre-1940s creative atmosphere. Walt was affected by what he saw as an intimate failure on the part of his new family. His mistrust of labour unions pathologised into paranoia and he became increasingly obsessed with the perceived threat of communism. This paranoia manifested in an aggression he directed at supposed threats to the American dream, which he so perfectly encapsulated.

The research of several writers (Wasko, 2001, Schickel, 1968, Watts, 1997) suggests that Walt's political leanings were very much a reflection of his own personal values. He was an attendee at American Nazi party meetings, an opponent of unionisation and communism and a staunch Republican supporter. Indeed his ideological transparency with Ford also endeared him to Leni Riefenstahl, whom Walt met briefly on her Nazi-goodwill mission to Hollywood (Leslie, 2002). In fact, Walt was the only Hollywood producer to agree to meet her.

The struggle with unionisation at his own studio gave fuel to his political leanings and provided an outlet for his now deep-seated resentment of his workers. He became an instrumental figure in the Motion Picture Association of America (MPAA), which would produce the notorious Hollywood Blacklist: a list of industry professionals labelled as communists. This resulted in numerous professionals being exiled from Hollywood, never to work in the American film industry again. Among those named by Walt as communist conspirators was David Hilberman, a veteran animator at the studio and one of the Disney strike leaders. Although there existed no proof of his supposed communist affiliations, Walt's accusation proved significant enough to have his name added to the blacklist. As a result he would never work in Hollywood again (*Secret Lives: Walt Disney*, 1995).

The unionisation of Hollywood represented a move by people to challenge and democratise established American institutions. Instrumental in this process was publicising certain inconsistencies and inequalities implicit in American society. While Hollywood had a reputation for being morally corrupt, Walt Disney and his studio were universally praised for their cleanliness and strength of morality; in fact Walt himself was considered unanimously by the popular press as a Hollywood 'golden boy'. Many of the major Hollywood studio heads were Jewish Americans who had moved to California from New York. They were urbanites and culturally a minority in the United States. Walt was the image of the average American: conservative and Christian, who could claim to both suburban and rural upbringing. What Disney biographers seem to agree upon most clearly is that Walt was so successful in estimating audience reaction as he himself represented the embodiment of mainstream social values. Thus the image of Walt Disney became sacrosanct within American culture. In the 1930s he had become a shining example of how the average American can achieve his dream, and in the process integrated himself into the wider American iconography. The image of unhappy workers at his animation factory was an attack on the great American psyche, which is perhaps why it had so little effect on mainstream perceptions of Disney as a studio. As Mattelart and Dorfman (1991) discuss, Disney had already established itself within American hegemony from early in the company's inception. It can be supposed that the public was more than content to disavow the cruel realities of Disney that the strike pointed to (Smoodin, 1994). The perverse duality that kept the company popular is also what acts as a cultural protection for the image of the organisation itself. Long (2008) describes that this denial is implicit in the structure of perversion and functions as a defence of the narcissistic integrity of perverse structure; this defensive position being fetishistic in nature.

The collective imago of Disney is a construction that can be seen as a cultural fetish; constructed as an absolute, whole and altogether irreproachable image. In order for its image to assuage collective anxieties it must disavow certain realities. This disavowal is carried out in the unconscious but expressed in the field of hegemony. In a similar way, in *Looking Awry* (1991) Zizek discusses Stalinism's perpetuation the image of Stalin as servant of the people, yet by the same measure he embodied all manner of physical and Real cruelties. The image of Stalin is erected as unquestionable to hide the perverse duality of the monstrous institution, in this case the government. Disney's role in American culture is similarly integral and precarious. This defensive mechanism is what bars the public from the 'true' industrial process behind a façade of innocence.

Although Roy Disney settled with the strikers and the company gave into their demands, Disney never publicly admitted guilt or wrong-doing. No damage was done to the company's image; the collective American consciousness accepted the disavowal the company offered. This is an overt expression of what Gramsci refers to as the war of position, in which competing ideologies are suppressed, not just by those in power who this suppression serves (Disney, Hollywood and the American government), but by the greater American public, who were disinterested in conceptualising Disney as anything but harmless family entertainment.

There are many accounts in critical theory of the Disney company maintainance of an acceptable image for society, despite the many dualities that have been exposed in the company's image. Even within critical discourse Disney has long been perceived as a difficult subject for academic discussion to engage with, though this has changed significantly in recent years with the informal establishment of 'Disney studies'. Writers such as Schickel (1968), Giroux (2000), Elliot (1993), Mattelart and Dorfman (1991) all came to academic or even political conflict as a result of their critiques of Disney. This is a clear expression of disavowal operating to protect the structure of dominant ideological positions by preserving Disney's fetishised image. While Mattelart and Dorfman were exiled from Chile for their socialist leaning, their book *How To Read Donald Duck* (1991) was burned along with other leftist texts that were associated with Allende's government and therefore threatening to the American-backed Pinochet coup. The text was prohibited in Chile while the Pinochet government remained in power (Kunzle, 1991), and Disney sought to ban its import into the United States (Byrne and McQuillan, 1999). Thus American and capitalist hegemony can be seen to be intimately tied to Disney, to the point that to discuss one necessitates a discussion of the system as a whole. The perverse mechanism is not just an abstract dynamic within the company; it is an intrinsic hegemonic principle within the society it exists in. Perversity is not just an aspect of the individual and the organisation, it is a fundamental structuring principle of mass culture.

Within this hegemonic exchange there is a cultural exchange at the level of fetishism. The argument here thus starts to coincide with Althusser's (1971) position that ideology becomes implicit in the product, and this product then goes on to aid the subject in constructing the ego. This mirrors Baudrillard's position that simulacra are implicitly ideological. Media corporations such as Disney thus exemplify the ideological state apparatus that Althusser discusses. The ideology implicit in these apparatus is mirrored in the subject who engages with them via the regressive cinematic apparatus. Thus the fetish should express a dynamic shift in the 1940s, which Eric Smoodin (1994) has drawn attention to in his discussion of the cartoon body as an ideological currency of the period.

Chapter 11

World War II and Propaganda

This chapter shall offer textual analyses of the propaganda and educational films produced by Disney during World War II. These textual analyses can be situated within their industrial and socio-historical context and the points collected in these analyses can be related to the greater process of hegemony, and integrated into a theory of the cartoon body as begun in previous chapters.

During World War II there was a tremendous drop in box office attendance. This, coupled with closed foreign markets, led to a severe crisis for many Hollywood studios. Many studios began working for and with the government to provide alternative sources of income. Disney likewise became involved in the war effort, even renting part of its studio to the United States Military. Although this would be a difficult time for Hollywood studios, the tactics they employed in recouping their losses at home would greatly benefit the American film industry after the war. Ensuring that their films were able to recoup production costs at home meant that foreign markets could be exploited purely for profit, which similarly led to Hollywood's domination of European markets after the First World War (Kolker, 1999). Disney survived this period both through its ability to diversify its products and by working closely with the American government. Its production of propaganda was particularly important, as it provided the company with the grounds to experiment with and perfect the manipulation of American hegemony for commercial ends: to position itself centrally in American culture, tradition and consumerism.

It is important to clarify what is meant by propaganda and for the sake of this discussion to review psychoanalytic accounts of propagandist film. While many of the authors mentioned here discuss propaganda, the majority of them specifically analyse fascist propaganda and the continuity between propaganda and fascist modes of thinking. Ernst Kris (1944) sees an essential division between the propaganda of democratic and totalitarian nations. Fascist propaganda focuses on the idealisation of the leader, while democratic propaganda distributes this idealisation between the subject's ego and the leader. In both cases the super-ego is projected onto a source outside of the subject, either onto the leader or the nation.

While the ideology underlying the Disney organisation is unquestionably right of centre, the appeal to the subject is always done to instigate an idealised democracy, within which the collective American ego is sacrosanct. There are overlaps in this appeal between the propaganda of Disney and that of fascist Germany: in both cases there is a concerted attempt to homogenise the audience in order to produce a uniform response. Kris (1943) claims that democratic propaganda distributes identification between the ego and the super-ego more evenly than in the case of fascist propaganda, which seeks to emphasise the totalitarian voice of the super-egoic leader. He also draws the comparison between ritual dance and propaganda, both of which Freud (1922) suggests to have the capacity to regress the subject to emotional states that overbear rationale. In this state the 'leader' or master takes the position of the super-ego, making an intra-subjective address to the subject. Thus order comes from within rather than from an external agency.

In his discussion of the emotional appeal of propaganda, John J. Hartman (2000) describes the propagandist film as an attempt to propagate a set of ideas or ideology by an interested group. While defining propaganda in terms of ideological propagation is useful in that it situates this form in a continuum with mainstream media, it is also necessary to delimit the concept. Propaganda achieves ideological complicity through an emotional rather than rational address to the viewer, although 'rational' arguments are made to appear as central to the form. The propaganda film aims to regress its viewer to simplistic emotional responses to establish a threat and make it appear manifest. This threat causes a regression in its recipient which is marked by extreme binary thinking: *this is right, as opposed to that which is wrong.* The solution to this threat is the ideology being sold, which becomes manifest in a group, an individual or an organisation. The propaganda film blends reality and fantasy with the result of creating a daydream in which "images connect with primary process" (Hartman, 2000, p336). Thus the propagandist provides a space in which fears are played out, the resolution of which is dependent on ideology as a product.

The concept of crowd regression has its origins in the controversial work of

Gustave Le Bon (1895). Le Bon proposed that crowds become dependent on images and illusions to guide their actions. The leader must thus supply these illusions to garner support. Freud's (1922) *Group Psychology and Analysis of the Ego* describes the group's motivation as stemming from a regression to erotic ties as opposed to reason or perception. Freud (1922) suggests that the leader takes the position of the ego ideal, taking residence in the subject's unconscious life as an apparition of the primal father: the dominating, irrefusable father of the primal horde. Propaganda is thus a regression to a ritualistic form of communication in which emotion is sanctioned by an agency of social control: an externalised super-ego. Adorno (1951) suggests that the subject idealises the leader or the ideological entity as a substitute for self-idealisation. The libido that would normally find expression in Freud's (1914) primary narcissism becomes attached to the leader, forming what is essentially an artificial regression (Adorno 1951). The subject loses their own ego ideal, for which the leader acts as a substitute.

Adorno, Lowenthal and Massing (1946) collectively discuss the capacity of unconscious conflict to bypass logic in their analysis of American fascist propaganda. Adorno claims that there are three characteristics of this propaganda:

1. It is personalised and non-objective: it brings the individual into relation with their needs in the image of a small man transformed to potency.

2. It substitutes means for ends: discussion of what needs to be done as opposed to what this will ultimately accomplish.

3. Propaganda is *ultimate content*, it provides a simplified solution to the problems of gratification.

Adorno takes note that propaganda can function as gratification in itself, and constitutes an irrational wish fulfilment. He compares the propagandist film to the viewer's engagement with the soap-opera, in that it depends on a gratification through vicarious catharsis in seeing a problem approached and a resolution offered. This is contrary to an important and obvious principle in the propaganda film. Rather than offering catharsis in viewing a problem resolved, the effectiveness of the propaganda film is often dependent on the viewer's frustration with a problem. This frustration is what motivates the viewer to leave the auditorium and affect change themselves.

Kris (1943) suggests that the propaganda of the Western world had become self-conscious in the 1940s, reacting against the propaganda of the First World War it now had to to rely on an appeal to consumerism and an awareness of the failings of jingoism. He describes the Second World War as the war in which propaganda essentially failed to rouse the conformity of the first war. In discussing the old and new propagandas (new referring to the 1940s), Kris seems to advocate a form based on a "strategy of truth" (Kris, 1943, p386). This is evident in the propaganda films of the 1940s, which offer a melange of truth and fiction, conflating the two to produce a false reality, or what Kris and Speier later describe as the production of a "staged reality" (Kris and Speier, 1944, p13). The concept of the hyper-real can be shown to be structurally transparent with that of the staged reality discussed within propaganda, which can be shown to carry simulacra that colour and affect culture through the process of hegemony. This is particularly blatant in the pseudo-documentary form, such as *The Reluctant Dragon* or *Victory Through Air-Power* (1943). It can thus be demonstrated through the analysis Disney's propaganda films produced during the war, that the viewer's negotiation between gratification and the super-ego is dependent on the regressive aspects of the Disney form.

The Production of Canadian Propaganda

Although America did not formally join the war until 1941, Disney studios had already begun making films to support the war effort for Canada, which had joined the conflict alongside the United Kingdom. This first batch of propaganda films seemed a long way removed from the studio's previous output: the innocent cartoon shorts of the 1920s and 30s.

Most of the Canadian propaganda films were produced to promote the purchase of war-bonds. This was a government savings scheme that encouraged the population to invest their money in the war effort, under the promise that these savings would be partially repaid after the war ended. The first of these was *The Thrifty Pig* (1941), which was a revamped version of *The Three Little Pigs* (1933). The story is much the same as the original, except that now the big bad wolf wears a Nazi armband and a German officer's hat. He chases the two lazy, child-like pigs until they flee into the house of the wise thrifty pig, who cleverly built his house out of war bonds. Just as in the original, the two lazy pigs are infantilised and the wise pig represents the gruff, prudish voice of the conservative working man. The wolf is shaggy, hairy and dark; his mouth drips with saliva. He is similar in appearance to the black shaggy helpers discussed in *Pinocchio*; indeed hair, shagginess and gruffness can be seen to signify a negativised maturity. The wolf's voice is much deeper and more adult-like than those of the pigs.

When the wolf comes to eat the pigs at the house made of war-bonds, they defend themselves by hurling the bricks (i.e. the bonds themselves) at the wolf until he runs howling from the house. The short concludes with a string of aggressive and obvious propagandist images. Allied planes attack German planes which are riddled with bullet holes and sent crashing. Allied warships fire on German ships which explode and sink. This final section is set to stirring instrumental music and features a mature male voice goading the viewer to victory. These images in the context of the re-worked Disney cartoon have quite a jarring effect. They are of a different kind of animation, far more realistic in their appearance. In striving for overt realism they create an abrupt contrast between the animated sequence and the string of propaganda featured at the end. It is interesting then, that this scene can be described as aesthetically hyper-real. The blending of animation with an uncanny attention to realistic detail gives us an image that starkly contrasts with the Disney animation that has come before. This is a different kind of hyper-real imagery from what has been discussed in *The Three Caballeros*. *Caballeros* transposed animated characters into a space in which they could interact with real characters. These propagandist images accomplish the creation of a similar space by subtly blending reality and animation, which creates all the more perfectly the third phase of simulation.

The purpose of the creation of this space seems radically different in context. For *Caballeros*, the hyper-real space makes available the foreign and exotic body, a space where fantasy can be played out in the safety of an innocuous animated medium but with a tangible and 'real' object. The propaganda sequence, however, creates an image of victory again in the safe space of animated fantasy, but drawing on reality to create a perceptibility and tangibility to the image. In comparing *The Thrifty Pig* to succeeding shorts a clear pattern emerges that denudes the mechanism and structure at work in these early propagandas.

The Seven Wise Dwarfs (1941) follows the same formula. This short starts with a reanimated seven dwarves working in their mine but humming a slightly different tune. Instead of "from off to work we go ..." (*Snow White and the Seven Dwarfs*, 1937) they sing, "We'll do our part with all our heart". They bring their precious gems into a contemporary-looking North American town to invest their hoard in war bonds at the bank and post office. Again a familiar cartoon image is brought into contact with contemporary political and social themes, and is finally set against the concluding hyper-real images of victory and war in the violent end sequence. The space created, albeit crudely, is hyper-real and protagonist. Similar to Donald Duck and the three pigs, the dwarves are child-like and infantilised. The target of the short is clearly adults with money to invest in war-bonds, thus the short represents an attempt to infantilise and simplify the position of the adult subject.

This infantilised position is put in a context that is both cartoon, supposedly innocent, and adult through the themes and images of war-bonds and warfare. All the time the address to the viewer is enunciated from an authority (the government war-bonds scheme) to the position of the child. *Donald's Decision* (1942) was an altered version of *Donald's Better Self* (1938), in which Donald struggles between an angelic and demonic version of himself. Donald's evil self is identical to him, except that he is dressed in a red devil costume and has a gruff, leery man's voice. His angelic self is another version of Donald wearing a white robe and halo. He, and he is referred to as a 'he', is voiced by a woman, and is made to sound maternal and innocuous. This short is interesting as it initiates a binary opposition between authorities: there is a bad authority and a good.

A commanding voice comes from Donald's radio to encourage citizens to invest in war bonds. The angel tells Donald to go to the bank right away, while the devil insists that he spend the money having a good time. The angel tells Donald that he must "defend the country that makes good times possible". Rather than making the choice between enjoyment and duty, the two are tied together. Thus Donald is directed to defend his capacity to enjoy. This authority insists that Donald must *usufruct* his gratification, as opposed to the bad authority who insists that Donald foreclose law and gratify himself regardless of consequence, in this case the consequence to the country.

Usufruct, as Lacan (1972) uses the term, refers to the command by the super-ego to enjoy in part, to make enjoyment possible in the context of society. This enjoyment in part allows the subject partial gratification as they are not permitted to venture into excess. It is this principle that underlies the seeming paradox of the super-ego's command for the subject to 'enjoy'. As stated earlier, the super-ego does not strictly adhere to the Law and the prohibition of boundless gratification embodied in the pleasure principle. The super-ego has the capacity to brutalise the subject, to bring them into contact with jouissance and thus transgression (Lacan, 1972). It is thus possible to split the function of the super-ego between positive and negative affects on the subject, and indeed this is what the viewer starts to see in Disney propaganda films.

The 'good' super-ego is represented by the angel and the voice from the radio.

174

They command the subject to enjoy in the context of patriotism and national duty (as extension of the Law). The devil, however, pushes Donald to the excess of enjoyment, free of the social contract. What is of course ironic is that Donald has traditionally been associated with the id, a character unaccustomed to boundary and any paternal 'no'. Thus the short is also demonstrating that even the demanding child can be brought into line with the command, just so long as that command offers some enjoyment. The devil is not able to argue with the angel's interdiction and attacks while saying, "I'll have to blitz him!" The reference ties the association of this immoral authority to the perceived foe: Nazism. The angel defeats the devil and walks Donald past an array of recruitment posters to the post office.

What is peculiar about the short is the choices made regarding these voices of command. First there is the booming master's voice on the radio, followed by the calm sensible mother and finally the leery despicable voice of the devil. Donald's voice is incoherent and childish as always. He is the babbling inarticulate child, barely comprehensible except for his indignation and tantrums. The mother's position in the film is to coax the child to stand up against the enemy by accepting that to continue to enjoy and indulge itself, the child will need to delay and usufruct gratification. The voice of the mother reinforces the paternal quality of the voice on the radio but also creates the object for the child. Embodying and referencing the big Other, the female voice offers Donald a point of gratification, though it is strange that this voice is positioned within a clone of Donald that is clearly referred to as a 'he'.

Perhaps the crudest of the films commissioned for the Canadian government was 1943's *All Together Now*, which featured the whole host of Disney characters. It involves a parade in front of the Parliament. Among the demonstrators are: Pinocchio, Geppetto, Felix, Donald and his nephews, Pluto, Mickey and his band, Goofy, the seven dwarves and Snow White. They all bear placards which state, "All together for war savings, 5 for 4, help win the war". After they finish marching past the Parliament the viewer is returned to the aggressive and hyper-real propaganda that concludes all of the Canadian shorts.

The quality of these films is universally poor relative to Disney's high attention to detail and perfectionist reputation. While the images in the final section of the shorts were clearly contrived and constructed to be manipulative, the rest of the content appears haphazardly strung together with old animation cels. The Canadian government evidently paid for the use of

Disney images but not Disney's creativity. It was not until the United States joined the war that Disney propaganda took a life of its own and the trends begun in these shorts became conventions of a Disney sub-genre.

The United States Enters the War

In December 1941 Japan bombed Pearl Harbour and the United States formally entered the war against the Axis powers. The day after the attack took place the US Army commandeered part of the Disney Studios for a period of eight months. It was estimated that over 93% of the work undertaken at Disney in 1942 was for the government (Wasko, 2001). This allowed the relatively small studio to survive in a time when many of the Hollywood majors were faltering. While the subjects of the government films ranged from overt propaganda to education, military training and military strategic proposals, the quality remained a testament to Walt's staunch nationalism. The propaganda films took two different forms: the first films were self-contained stories or parables of the war, while the second were slapstick misadventures of Donald in the army.

Despite his childlike nature Donald was chosen to represent the American going to war, whereas Mickey only makes a single appearance in a heroic picture in *Out of the Frying Pan, into the Firing Line* (1942). The image of Mickey is carefully used in this instance, to allude to the sacred mouse being part of the war effort. Perhaps his already heroic status would perhaps be too much to be shown in these films. How could Mickey be shown in light-hearted propaganda? Possibly he would have to be depicted as a humourless hero, earnestly fighting the enemy. The images would be far too pointed to be shown to a public so wary of the propaganda of the first war. The realisation that something sacred and uniquely American was being put in an appalling context would have stirred the populace in the wrong direction. Ironically the slap-stick childlike nature of Donald is precisely what enables him to be presented in this context and to sanitise it with humour. His comedic mishaps had the capacity to disarm the viewer into a false sense of security regarding these issues surrounding conflict.

Eric Smoodin (1994) notes that Warner Brothers' *Private Snafu* films were similar in content, presentation and purpose. Created specifically as military instructional tools, *Private Snafu* featured an infantalised sexually precocious soldier, whose naive blunderings provided the viewer with a 'what not to do' in various situations. *Booby Traps* (1944) features Private Snafu lumbering through a battle zone and being seduced by various trappings disguised as temptations. The first of these is a shower, then a camel and then a harem,

176

complete with semi-nude women. The purpose of these shorts was instructional. They were part of a military film bill called the *Army Navy Magazine* which featured news reels, propaganda, educational films and animated shorts. Thus, *Private Snafu* would typically be placed at the end of the bill and act as a fable, demonstrating what will happen to soldiers if they are not obedient and attentive in their training. The tone and implicit address is to the soldier as a child. Just as in the Disney propaganda shorts thus far discussed, the viewer is placed within an infantilised position where they are subjected to commands from a paternal authority. The use of sexualised imagery in cartoons became far more commonplace in WWII and can often be seen to complement this paternal authority.

Adorno (1946) noted that innuendo is a common trope in propaganda. Likewise, Smoodin (1994) suggests that patriotism, and indeed the exoticism of ethnicity, provided a safe context with which to explain away the transgressive content of these cartoons. Thus, the pairing of sexuality with the command of paternity (to patriotism or to objectify the exotic) reduces its transgressive nature. In the 1940s cartoon sexuality was still regulated by the Production Code and the Hayes office. The Hayes code was the regulatory instrument within Hollywood that connected conservative sentiment in the government to the entertainment industry. In a sense, it represented a super-egoic regulatory system within the structure of Hollywood film production itself. Up until the 1940s Disney had still regulated its content to omit any obvious expression of sexuality. As discussed earlier in Chapter 3, this omission is what enabled the production of such transgressive narratives seen in classic Disney. The shorts that Disney would produce during the war were transgressive in a more formal sense but still managed to be sanctioned by the super-egoic authority of the Hayes code. Perhaps this is what allowed Disney to later become so instrumental in the greater American hegemony.

Donald gets Drafted

The first of the Donald series of propaganda shorts was *Donald gets Drafted* (1942). The short starts with a catchy army song: "the army's not the army any more, it's better than it's ever been before!" Donald approaches a draft office and looks at various recruitment posters that show soldiers enjoying all kinds of niceties in company of attractive women. Each of these contains a different slogan: "breakfast in bed!", "everybody is pals!". "fall in, it's time to fly", "pretty hostesses, join now!", "be irresistible! join the air corps". The obvious inference in this rather crude attempt to bait youth into military service is that it will make them attractive to the opposite sex. As Donald

177

stares at this last poster, the image of the soldier turns into an image of himself, held up by the two beautiful women. The women are curved, their faces are simple and devoid of detail, big eyelashes and smiles, indeed their figure has been reduced to a sexualised set of shapes. Thus the objectified form of the women is offered to the child by the externalised super-ego: join the army and you will be allowed to enjoy.

Convinced by the posters, Donald proceeds into the recruitment office, happily waving his draft papers. The term 'drafted' in the title purposefully misleads the viewer as Donald is a willing volunteer. The short attempts to make the association between the draft and voluntary service, or between paternal command and personal choice. The narrative sets up the viewer as a dupe, associating duty with gratification under the title of involuntary servitude. *Donald gets Drafted* engages the viewer as an infant; the viewer is patronised just as Donald is. He wanders from sign to sign haplessly, persuaded by their gaudy jingoism. The duck is fixated on the content; engaged on the part of the viewer. As Donald sees the posters he stands with his mouth open, grabs his heart and lets out a sigh while fluttering his eyelashes. He runs from one poster to another, wide-eyed and excited. Although his appearance is implicitly childish, the excitement he derives from the posters is obviously sexual and adult. If the short was intended to be in some way satirical then this is certainly not apparent in the viewing. The naive heavy-handedness of the call to arms overbears any possible ironic or oppositional reading of the posters and the enthusiasm with which Donald signs up for the army. In the draft office we see Donald gyrating, making rhythmic dancing motions while blowing an imaginary flute: he is an un-trousered, impulsive pleasure-phile blowing his flute, just like the happy-go-lucky pig in *The Three Little Pigs* (1933). He is the instrument of the viewer's gratification; both the object of gratification within the scenario and the point of identification.

As Donald enters the draft office he blurts out, "I wanna be a flyer!" He then opens his arms and pretends to fly about the room. He signs on the bottom of a form and asks, "Now, can I fly!?" The absolute infantile nature of Donald in a very adult situation is quite unsettling, but likewise the sadistic context of war and the draft seems to fit well with his infantile aggressivity. This is an uncanny image of the sexually charged child entering into a contractual agreement: one granting him access to the pleasure of which he has fanta-sised. It is uncanny due to the real-life human setting of the draft office with a child signing a contract that puts him at the service of a military at war. In the next sequence Donald is sent to be inspected by the medical staff, who (in slap-stick form) examine him roughly and pass his every failed test. This part of the short once again creates a failed parody: instead of underlining the relative ease with which young men could pass the army medical exam, it seems to make light of the formality of the process, making it seem less intimidating. This is of course laden with the idea that anybody can pass the army medical exam.

Donald is stripped of his clothing, looks down at his groin and blushes while trying to cover his non-existent genitals.

The duck's embarrassment
(Image by Paul Byrne)

With his belittling sailor-suit removed he is left exposed, his unbridled id left for all to see. He is forced into an army uniform which is at first too big for him, then shrinks too small and traps him until finally expanding to fit. As previously mentioned, Tasker (1993) suggests that the uniform has the capacity to stabilise the transgressive body, containing it within patriarchically endowed signifiers. Thus the image of the army uniform contains Donald's sexually precocious and aggressive temperament. Although the uniform is a poor fit (being to big for a child's body), it can be shrunk down to his size until it literally contains him. Donald's body is indeed transgressive: though he is a childish force of demand, the un-socialised expression of the id, he is castrated. His absent organs are testament to his castration and evidence of paternal castigation that has gone unheeded. His embarrassment is an ironic reminder of the question 'what have you got to be ashamed of!?' He is the image of the castigated, impetuous child, as if to suggest that he has transgressed the pleasure principle and been suitably castrated, and yet is still an icon of transgressive demand.

The rest of the short follows Donald's trials and tribulations through boot camp. It follows the classic Disney short formula of the novice in conflict with the authority figure: the aggressive mean-spirited cat, who this time takes the role of the drill Sergeant. He dominates Donald and derides him, exclaiming, "You'll make no soldier!" to which Donald responds: "I quit!" Of course Donald is not allowed to quit and continues to battle the Sergeant for his right to enjoy himself. The short ends with Donald being disciplined in isolation, peeling a never-ending mountain of potatoes to the happy jingle of "The army's not the army any more ..." Yet despite this ending, the image of army life is left relativity untarnished: all of the negative connotations surrounding the military are attached to the Sergeant, the obstacle to Donald's care-free fun. Thus the tensions of the viewer regarding such matters as conscription and military training are exorcised through the catharsis of Donald's conflict with the Sergeant as opponent.

In *The Disappearing Private* (1942) Donald is once again in conflict with authority via the Sergeant. Given orders to paint a cannon in camouflage, Donald accidentally paints it with top-secret invisibility paint. After this Donald makes himself invisible and escapes the Sergeant, who is in turn driven mad while trying to apprehend him. At the end of the short a General arrives in his car to see the Sergeant in a state of confusion and believes him to have lost his wits. The ultimate authority of the positive super-ego (the General: representative of the army) unknowingly sides with the insolent child (the invisible Donald) and chastises the castrating and brutal authority of the negative super-ego (the Sergeant, who frequently makes threats of violence against Donald). In this way the paternal authority embodied in the military maintains its status free of denigration and the demanding child is free to enjoy. This enjoyment is essentially free of the Law as it maintains 'respect' in regard to the super-ego. The super-ego is thus split to maintain its integrity and capacity to command while denigrating the image of curtailment to the child's gratification. This narrative binary opposition set up within the space of the super-ego is a particular convention of Disney's propaganda. The command to enjoy is the currency that motivates the viewer within this space.

Several shorts also featured Pluto, Mickey's faithful dog. In *The Army Mascot* (1942), Pluto is lured into a military camp after seeing two army mascots, a

Fetishised reward and Salivation
(Image by Rupert Norfolk)

giant bull dog and a small chihuahua, being fed large portions of meat. Enjoyment and gratification is the key to the narrative. Pluto sneaks into the camp and tries to usurp a goat, who is the mascot of a different division. He struggles against the goat to win the soldier's attention and finally gets taken as their new mascot, winning their approval by chewing an entire bar of tobacco. At the end of the short, he stands with his chest out at attention while the soldiers bring him his reward of meat. The short represents another route to viewer compliance and seduction, ironically involving a Pavlovian approach to reinforcement: patriotism will be rewarded with gratification. The dog's salivation and desire for the meat is indisputably sexual: he relishes the smells and sights. The meat itself is utterly fetishised, overwhelmingly objectified for the viewer, offering total oral gratification.

In reference to fascist media, Hansen (1993) discusses Benjamin's reference to the phantasmagoria; a sensuous gratifying commodity that acts as a "mental drug and utopian wish-image" (Hansen, 1993, p37). This is the utopian currency of the fetish, the little thing used both in service of gratification and idealisation. This supports the alienation Benjamin sees as integral to consumerist gratification. By positioning the viewer as the one full animal in the Disney cast (as opposed to anthropomorphic half-children), the *mise-en-scène* moves from the voyeuristic look that is so prevalent in other Disney films to an enclosed fetishistic space. A fetishistic *mise-en-*

181

scène features in few of the Disney shorts as markedly as this, with the exception of other Pluto films that use a great deal of close-ups to emphasise reward. The presentation of a reward contingent on the approval of a mass (i.e. the men in the army) fits neatly into the broader context of the structure of gratification within propaganda. The narrative drives the viewer's desire towards Pluto's end: the obliteration of distance between dog and object. The viewer is made compliant as gratification depends on a cathected reward. In effect something has been given value and has attained this value through engagement with the short's simplified ideological system: the hungry dog gets the bone, on condition of appeasing a larger super-egoic mass, namely the U.S. Army.

This is also the case in *Out of the Frying Pan, into the Firing Line* (1942) which features Pluto and Minnie Mouse. Minnie is about to give the last of her bacon grease to feed Pluto when a voice from the radio commands "Don't throw away that bacon grease, housewives of America!" The voice then explains that the war effort needs excess cooking fat for munitions manufacturing. After explaining and illustrating through a series of violent images, the voice states that helping the war effort will aid those loved ones on the front lines. The short then cuts to the aforementioned image of Mickey in combat fatigues. When offered the bacon grease a second time Pluto refuses it, bringing the grease to a participating butcher who rewards him with sausages. Thus a short-term pleasure (the grease) has been substituted for a more long-term gratification (the sausages).

Likewise *The New Spirit* (1942) has Donald listening to an address from a radio, which asks the listener to do their part for the war effort by handing in their income tax on time. By paying taxes promptly the war effort can use its "taxes to beat the Axis". The short is intensely visual, demonstrating the different weapons to be manufactured and enemies defeated. Donald is patriotic and enthusiastic to do his part – so much so he runs from one side of the country to the other to deliver his tax forms. In both films the weaponisation of America is fetishised; close-ups of weapons, ships and explosives focus the viewer entirely on their potent phallic nature.

Films such as *The New Spirit* (1942) received favourable and unfavourable readings among the divided American public. Smoodin (1994) suggests this as evidence of resistance to the ideology of consensus that wartime Hollywood was working to create in tandem with the American government. During the war this ideology of consensus became central to the work of propagandists. This image of homogeneity was intended to smooth over the divides within American society of the time. German and Italian Americans favoured an isolationist stance to the war whereas Americans from English or Central European backgrounds favoured intervention. Sentiments towards the war were also divided along race and class lines, with the unionisation of America creating vast gulfs in mass consent. The government needed to manufacture an image of America as a unitary body: an image of individual difference that was in effect homogeneous and would render a unitary response. Films such as *The New Spirit, Out of the Frying Pan* and *Donald Gets Drafted* can be seen to perform this task subtly, while the progressively inflammatory propaganda that the studio produced builds on the success of Hollywood to create this image of consensus which crowns the hegemonic victory of the 1940s war-effort over individual difference. Thus the regulation of desire through consensus achieves what the Hayes code could not through censorship guidelines. The command to enjoy over-rides the forbiddance of individuality and the perceived excess of personal freedom.

The Cartoon Body: Sadism, Exaggeration and Manipulation

There are several of Disney's propaganda films that are particularly striking in their use and manipulation of the cartoon body, and the strength of their message. *Education for Death: the Making of a Nazi* (1943) and *Der Führer's Face* (1942) were perhaps the most effective of the propaganda films produced and demonstrated a definite shift in Disney's aesthetics. Each of these films epitomises the trends thus far discussed: the dividing of the super-ego into good and bad parts, and the command to enjoy being utilised to create a homogeneous response to the war. Coupled with these formal qualities is the manipulation of the image to provoke aggressivity in the viewer, the formation of a sadistic gaze.

Education for Death takes the image of the innocent Disney-child and shows them being warped by the evils of Nazism. The child is perverted by Nazi propaganda, slowly transforming from a sympathetic boy into a mindless and faceless machine of war. This short represents the struggle between two authorities, presenting a positive propagandist argument that discusses the evils of the negativised enemy propaganda. It does this effectively through the setting for the message; here Disney animation ultimately disarms the viewer and the critic alike. What separates these shorts from those already discussed is the extent to which the derision of authority and the opposing authority-figures is depicted visually. *Education for Death* starts with a meek and shadowed couple in a great hall. They are being forced to provide proof

183

that their newborn child Hans is of perfect Aryan descent and given a name that is permissible. The figure of authority here is not he who provides the name, instead it is the man that checks against a list of forbidden names, that range from Jewish names to those of allied politicians. Yet even he is not the provider of true law, the beurocrate mearly represents malevolent limitation. Rather the Law is provided by the looming American voice from beyond the film's diegesis. He provides the words and commentary to the story, that situate and interpret the images for the viewer.

The next part of the film takes us to Hans' classroom. The teacher is fat and caricatured, with exaggerated and feminised curves. Barbara Creed (1993) comments that the caricatured feminisation of the male form is often performed to produce a grotesque body, one that is "capable of being penetrated", and thus made passive (Creed, 1993 p19). The form of Hans himself is a typical Disney child: a caricature of infancy with a large head and small body. His giant blue eyes and baffled expression only add to his status as a figure of innocence. The teacher aggressively relays a story of a fox killing and eating a rabbit and asks Hans what he thinks. The little boy replies in German, "The poor rabbit!" and is scolded for his meekness.

He is made to sit in the corner of the class wearing a dunce's hat, a specifically American gesture to inflict shame on a bad child. The other children, while innocent in their design, are quite monstrous in their animation. They have furrowed brows, small eyes and bare hateful, angry expressions as they all start to shout: "Death to the rabbit!" "The rabbit is weak!"

As they start to jeer they take on the ugly appearance of the agitating children in *Dumbo* and Lampwick in *Pinocchio*. Hans' demeanour alters under pressure of his peers and becomes as monstrous as they are, saying that he now hates the rabbit. What is seen here is a very simple narrative repositioning: the innocent Hans is corrupted by the cruel intentions of a monstrous authority figure, who has already corrupted his fellow classmates. He is driven to conform and thus becomes a Nazi. The image of Hans changes and somehow loses its Disney-esque innocence. This loss is firmly shown to be the result of the malevolent authority of the Nazis. Hans' innocence is an idealised image of infancy, made to mass-appeal. This is done in order to draw the viewer into a position of idealisation and then show how the monstrous entity – the intrusion of the malevolent authority figure – corrupts the child into a fusion with an alternative ideology. First this malevolent authority (the name checker) steals Hans away from the maternal care of the Other and second, the authority (the teacher, speaking for Adolph

Hitler, who is similarly caricatured and monstrous) institutes Hans into a false symbolic order.

This propaganda film's use of authority figures is intrinsically sexually manipulative. It plays on the viewer's fundamental anxieties two-fold: the image of the demonised symbolic father is conflated with that of the negative mother: she who envelops the child and is outside of the 'good' paternal authority. This amalgamate entity of primordial maternity and symbolic paternity is shown to warp the child to negative designs: in this case producing the Nazi super-soldier, blinkered, muzzled and in chains, marching towards a death in the oblivion of the violent horizon.

The subject fears what the malevolent symbolic father/archaic mother represents, which is why he/she is such a contentious figure in its cinematic appearances. The propaganda film is playing to the ambiguities of the father. The authority figures of the film are derided while at the same time the voice from beyond presents a master's discourse: a running commentary on the film's events, reassuring to the viewer. Like *Fantasia*, the viewer's interpretations are wholly guided by a voice from beyond that precludes the image. This voice originates in the realm of the paternal authority and the positive super-ego: that which vanquishes the overwhelming mother and enables enjoyment. Thus, when the viewer attains a sexuated position within the film, it is one that the voice directs to aggressivity, to brutalise and punish the negative conflation of negated masculinity – embodied in the feminised nuances of the teacher's curves.

Kris (1943) comments that caricature itself carries regressive aspects that have the capacity to incite the viewer to aggression. Closeness draws the viewer in while regressive qualities alienate, becoming 'too much', too close and ugly. In this case the body of the teacher is touched and manipulated by the gaze of the maternal super-ego, a gaze that simultaneously feminises and regresses the masculine form. This aggressivity is well described by what Carol J. Clover refers to as a *sadistic gaze* that operates in horror film (Clover, 1993). The sadistic gaze seeks to punish the maternal and the feminine for the trauma its body represents, while likewise evoking aggression in the direction of the gender-transgressive monster or villain.

Der Führer's Face was likewise rousing and affective in its play on authority. It was perhaps the most commercially successful of the Disney propaganda films and was even awarded an Oscar. It was deemed so effective that it was translated and dropped behind enemy lines to demoralise German civilians. *Der Führer's Face* was similarly manipulative but takes the imagining of sadism and gender conflation to a greater intensity; rather than an exercise in mastery it takes an associational and experiential route to stir the viewer. It does this via a play on caricature to rouse affect.

The short begins when Donald Duck awakes to find himself living in Nazi Germany. Outside his window there is a parade of monstrous Nazi caricatures. Their bodies are warped and misshapen in such a way that when they collide together they slot into each other's shapes. Each character has a differently emphasised part of the body. The first is long and skinny with his face covered by his helmet; only his long nose and mouth are visible. The next figure has a huge upturned chest and giant arms, but beats a tiny drum located at his groin. The third is a little fat man blowing an over-sized trumpet, the fourth has a giant backside and plays a small whistle. The last is also tiny but hits a giant drum.

They are all distortions of the human body, their physical qualities exaggerated to the point where they are objectified to a negative extreme. Their body parts are stretched and cathected but not in such a way that makes them attractively engaging for the viewer, rather the opposite. The mix of the engaging material of the animated form combined with the too-muchness of the caricature plays with the erotic position of the viewer; driving the form to the abject. The gaze is manipulated by the caricaturist so as to demarcate the negative characters. The third Nazi in the parade is fat and bulbous, his face is curled upwards and baby-like. He has long eyelashes, which he flutters while swinging his hips side to side, the image of the over-indulged child fused with sexed androgyny. Taking something close, familiar and innocuous, while warping it with something sexually powered and threatening – the over-feminised male – thus creating a disturbing uncanny apparition (Kaplan, 1990).

The fat and bulbous Nazi sings: "Vee bring the new world order," and blows into a whistle. As he blows his neck stretches and head distorts, until his head itself becomes phallicised.

While Eisenstein draws attention to the familiar sight of elongated necks in cartoons, he is hesitant to draw direct comparison to the penis, but rather skirts around the phallic nature of the image by referring to it as "a sensuous process in cited metaphors" (Eisenstein, 1941–1946, p57). In fact he goes so far as to say that the elongation of physical features and the plasticity of the cartoon body is itself gratifying, though he fails to speculate why.

The characters are mutated distortions of Disney's human characters, uncanny and warped. It is interesting that this character's head and neck

The grotesque phallus.
(Image by Paul Byrne)

become phallicised as a warped symbol of potency. It is a potent condensation, one that combines the overpowering phallus with the mutated feminised-male baby. This sickly parade makes its way to Donald Duck's house. He is made to get out of bed at gun point while his alarm clock calls out "Heil Hitler!" Donald gets up and puts on his clothes, which are made from coarse paper. He soaks a single coffee bean in hot water and saws off a slice of wooden bread for breakfast.

This was a direct appeal to the anxieties of American consumerism. The image puts Donald in a state of destitution at the hands of the malevolent authority, here completely encapsulated by the marching band, who also contains semblances of Mussolini and Emperor Hirohito. Donald is then brought by the marching band to a munitions factory where he begins slave-like work: screwing caps onto bullets, shells and bombs. In-between making shells he is forced to give the Nazi salute to images of Hitler which litter the factory and the assembly line.

As his load of work becomes greater, he is forced to work faster until he is literally bowled over with work and crumbles into a hallucination and cartoon jouissance. Here instead it is the negative authority of the maternal super-ego (Zizek, 1992) that provokes the subject to jouissance. This is the transgressive aspect of the super-ego, that imposes its own law: the law of jouissance discussed earlier (Loose, 2011). The law of jouissance is structurally transparent with the desire of the primordial mother, as it is a law that drives the subject to transgress its limits and obliterates subjectivity. Hence a value typically hidden beneath Disney ideology is used strategically to instil repulsion in the viewer.

Using the principles laid out in Thompson and Johnston's (1984) guide to animation, bad characters are typically warped to emphasise malevolence while maintaining appeal. This is not the case in *Der Führer's Face*. Here the body of the malevolent has been distorted to emphasise the phallic: the musical instruments, the distorted phallus-head and the weapons of the marching band. This is similar to what Zizek (1992) discusses in terms of the distorted face of the elephant man in David Lynch's 1980 film of the same name. Here the face of the elephant man, with its elongated and phallic nose, becomes the grotesque object of the maternal gaze, being both phallic and primordial in its representation of *being* the phallus.

The feminisation of the masculine forms of the marching Nazis further unsettles the viewer, blending sexual difference in a manner that references the primordial (i.e. *phallic*) mother. The grotesque nature of the manipulated and exaggerated bodies is in continuum with the *monstrous feminine* discussed by Kaplan (1990), who finds this monstrous image of primordial maternity in the body of Nola Carveth in *The Brood* (1979) and the enveloping alien Queen in *Aliens* (1986). By driving Donald into the factory the Nazi marching band envelops the duck into a disastrous relation to the monstrous form of Nazi Germany as summarised in the bodies of the marching band itself.

As noted earlier in the discussion of *The Three Caballeros*, Donald frequently slips into hallucinatory states when overpowered by his libidinal excesses, bringing the viewer with him. While this usually occurs during his sexual pursuits, it happens here when his workload becomes overpowering. Sex and work appear as excesses for the id-driven Duck. As mentioned earlier his form can be viewed as the embodiment of punished transgression and yet he proceeds to transgress. It is as if the constraints of adulthood are so beyond him that limits of obligation overpower his senses and drives him to distraction. The sequence ends with Donald waking up again in his own bed, clothed in American flags. The shadow of a miniature statue of liberty in the window gives him a start but on recognising it he hugs the statue saying: "Am I glad to be a citizen of the United States of America!"

While the film might seem naive to the contemporary viewer, the scenario that the short constructs is insidious and subtle. The malevolent authority is constructed within the borders of the sexualised though misshapen body; this authority forces the transgressive body to threaten the limits of the good (American) Law that moderates work and leisure. This transgression produces a similar hallucinatory state to the cartoon jouissance previously noted in Donald's sexual pursuits. In the end the transgressive body is saved by a return to the true (American) patriarchal Law, signified by the small statue.

Propaganda, pornography and utopia

As John J. Hartman notes: "Propaganda, like pornography, is one of those difficult words to define. One person's propaganda is another person's persuasive argument" (Hartman, 2000, p329). In his discussion, Hartman makes continual reference to the similarities between pornography and propaganda. "The intention of the pornographer is to appeal to what has been called the "prurient interest" of the viewer by tapping the conscious and unconscious fantasies to elicit feeling of sexual excitement. In a similar fashion, the political propagandist attempts to make use of existing cultural myths" (Hartman, 2000, p 335). Hartman's relation of propaganda to pornography points to an inextricable link through similar structural conventions. Like pornography, propaganda provides a utopian image that initialises a regression to a baser position in the subject's erotic development.

In his discussions there is a clear political dimension to Eisenstein's (1941–1946) analysis of Disney's capacity to reach its audience. He attempts to emphasise the transgressive nature of Disney in terms of American governance and economic systems. By making this transgression synonymous with utopian socialism, Eisenstein ignores that utopia is itself a regressive simplification of gratification and transgressive in itself. Pornography provides a reductive, simplified and transgressive position in relation to gratification, indeed pornography is by its nature utopian. Propaganda is likewise a move towards utopia, thus both can be defined as a simplification that is structured by what Zizek discusses as a coincidence of the gaze between subject and object (Zizek, 1991).

Zizek defines pornography by the coincidence of the gaze: the attempt is made to capture the viewer as object rather than as the subject who bears the intra-diegetic look. The address is made to the subject *as object* in both pornography and propaganda. The act within the diegesis makes an appeal to gratify the viewer, who is positioned as the recipient of a sexuated address. The intra-diegetic desire that the viewer identifies with in narrative film is therefore reflected back to the viewer. Zizek notes that in the majority of pornographic imagery the male porn-star looks away from the camera at the female body, while the female porn-star looks at the viewer. This look belies the address to the viewer, the movement of desire that puts the viewer at the point of object and the film at the point of address. This look can be seen structurally within propaganda, and is reminiscent of J.M. Flagg's "Uncle

First World War propaganda: the address to the viewer as object (Flagg, 1917)

Sam Wants you for the U.S. Army" (Flagg, 1917) posters as well as the images of Donald at the start of Disney shorts.

Private Snafu frequently looks at the camera to disclose his next action, as does Donald. The viewer becomes the passive object – instrumentalised in their own gratification. As their gratification must drive them to act after the propaganda film has disclosed its message, they must be left unsatisfied so that they must take the action to satisfy themselves. The act within pornography and propaganda eliminates the distance between subject and object. Thus the medium itself acts as a fetish – omission of desire in favour of utopian address. The address is indeed utopian as it presents an idealised space in which viewer satisfaction is central, guaranteed and liberated from anxiety.

Pornography and Disney both provide a point of reference that seems outside the typical 'male' gaze. Perhaps this is what is referred to in Kris' *staged reality* (Kris and Speier, 1944, p13) and Adorno's *ultimate content* (Adorno et al., 1946, p126); it is a product that claims to offers a direct gratification in the Real (as it is dependent on its audience taking *action*). Likewise Disney propaganda presents the 'act' in the form of a persuasive and emotive argument. We view the scenario unfolding that presents a utopian vision of sexual positioning – of utopian enjoyment within bounds that the paternal super-ego offers. The paternal super-ego is the authority figure in propaganda. He is idealised, untouchable and can be seen in the faceless hands that push Donald about in the draft office, the voice from the radio that commands attention, the general who interdicts and brings the Law, and the extra-diegetic voice that tells us what evil has befallen Hans.

Zizek's maternal super-ego is precisely what is repugnant, and used as a counterpoint to the paternal agency. It is the agency of the primordial mother, the authority in place before the actualisation of the paternal signifier in the Oedipus Complex. Thus the maternal gaze distorts the elephant man and warps the phallic features of the enemy which comes to reference her own transgressive body – the Nazi marching band, the jeering children and the caricature of Hitler – gross distortions touched by the maternal gaze and the feminine. Within Disney the paternal super-ego offers utopia, while the maternal super-ego offers ruin.

These shorts provide an insight into a unique and extremely provocative period in Disney film-making, the ominous climax of which was not another propaganda film as such, but rather a feature film made to aid policy makers in re-strategising the actual conflict. In the early 1940s Walt met with Major Alexander Seversky, an ex-Soviet fighter pilot who had defected to the United States and joined the American Air Force. Seversky had written a book entitled *Victory Through Air-Power*, advocating the strategic rather than tactical use of bombers in the war (Schickel, 1968). Strategic bombing refers to the use of aircraft to deliver bombs to targets within enemy territory, to cripple production, destroy supply lines and demoralise civilian populations. Walt thought this message to be of great importance to the American war effort, so much so that he chose to personally fund the making of a *Victory Through Air-Power* (1943) film. The film was then used to promote the ideas espoused by Seversky to the general public, to politicians and to the military. Much like *Der Ewige Jude (1940)*, *Victory Through Air-Power* was a pseudo-documentary: a staged reality. It offers the viewer the confirmation of threat in a scientific presentation, using charts and statistics to make its point (Hartman, 2000). It is emblematic of Kris' 'new' propaganda, one loosely based on established facts.

The film promised that by shifting the use of bombers to targets within the opposing nations, America would be able to limit its casualties and end the war swiftly. In his discussion of the film critic James Agee (1943) comments that there is a marked avoidance of the issue of civilian casualties. This is pornography in its simplest sense: a utopian vision of sadistic climax that accomplishes gratification in the form of victory. *Victory Through Air-Power* likewise encapsulates Adorno's (1946) criteria of American fascist propaganda. The desires and death of the other (at least the other as enemy) are removed from the fantasised scenario to provide a clean and clear image of warfare; means eclipse ends and consequences.

191

This is the pornographic utopian vision of warfare; the simplified gaze makes an address to the viewer as object. The cartoon body acts as both the fetish that calms and the transgressive form that elicits sadistic punishment. The polemics of right and wrong are cleanly differentiated into an oppositions between positive paternal and primordial maternal. *Victory Through Airpower* represents what Hansen (1993) describes as technology's capacity to facilitate mass destruction, by situating it within an abstract and hyper-real (though she does not use the term) context. This is the essence of what Benjamin and Adorno acknowledge as the capacity technology has for servicing collective hegemony to the monstrous ends of war (Hansen, 1993). The core of this for Benjamin is technology's capacity to reorganise humanity's relation to nature: as prosthesis it can support a psychical shift necessitated by political action to the ends of utopian visions of war and its outcome. Through its presentation as hyper-real, both tangible and intangible, it can convince an audience of a Disneyified reality of war. It is this effort and address that prevails within the struggle for hegemony, paving the way for the ideological homogenisation of opinion that was required to go to war and commit to the ethical ambiguities of service, death and holocaust.

Chapter 12

The Consumerist Utopia

The purpose of this last chapter is to describe the narrative and structural changes that took place in the 1950s and 60s, before the company would loose its figurehead in 1966. While there is a tremendous wealth of critical study of Disney theme-parks, this area shall be referenced but not discussed in detail. While in-depth studies of these aspects of Disney are important, the project of this text is to create a theoretical artifice: that of the archetypical consumer who interacts within the Disney apparatus. This apparatus has been addressed primarily in terms of the viewer who engages within the Disney cinematic apparatus and how this engagement provokes consumption, ideological or otherwise. It is in this context that Disney theme-parks and television will be referenced, as they represent avenues of expression for this compulsive consumption. It is this idealised consumption that can be identified as the core of the Disney apparatus and the object of Part Three of this text: the consumerist regressive utopia.

After the wartime period a different Disney took shape. Walt would never participate in the studio's creative process as he had done before. The studio had lost a great deal of its drive and edge with the bitterness over the company's handling of labour disputes. Walt himself became a different character in the studio, being nicknamed 'the wounded bear' by his staff, who were increasingly subjected to his aggravated mood swings (Watts, 1997). His interest in feature-length animated films likewise dwindled and between 1942 and 1950 there were no feature-length animated films made at the studio. The films of the South American 'Good Neighbour' policy were feature-length collages of shorts, as were *Make Mine Music* (1946), *Fun and Fancy Free* (1947), *Melody Time* (1948) and *The Adventures of Ichabod and Mr Toad* (1949), the films made immediately after the war. The commonalities shared by these compilation features were perhaps their marked blandness and lack of charm when compared to the animated films of the classic era of Disney film-making. The five years after the war saw a dramatic change in the content and style of media being produced at Disney. Work on big features such as *Pinocchio* and *Bambi* was labour and finance intensive, whereas the newer films were comparatively low-cost to produce and able to generate sizable returns as the entertainment market itself was changing (Wasko, 2001).

Disney also began to venture into more live-action features, the first of which was *Song of the South* (1946). *Song of the South* maintained the live-action/animated blend of *Caballeros* and featured the adventures of Brer Rabbit as told by Uncle Remus, an African-American folk figure. Walt claimed he was realising a childhood desire to see these stories on screen and emphasised the personal nature of the film. It featured a young boy named Johnny who leaves city life to go to live with his mother and grandmother in a Southern plantation after his mother and father's separation. There he feels alienated and out of place, but makes friends with Uncle Remus who tells him stories and offers him reassurance. Johnny's mother becomes uncomfortable with Uncle Remus' influence on Johnny and expels Remus from their plantation. Johnny chases after Remus but is attacked by a bull and falls into a coma. When Remus comes to visit Johnny in hospital, he is woken by the story-teller's voice. The film ends with Johnny's parents back together and Remus telling his stories to a host of children.

The film was unrepentantly sentimentalised, and sold the image of the nuclear family surviving in the face of uncertainty. Wealthy characters are powerful but impoverished characters (Brer Fox and Brer Bear) are depicted as foolish. Yet the stories depict a conventional Disney narrative of the triumph of the weak over the strong (Watts, 1997). While this formula was central to the Disney of the classic era it was not so successful in the late 1940s climate of success and growth. The film also came to controversy over its portrayal of Southern African-Americans as simplistic and ultimately subservient to the desires of white protagonists.

It was also in this period that Disney produced a number of low budget nature films titled the *True Life Adventure* series. *Seal Island* (1948) was a nature film shot on the Pribilof Islands that was the most successful of these films. The 30 minute short-feature won an Academy award and soon became a template for other successful and relatively inexpensive ventures for the studio. The success and critical acclaim of *Seal Island* spawned a whole series of Disney nature films that shared the low-cost but high-yield return. The success of these films generated enough income and acclaim to revitalise the studio.

194

Like the animated films, the nature series relied heavily on anthropomorphism to engage the audience. Schickel (1968) suggests that anthropomorphisis appeals to the child-like tendency to project one's own ego onto the outside world. The external object of the child's affection and attention becomes a recipient of his or her own character and personality. To project human qualities onto the animalistic can be seen as a natural extension of the child's egoism. Mollenhoff (1940) and Eisenstein (1941–1946) also saw great import in Disney's use of anthropomorphism, referencing animism as central to its understanding. Freud (1919) positioned animism as implicitly uncanny in character. Animism, he posits, mirrors early structures of mental topography and holds a utopian quality in its figuration of existence. This figuration involves the super-ego's directive to project the negative aspects of the psyche onto some objects and the positive onto others, a radical binary opposition between figurations of authority and the uncanny. Indeed Hansen (1993) discusses the encounter with Mickey Mouse as having a definitively uncanny character. For Hansen, he is a peculiar hybrid of the familiar and the strange, all the more emphasised by his hyper-real and utopian quality. As a fetishised homunculus Mickey is utopian in form and appeal, his body itself suggests a harmonious unity that is beyond realisation: being capable of representing both the ideal ego and ego ideal. Perhaps this is why Benjamin saw Mickey Mouse at the precipice of fascism and its prevention: he has the appearance of offering solution to all extremes that seemed savagely out of control in the first half of the 20th century.

For Disney, the 1940s ended with much unresolved tension between the staff and management at the studio, just as the world struggled with its own negotiation of totalitarianism. The films produced after this period bore the mark of an altogether different product. This was perhaps the result of several factors: the alienation the staff felt within the company, animation itself becoming a sideline for the company, and the cultural upheaval that defined 1950s America. This is a period of modernism and industrialised art, a form that packaged all things Disney: film, television, merchandising and music. Industrialisation brought Disney to a wider audience, a move that ensured the company's solvency. Yet many characterised this period as essentially devaluing the artistic merit of Disney films (Wasko, 2001, Schickel,1968), while others emphasize that it ensured the company's reach into American culture and society (Watts, 1997).

In the 1950s Disney cartoon shorts were being surpassed by the narrative and comedic superiority of Warner Brothers shorts, but the Disney company

195

soon lost interest in this competition. The success of Warner Brothers' and United Artists' new series *The Pink Panther* was owed to a different sort of animation, the kind Disney had experimented with in *Victory Through Air power* (1943) and the *Baby Weems* segment of *The Reluctant Dragon*. This was a more simplified form of animation: cartoons for cartoons' sake, that did not attempt to become the advanced simulations that the Disney studio had obsessed over for so many years. Disney shorts were also becoming increasingly difficult to make profitable. This and the unwillingness of the studio to take the risk of making animated features saw a marked change in the studio's output into simpler and less production-heavy animations. Walt himself relegated creative control to others at the studio, such as Bill Walsh who produced a number of live-action features for the company, most notably *Mary Poppins* (1967). during this time Walt began to participate more actively in the company's move into theme-parks and television (Watts, 1997). This was a move that consolidated Disney's creative output into what is described by Alan Bryman (2004) as *hybrid consumption*, a consumerist synergy that shall be discussed later in this chapter.

The 1950s saw middle-class privileges expand further than in previous decades. The middle-class family was the ultimate unit of consumerism. As discussed in the previous chapters, the ideology of consensus and unitary response was at the heart of American hegemony in the 1940s. The creation of a middle class was instrumental in this process as it removed divisive boundaries between the working and upper classes. Thus the sentimental modernism of *Fantasia* eventually becomes expressed in the blurring of high and low brows (perhaps marking the creation of a cultural uni-brow?), in order to effect a homogenisation that would render American society commercially exploitable (Watts, 1997). Thus the familial aesthetic of this period espouses an ideology of consumption underwritten by a commercial hedonism.

In his aptly named *The Strategy of Desire* (1960) Ernst Dichter advocated the new hedonistic approach to consumerism that would support the economy and institute the nuclear American family as the new consumerist unit. He argued for a consumerist utopia, in which pleasure and leisure are moral acts, supplanting what he perceived as a Victorian puritanism opposed to commercial indulgence (Dichter, 1960). Baudrillard (1968) argues strongly against this position, which he sees as prevailing to present day. He suggests that this commercial hedonism essentially submits an infantilised consumer to an involuntary servitude to economic systems. He proposes that the re-figuration of consumerism in the 1950s and 60s ushered in a return to an Oedipal structuring of society that infantilises the consumer while paternalising the corporation and the marketeer. This commercial hedonism represents a hidden imperative within the wholesome family values of the Disney product of the 1950s and 60s period. This marked a cultural redirection from self-control towards gratification within the confines of the commercial, an attitude that idealised limitless pleasures.

Smoodin (1994) suggests that *Nifty Nineties* (1941) can be seen as an early forebear to 1950s American consumerism. The short features Minnie and Mickey in an 1890s suburban setting. There is a surprisingly sexual quality to Minnie's appearance; her buttocks are greatly exaggerated to reference the cinoline worn by women of the time. After passing her, Mickey turns on his heel and leers in her direction, after which hearts resembling Minnie's buttocks float into the air. He picks up her dropped handkerchief and bribes her with sweets to join him to take in the vaudeville. Mickey and Minnie are shown driving together through a suburban street; they pass Donald and Daisy Duck on a bicycle with their three nephews. This produces a new image of both Mickey and Donald in a more domesticated and sexually conventional context. It places the viewer in a familial setting that is instantly recognisable as a sentimentalised America from previous idealised decades. However, the short still bears the wartime hyper-sexualisation of the cartoon body in the form of Minnie's exaggerated buttocks. Despite Walt's perpetual insistence that Mickey and Minnie were just good friends we now see an obvious, if traditionalised, sexual exchange between the two. Mickey's free time positions him as an icon of the leisure class in a time normally associated with frugality and Puritan abstention. Thus sentimentalising the past promoted the sexualised consumerism of the future.

This period marked the rise of the American "middle-brow" (Schickel, 1968, p277), or the fusion of the most obvious elements of high and low culture, consumed and proliferated by an expanding middle class. The dominance of the middle class came about from the prosperity and comfort that the increasing automation of manufacturing presented. This forged the base for the consumer economy that provided Americans with a strong focus on individualism and leisure.

Disney grew with the proliferation of the leisure ethic; its diversification into other areas of entertainment responded well to the consumers' increasing demands for differentiated family activities and commodities. This "new consumerism" (Watts, 1997, p362) was defined by the increasing commercialisation of leisure. Record labels, newspapers, magazines, advertising, radio, television and film production became increasingly incorporated and integrated until a whole world of homogeneous yet diversified consumables became available to American society. In this way the culture industry became the dominant force in American hegemony. The industry's strong ties to governmental conservatism through corporate interest groups left little room for dissenting opinion against the absolute commodification of enjoyment. The increasing emphasis on consumerism and individuation fed the anti-communist paranoia that was another defining feature of the 1950s. By linking happiness and family values to consumerism American culture set itself diametrically opposed to the perceived values of communism. The connection between happiness, consumption and leisure was clearly to the advantage of the commercial world that was able to exploit the radicalisation of consumers against a perceived red threat. For Disney the 1950s provided an ideological perfect fit: not only was entertainment seen as a necessity to the American way of life, but consumption itself came to symbolise an American pastime that could bolster the economy and strengthen the nation. It is no surprise then that Walt's decision to diversify and branch out into television, distribution and amusement parks allowed the company to grow into one of the most successful Hollywood majors. Indeed, Byrne and McQuillan (1999) note that Disney has been able to maintain its hegemonic influence across the decades since its inception. In fact this influence has solidified and grown to the point that the company is an inescapable part of children's media, family entertainment and westernised culture.

Television and Disneyland

Perhaps the most significant event for Disney in the 1950s was its move into television. Christmas 1950 saw Disney's first television production on NBC: *One Hour in Wonderland* (1950). The Christmas special was a fusion of live action and animation and featured a promotion for *Alice in Wonderland* (1951).

Disney is credited to be one of the first Hollywood studio heads to recognise and fully exploit this new medium (Wasko, 2001). Disney's weekly series *Disneyland* began in 1954 and was screened on ABC. In the programme Disney recycled its old cartoon shorts, screened new material and promoted future productions. *Disneyland* also had live-action segments, the best known of which was *Davie Crockett*, a mini-series featuring the adventures of a fabled American historical figure. Prior to the series' release, Disney purchased large numbers of raccoon skins to manufacture copies of Crockett's signature hat, successfully pre-empting the audience's demand for related consumables (Elliot, 1993). This move was the company's first foray into what shall be discussed in relation to Disney theme-parks as hybrid consumption.

By 1961 the series would switch provider to NBC and change its name to *Disney's Wonderful World of Colour*. As with *Disneyland*, the new series featured Walt as main story-teller and creative mastermind to the Disney process, though his appearance was seen by some as indulgent and shamelessly self-advertising (Watts, 1997). The series was also ill received by some of the majority of American households who still owned black and white television sets, as it was felt that Walt was attempting to push the new technology (Smoodin, 1994). While the television series clearly offered commercial possibilities for the backlog of Disney content, another equally important function was its ability to promote and advertise the upcoming *Disneyland* theme park in California and later *Walt Disney World* in Florida.

With Disney's move into television came the resources to realise Walt's most ambitious plans: the creation of a physical leisure utopia. The partnership with ABC forged through Disney's venture into television would enable Walt to raise funds to build *Disneyland*, Disney's first themepark. ABC contributed $500,000 into the venture and became a 35% owner of the park (Wasko, 2001). Walt started a company called WED (Walter Elias Disney) Enterprises to manage and develop the park as a separate financial entity. The television series *Disneyland* was used in conjunction with the development of the park. It served as a promotional device and like the park was divided into four parts/zones: Fantasy-land, Adventure-land, Frontier-land and Tomorrow-land.

The park was designed and built to Walt's personal specifications. He sent several employees to research existing parks and report back their findings. The chief divergence between his park and others would be its exclusion of typical rides, such as the roller-coaster or Ferris wheel. Beer and hot-dogs, which were associated with the carnival and theme-park experience, would likewise not be available (Bryman, 1995). It would rather be a theme-park built on attractions, organised along lines of clean living and family-safe entertainment. As noted before, the central hub of the park would be Main Street USA, modelled on down-town Marceline, the locus of Walt's childhood fantasies. No other area in the park is accessible without first venturing into the Main Street area. The park is likewise encircled by a miniature railway, another important vestige of Walt's fantasy life. Main Street is also home to the famous audio-animatronic Abraham Lincoln, a robotic artifice who recounts his life for the audience. Like the television series, Disneyland had the effect of opening another route of gratification to the viewer, who now could become an active participant in the hyper-reality of Disney. The new domain was an absolute simulation, a pure simulacrum; a streamlined fantasy-scape built to encompass an audience in a consumable reality. It became a domain for the 1950s family to consume as a unit, another move towards a utopian realisation of the Disney entity in which its structure (of fantasy, mythical biography and fetishised commodity) could be walked through. In its essence, this structure expresses itself in what Bryman (2004) refers to as hybrid consumption.

In *The Disneyization of Society* Alan Bryman (2004) suggests that the Disney enterprise is supported by a system of consumerism he terms hybrid consumption. Hybrid consumption is a process that connects different forms of consumerism: media, merchandise and theme-parks. The result of this mode of consumerism is a blurring of lines between buying merchandise and viewing the film. Thus spending money on merchandise becomes associated with the experience of the gratifying Disney fantasy. In this way the perverse relation between Disney and consumer is actualised in the Real by the practice of buying material produce. Hybrid consumption became so effective for Disney that the company has become a figurehead for this kind of marketing. Disney has now become synonymous with a global process Bryman has dubbed 'Disneyization', the main goal of which is "increasing the inclination to consume" (Bryman, 2004, p4). Bryman argues that Disney is not just a special way of manipulating and presenting stories; it is also a unique way of marketing to the subject as consumer. This move towards encouraging a *compulsive consumption* is remarkably close to what Peele (1985) defines as the core of addictive behaviour. Likewise, Loose (2011) draws attention to the creation on the law of jouissance (the structuring principle of addiction) as a radical alternative to social structures organised by paternal Law. Loose notes the law of jouissance is itself dependent on the creation of symbolic institutions that provide the structure within which the addict may operate. While this structure is constructed via socio-symbolic interactions (persons interacting to produce an organisation that supplies the addictive thing), they allow the subject access to self-administration of their jouissance in absence of the social bond. The Disney world of hybrid consumption thus offers an alternative structure within which the subject attains gratification independent of the social bond; a fantasy of gratification free of the constraints of Law.

200

Feature-length Films of the 50s and 60s: Familial Sexuality

Feature-length animation as it develops in the 1950s and 60s is paradoxical both a recipient of the family-friendly aesthetic and increasingly imbued with a subtle yet visible sexualisation of form. The development of the character tropes discussed in chapter five is particularly interesting. The films of this period become more subtly sexualised and in the same measure become more Oedipally conventional. While the vestiges of this trend can be seen in the post-war compilation shorts of the late 1940s, it is most evident in the 1950s and 60s Disney animated features. The similarities and discrepancies between the representation of the body between the classic era and the 50s/60s period will be discussed here. These films will not be analysed in the same depth as those in Part Two as they are far more homogeneous and stable in their narrative formulations and formal qualities.

In 1950 Disney had begun production on *Cinderella* (1950), its first feature-length animated film in eight years, while simultaneously starting work on *Alice in Wonderland* (1951) and *Peter Pan* (1953). *Cinderella* and the other Hollywood features of the 1950s were built on themes of maternal mistreatment: the mother as a domineering and cruel figure. Ann Kaplan (1990) considers that these mothers were emblematic of a masculinist unease with woman's appearance in the American workforce during the war. This represented a change in gender roles that produced an uncomfortable encounter with phallic women, empowered through stereotypically male cultural practices. Kaplan discusses *Now Voyager* (1942) as exemplifying this masculine unease with the empowered woman and considers it to behave sadistically to the *negative* mother. In *Now Voyager* the mother, Mrs Vale, is an image of phallic potency, empowered through her subjugation of her child Charlotte. Charlotte seeks a father figure in order to free herself from the negative mother, the archaic Other who seeks to transgress the paternal law (or ignore it) and maintain affective fusion with the child. The surrogate father of the text is Charlotte's psychiatrist who is also her love interest. He seeks to punish the negative mother for her relation to her daughter, and offers Charlotte entry into the symbolic by way of proposal and romance (Kaplan, 1990).

Cinderella as a text is similar to *Now Voyager* as it too behaves sadistically towards the image of the mother. Cinderella's step-mother is ugly, foreboding and irrational. She refuses Cinderella's wishes to leave the house and meet the prince, as her control is to be an absolute authority in Cinderella's life. Although it is in actuality the desire of the child that binds it to the mother,

201

Camp and the Villain
(Image by Rupert Norfolk)

the question becomes one of positive and negative maternal images. According to Kaplan (1990) the positive mother is required to be subservient to the paternal whereas the negative mother mirrors the desire of the child (the desire for the child to be with the mother). The negative mother is abject, with the capacity for ugliness that begets a phobic object. She is the mother that the child must struggle against in the process of individuation. The theme of abject and evil maternal masses and conventionalised paternal authority becomes commonplace in the Disney of the 1950s and 60s. *Alice in Wonderland* is beset by the aggressive bullying and engulfing Red Queen. *Sleeping Beauty*'s (1959) witch Maleficent is put out by not being invited to her betrothal, a right she deigns to have. In *101 Dalmatians* (1961) Cruella is just as much a negative mother as she strives to *adopt* the Dalmatian pups, before cannibalising the child (puppies) by turning them into a fur coat. *Peter Pan* is perhaps light on representations of negative maternity; rather Peter is conflicted by jealous romantic interests. The maternal Wendy is pitted against the Indian princess and the impulsive and jealous Tinkerbell, a malicious fairy in her own right. Instead the story relies on the feminisation of Captain Hook, to produce a camp rendition of the classic character, whose caricatured curves reference an implicit feminisation of character.

Camp was a characteristic attributed to many of the 1950s and 60s Disney male villains, expressing the studio's implicit conservatism and valuation of stereotypically masculinated forms. This was likewise visible in the gender-non-specific Siamese cats in *The Lady and the Tramp* (1955), and in Shere Khan and Kaa in *The Jungle Book* (1967). The scene in which Kaa and

Kaa and Mowgli
(Image by Rupert Norfolk)

Mowgli meet seems rife with inference; that the phallic python represents some form of misconduct with the infant Mowgli – an absolute distortion of his role as Mowgli's co-mentor in Rudyard Kipling's (1894) original text.

The figures of the heroes and heroines within these films become similarly homogenised in this period. Narratively the main protagonist moves from a position of care-free self-indulgence to being an integral member of the family unit. Whether this be the child, mother or father, the end position is the same: becoming part of an adoring mass of the family. Thus *Peter Pan*'s Wendy negotiates her dreams of Neverland only to find that her place is back in the real world as a maternal figure of responsibility for her two younger brothers (Byrne and McQuillan, 1999). Mowgli defies the words of the panther Bagheera and seeks a vagabond's life of pleasure, until he is forced into the life and death world of responsibility and must leave the jungle, spurred on by the advances of a young girl.

Both *101 Dalmatians* (1961) and *Lady and the Tramp* (1955) offer virtually identical narratives which feature the passage from care-free bachelor life to fatherhood and family-life. The role of the father within these films is likewise tied to the creation and propagation of the family unit. The King in *Cinderella* strives to arrange a marriage for his son and Cinderella. The narratives of both *Lady and the Tramp* and *101 Dalmatians* end in the

203

creation of the family unit, as does *The Jungle Book* with Mowgli's return to humanity. Again, the only film not strictly organised in relation to patriarchy was *Alice in Wonderland*, which the studio found particularly hard to Disneyify for the American audience due to the surrealist strength and uniqueness of the original text. Walt famously did not enjoy *Alice* as a film, complaining that it "was filled with weird characters" (Walt Disney, cited in Schickel, 1968, p295). American audiences were likewise not taken with the film, which performed quite poorly upon release. Although things were going so well for Disney in the 1950s that when *Alice in Wonderland* failed at the box-office, the effects were little felt by the studio. *Peter Pan* did not perform much better at the box-office than *Alice*. Perhaps because of the strength and non-linear nature of these texts, they were harder to rework into specifically Disney films. Their literary reputation also limited what Disney could alter with regards to the story and the characters.

Peter Pan also had issues with placing the child into a familial context. The film appears at times to be structured by the struggle between Peter, the self-centred hero reminiscent of Disney's classic era, and Wendy, the maternal heroine emblematic of the new Disney family. Peter is the impulsive child, uncastrated and wilful. He is driven by whimsy and adventure, which contrasts drastically with Wendy's journey of maternal self-realisation: adopting the lost boys and indeed Peter himself. The sexualised Tinkerbell with her fetishistic buttocks (reportedly modelled on Marilyn Monroe...the fairy, not the buttocks) is the opposite of Wendy's homely figure, and serves as a vessel for Peter's sexual precocity that he eventually surrenders in his pursuit of the familial paradise offered him by Wendy.

Despite the father's role in structuring the gratification of the child, the paternal function is as ridiculed and impotent as it was in the classic era of Disney. The father has the function of supporting the creation of the family unit, but he consistently appears as diminutive and ridiculous. This is most obvious in *Cinderella*'s King, who appears as an impulsive agitated child, dwarfed by images of his son.

The two kings in *The Sleeping Beauty* likewise become foolish and child-like – while planning their children's future family they become drunk, playful and giddy. The fathers in *101 Dalmatians*, *Lady and the Tramp* and *The Jungle Book* (a position held by both Bagheera and Baloo) are defensive of the child, constructive of the family but inconsequential in the child's castration. Thus the father plays a symbolic role in organising the gratifica-

The Father dwarfed by his phallic son
(Image by Paul Byrne)

tion within these films, while the gratification is still dependent on the creation of the archaic (maternal) adoring mass in place of a family unit.

The negativised maternal figure across these films was done in service of a more conventionally Oedipal structure, which mirrors Baudrillard's (1968) staunch critique of the new consumerism; namely that it was shaped by the requirement of re-situating the consumer in a structural relation to the corporation, this relation being dependent on paternity, and namely a paternal super-ego, to direct this engagement. As stated before, the maternal super-ego is used strategically to create a sense of malevolence while simultaneously providing the viewer with the illusion of penultimate gratification at the level of the archaic. The paternal thus has the role of mediating and structuring the social constructions the consumer negotiates in approaching this gratification.

The live-action films of this period were just as narratively conventional as the animated films. Most of these films were structured by the family under threat and surviving malevolence thanks to the ingenuity and goodly nature of the main protagonists. They were fables of the nuclear family, featuring predictable clichés and low budgets; they tended to be low in financial risk and high in returns. Walt refused to make the move into experimentation that many other studios were taking. While the majority of Hollywood film-makers were breaking the classic Hollywood narrative conventions, Disney was sticking to a more linear and now old-fashioned approach to film-making. By the 60s Disney was moving into live-action features and production on shorts was further waning. The predictability and caricatured typing of characters was to produce a simplified product on a par with the emotional caricature of the medium of animation. Essentially the studio successfully Disneyified live action.

In 1953 Disney created the distribution company Buena Vista to replace their connection to RKO, allowing Disney to control the most crucial aspects of the industry from production to consumption. When *Alice in Wonderland*, *Peter Pan* and other features failed to perform at the box-office, the effects were not much felt by the studio, which was all the more secure for its diversification and streamlining of the exhibition process.

Walt Disney's Death and Walt Disney World

In 1965 Disney began to plan a second theme-park that would be much larger than the first. Walt organised the purchase of 27,400 acres of reclaimed swamp-land in Florida (Bryman, 1995). Rather than a theme-park as a place to be visited, Walt Disney World was to be an immersive experience of fantasy. The park undeniably expressed Walt's obsessive perfectionism: it was to be clean, controlled and perfectly managed for the gratification of the middle-class family. Of utmost importance to Disney (Walt and the 'entity') within this endeavour was the ability to control a suspension of disbelief at the level of the Real; the creation of a pure simulacrum.

In Walt's early conceptions of the park he planned for Disney employees to live in EPCOT (Experimental Prototype Community of Tomorrow), a planned community that would potentially house up to 20,000 people. Thus Walt would be able to control every aspect of his employees' lives: where they lived, where they worked, what schools their children would attend. The original plan involved a giant dome being constructed over the park, so that he would even be able to control the weather. EPCOT was the locus of Walt's utopia, the ultimate realisation of the structural proclivities of Disney. Walt was forced to build the resort first, as the lenders obviously prioritised investment that would guarantee returns. After Disney died, EPCOT was scrapped, as the inheritors of Disney were wary of the large investment that would be required for a planned community. Although a Disney planned community would be created years later in the form of Celebration in Florida, it would be built under a radically different ideology to Walt's utopian modernism. Contemporary EPCOT is featured as an exhibition at Disney World; a sepulchre to the original conception, it appears as testament to Walt Disney's grandest designs.

Walt employed 'imagineers' to actualise the park, as he had done with Disneyland. As the name implies their purpose was to engineer the real aspects of this fantasy utopia, architecturally and mechanically. The new theme-park was an exercise in pure escapism. The audio animatronics are found in abundance and serve the purpose of simulating a Disneyified reality. The robots represented Walt's last attempt to fuse the animated and the live, to make dreams and fantasies that one step closer to being realised. The centre of these animatronic creations was Disney's Abraham Lincoln. Walt had developed the idea from the 1964 World's Fair; he believed it was potentially as important an art form as Lincoln was a man. Schickel cautions that the animatronic represented "dehumanization of art at its final extremity" (Schickel, 1968, p337). Mirroring Baudrillard's (1988) supposition that the simulation ultimately obscures reality, Benjamin made note of technology's capacity to radically alienate the subject in its mediation between humanity and nature (Hansen, 1993). It was in this mediation that Benjamin saw Disney's greatest potential and peril.

The desire underlying all Disney production, so simple in one man's eyes, is that everything one wishes can come true. It is a brutal solitude that follows the attempted realisation of these desires, a desperate pursuit of wish fulfilment followed by the cataclysm expressed in the cultural disavowal necessary to support this structure. The ideology of control and realisation of fantasy was central to classic Disney animations. The classic era represents the semiotic chora of the Disney entity, expressed so clearly in the architecture and management of Disneyland and Disney World (Wilson, 1991). Disney World represents a crystallisation of Disney values, and is perhaps the most fitting monument to the mythical figure of Walt. Perhaps this aspect of the park is what gave rise to the rumour that Walt's remains were cryogenically frozen and hidden underground in Disneyland (Poundstone, 1983).

This tendency towards control, expressed structurally within Disney, is conceptually identical to Loose's (2011) account of administration in the study of addiction. Administration in this context is symbolic in its structure, a product of the modernist project of industrialisation and consumerism. At its core, what is administrated is jouissance as product; a commodity that is ideological in nature and excludes the Other (Loose, 2011). But the reality of jouissance is a reflection of the archaic mother; engulfing and totalitarian in the utopia of affective fusion, so nearly encapsulated in death.

Walt Disney died on the 15th of December 1966 after an operation to treat his lung cancer. Contrary to the discussions of contemporary Disney films

207

by Byrne et al. (Byrne and McQuillan, 1999), the content of later Disney administrations changed yet the perverse and regressive apparatus of its products became distilled and static. The company would go through various changes after his death and would move between pragmatizing its productions and maintaining adherence to Walt's will as a figurehead of the company (Barrier, 2007). The succeeding inceptions of Disney with its different figureheads (Ron Miller, Michael Eisner, etc.) would oscillate through various formulations in its product until finally settling on the image and narrative style of the Disney classic era. Films such as *The Lion King* (1994), *The Little Mermaid* (1989) or *The Hunchback of Notre Dame* (1996) can be seen to feature the signifying material of contemporary day, yet the narratives still rely on the passage of the child from stable relation to the Other, to another stable relation to the Other in absentia of paternalistic interference. As is evident in *The Lion King*'s Scar, *The Hunchback*'s Frollo or the androgynous phallic consumption of *The Little Mermaid*'s Ursula and her father King Triton that attempts to prevent her love. All of these characters are pacified in the course of the narratives which all conclude with a return to a state of infantile adoration. Thus the image, ideology and style of Walt at his most iconic becomes frozen in time, until it appears as it is today as an autonomous entity, structuring the internal workings of a corporate leviathan.

Conclusion

It was stated in the introduction to this research that the end result of this text would produce the archetypical consumer; the image of the contemporary subject immersed in the complex structures of the Disneyified culture industry. This subject becomes evident in the structural disavowal necessary for the utopian apparatus that has been discussed over the three parts of this text. Before approaching a holistic account of this structure it will be necessary to relate what concepts have been discussed and produced over the course of this work.

The project of Part One was to create an analogical homunculus of Disney as an object of study. This homunculus acts as a metaphor for both the structure of Part One and the Disney entity itself. Part One began by creating a theoretical context with which to discuss Disney as a socio-cultural institution by interlocking several concepts, among which the perverse organisation and addictification. As discussed by Long (2008), there is a perverse structure underlying contemporary corporate discourse. This structure can be considered perverse as it allows those within it to profit at another's expense through a disavowal of social conventions. It accomplishes this by convincing the other of a direct route to jouissance – a route that is at its essence outside the Law and manipulative of the symbolic, thus dependent on a disavowal of the paternal order. The subject as other to this structure is instrumentalised and convinced of an unproblematic and self-administrative relation to jouissance. This jouissance is not the jouissance of the Other, dependent on the social realm, but rather the jouissance of the Real: that which is outside the symbolic. Thus, through interaction within the perverse organisational structure the subject's relation to the Law is supplanted by the law of jouissance, an anti-law that drives the subject towards transgression and ultimately subjective obliteration. This process Loose (2011) describes as the prerequisite to the problem of addiction. It can thus be said that the subject is driven by the promise of gratification to interact within the perverse organisation. This interaction can be seen to mirror the process of addictification which submits the subject to a relation to jouissance that is characterised by compulsive consumption (i.e. addiction).

With this theoretical context in place the next task of Part One was to describe and establish the essential indivisibility between the myth of Walt Disney the man and the Disney company, which can be demonstrated as emblematic of the perverse organisation and its reach into contemporary culture. This was accomplished through the use of biographical texts being to highlight and discuss organisational characteristics evident in the company itself and the myths that surround Walt Disney. These characteristics were formed from an early stage in the company's inception and are composed of ideological positions organised along a tendency to control viewer gratification and to increase financial gain. These characteristics were shown to be directly related to the mythical construction of Walt Disney, who is still maintained as the contemporary figurehead for the company and the ideological template for its practice.

Part One proceeded to discuss psychobiographical accounts that posited Mickey Mouse and Donald Duck as representatives of Walt's ego and id respectively. When related to the viewer, both can be shown to occupy a similar role, though they appeal to different aspects of the psyche that they can be said to mirror. Both Mickey and Donald are focal points for the viewer and receptacles of the gaze. This function is referred to as the homunculus: a complex vessel for psychical constructs. The homunculus functions as a mirror with which to construct the viewer's ego ideal and ideal ego; the perception of a unified form, idealised by its function as an internalisation of the gaze of the paternal super-ego. The homunculus is fetishistic, appearing as solid, phallic and yet genital-free, so as to take a dual relation and purpose to the subject: that which wards away anxiety of castration and has the capacity to connect the viewer to gratification outside submission to the paternal. The homunculus represents the primary unit of consumption in the viewer's relation to the Disney structure. It can be likened to the little part of Walt that was made consumable; to enable his own gratification in an attempt at commercial immortalisation. This can be seen to be successful in light of Walt's ideological apparatus surviving him into the present day.

Thus the analogical homunculus that was the project of Part One is constructed from the myth of Walt Disney, coupled with the organisational and economic structure of the company, and finally blended into animation in the form of Mickey and Donald, Walt's most primordial on-screen surrogates in the address to the subject as viewer and consumer. Thus the conceptual homunculus (on screen) can be seen as the core of the homunculus as preformationist organisational metaphor (for the structure of both Part One and 'Disney' as an organisational construct).

Part Two of this text sought to conceptualise the cinematic apparatus that forms the base of engagement and address to the Disney viewer. This apparatus was described as regressive in form; requiring the audience to regress to simplified organisations of enjoyment in order to attain gratification. This gratification was described as intrinsically transgressive, hence the medium is carefully regulated to disavow the paternal and thus censorship. To accomplish the discussion of this regressive apparatus, the four chapters of Part Two offered textual analyses of the Disney films that made up the classic era. The outcome of Part Two produces an account of mass-appeal rooted in regressive simplification and structured by the perverse organisational structures of Disney itself.

Chapter five's discussion of Disney character tropes created a terminology with which to begin the analyses of regressive narratives. Among these tropes were the *desired*, the *adoring mass*, the *demanding* and the *malevolent*. These tropes were related to the concept of the homunculus, as established in Part One. The homunculus is thus the central point to the viewer's engagement within this apparatus, a unifying aspect that enables a perverse disavowal to operate, supported by the fetish nature of the homuncule form. In recounting the narrative structure of *Snow White and the Seven Dwarfs* the viewer's negotiation of these tropes was illustrated, followed by the introduction to the concept of the *archaic* in Lacanian theory by referencing the Neben-mensch as the primordial Other (Lacan, 1959).

Chapter six followed this discussion with an account of animation principles, producing a lexicon of regression with which to compose the *mise-en-scène* of the regressive apparatus. This was further emphasised by the analysis of *Pinocchio*, which drew attention to the negotiation of the figures of the father and the separation of his roles so as to enable this regressive pleasure, while structuring this enjoyment. This was achieved by splitting the father's image between positive and negative functions in relation to the regressive state. The father as agent of castration is negativised whereas the figure of Geppetto is maternalised, being father in name only. The father by name thus enables the gratification of Pinocchio (Geppetto's union with his wooden boy in the maternal space of his workshop) while the symbolic functions of the father as agent of castration are projected onto the malevolent characters. Thus the symbolic father is relegated to his imaginary facsimile, which is then divided between positive and negative extremes, and is projected onto different character tropes.

Chapter seven followed with a discussion of eroticism and the cartoon form in *Fantasia*. The erotic or sensual form is submitted to a number of scenarios which develop and submit the cartoon body to conventions that create a regressive, simplified and perverse diegesis. Introduced in *Fantasia* was a unique feature within the regressive form of the classic period: the paternal super-ego is given a voice with which to direct viewer gratification in an effort to produce a consensus subservient to a dominant reading of the more abstract eroticised text. This was a clear expression of a conscious move on the part of Disney to limit possible audience readings in an effort to control and mediate gratification. This was expressed in the hegemonic potential of the film for unifying high and low culture in an effort to produce audience compliance.

The last chapter in Part Two was dedicated to the relatively similar texts of *Bambi* and *Dumbo*. The two films demonstrate a progressive increases of threat to the maternal form and the incestuous union of the child to the primordial Other within the adoring mass. The threat to this state can be shown to situate the anxiety associated with castration and likewise acts as a vent for the anxiety of jouissance associated with the primordial relation between child and Other. While the mother comes under threat and is even killed in *Bambi*, her position is never left truly empty, thus the narrative begins and ends in a utopian state of affective fusion with the Other. The

cartoon body as an image within this dynamic impresses an intrinsic ambivalence on the part of the viewer. This ambivalence is felt as a result of the
disparity between the viewer and the cartoon form as an ideal. This disparity
is similar in structure to the aggressivity and adoration intrinsic to the
homo-eroticism of the 'built body' in contemporary cinema.

Part Three aimed to unify the concepts developed in Parts One and Two,
and synthesise a psychoanalytic conception of the consumerist utopia central
to Disney as a socio-cultural construction. Chapter nine began this discussion with an account of hegemony as conceptualised by Antonio Gramsci.
It established that hegemony is a struggle for ideological dominance that
utilises the culture industry to perpetuate values that are negotiated by the
general populace. This section described Disney's capacity to regulate hegemony in aid of consumerist utopia and the expressions of this regulation
in the unionisation of Hollywood in the 1940s and the North American
cultural exports to Latin America. This chapter used *The Reluctant Dragon*
to illustrate Disney's early forays into mediating American culture towards
its own ends.

This was followed by discussions of Disney's ideological exports relating to
the American 'good neighbour policy' intended to garner Latin American
support for the war effort. This section takes *The Three Caballeros* as
emblematic of this process. The analysis of *Caballeros* also highlights what
is referred to as *cartoon jouissance*, or the representation of transgressive
pleasure in the cartoon medium that guarantees the disavowal of the paternal
in order to enjoy its transgressive content free of censorship and cynicism.
In this regard *Caballeros* can be seen as a failure as it did not receive the
readings the studio had intended due to its heavy-handed approach to
sensuality that verges on the vulgar.

Chapter eleven began with discussions of Disney's work on propaganda films
during World War II and reintroduced the concept of utopia as an organising
principle of audience homogenisation. This chapter discussed the structure
of audience compliance being reliant on a division of the super-ego into
maternal and paternal aspects. The maternal super-ego represents the internalisation of the phallic mother (the archaic Other), this is the negativised
aspect of the super-ego that pushes the subject to enjoy beyond the bounds
of the pleasure principle. This is opposed to the paternal super-ego, the
internalisation of the father and the function of the Law. These diametrically
opposed aspects are used strategically in propaganda films to elicit audience
compliance through narrative and stylistic choices. The aesthetics of ugliness

was further developed in this section to take on an ideological and psychical dimension. The ugly becomes associated with the archaic maternal and the punishing aspects of the super-ego, it is used in conjunction with the image of the Axis powers as enemy. This is contrasted against the paternal agency that commands the subject to enjoy as a precondition to their compliance in the fight against a constructed enemy. In this way the propaganda film manipulates psychical projections to garner audience homogenisation, a key theme in achieving the unitary response the government sought of its public. Central to this manipulation is the maintenance of a particularly Disney utopia that is structured by a positivised relation to the primordial maternal.

The discussion of polarised developmental aspects of the psyche would seem to necessitate mention of Melanie Klein and her work concerning object relations, which in part discusses the positive and negative aspects of the maternal figure (see Klien, 1952). The relationship between Lacanian and Klienian theory is often complex and would require a great deal more discussion then a simple mention here, thus it would be a beneficial area for future research to discuss, yet this theoretical overlap is not directly relevant to the present discussion.

The concept of unitary response was continued in the final chapter which discussed the creation of the new leisure class of the 1950s. The leisure or 'middle' class would have the capacity to homogenise the consumerist public of the 1950s era in opposition to the perceived new threat of communism. This new consumerism was articulated by Ernst Dichter (1960) to be a moral imperative, which necessitates a hedonistic approach to consumption that would usurp ageing Victorian frugality and puritanism. Disney was instrumental in hegemonising the new consumerism, as is evident in the feature-length animations of the time and the company's expansion into television and theme-parks as a means to engage the nuclear family as a consumerist unit. The synergistic utopia constructed by Disney in this period would found core marketing principles of corporations for generations to follow, and Disney still considered one of the most successful organisations of corporate media practice to this day.

A utopian vision of gratification is thus constructed; the consumerist utopia makes its address to the subject as consumer via a regressive apparatus, the core of which is the homunculus as an aspirational model of unhindered gratification. To create an account of the archetypical consumer it is necessary to situate the subject within this construct. It is this structural relation that defines this consumer.

213

It is the regressive apparatus that situates the subject within a relation to Disney as a structure. The subject as viewer engages within the regressive space in a movement towards utopian regression: archaic affective fusion with the primordial mother, a state that is outside the Law and the intervention of the father in the subject's access to gratification. This mythical state is sold as a fantasmatic scenario.

Engagement with this scenario involves a set of identifications and projections that fuse the viewer as subject and the screen as object. Central to this dynamic process is the figure of the homunculus, the recipient of the subject's projections of the ideal ego (the aspirational image of egoic solidity). As such it is an idealisation, a pure simulacrum. It is an ideological object that acts as currency within the Disney utopia.

This utopia is the foundation of both the Disney entity and the Disney product; it is the primal simplification that draws the mass audience, offering a pre-symbolic and pre-gendered appeal that crosses divisive social, racial and cultural strata. It is the realm of perverse simplicity that Mollenhoff (1940) and Eisenstein (1941–1946) equate with animism. Animism, Freud (1919) posits, is structured by a binary opposition that separates paternal authority and the uncanny, and projects these poles onto different figures, enabling an externalised polarisation of psychical elements. This animistic simplification can be seen at all levels of the Disney entity, from the caricatures of malevolence to the idealisation of the homunculus. Central to this structuring practice is a paternal authority that acts in service to a primordial maternal mass.

As stated, the homunculus is central to the viewer's engagement with Disney. The homunculus acts as a fetish for the viewer, in that it supports and enables a disavowal of the paternal function. As Dadoun (1989) notes, the fetish is divided between positive and negative functions for the subject. As a positive, it enables a defence against castration by covering the lack of the Other. It simultaneously protects the subject from being enveloped by the archaic mother, as it also maintains a phallic function and thus wards against her as a token of the paternal. As a negative, the fetish enables access to jouissance: transgressive and traumatic gratification that threatens subjective obliteration. It is therefore both protection from the archaic Other and a key to illusory access to her jouissance. This is not a jouissance of the Other (dependent on transgression of the paternal), but rather a jouissance of the Real.

It is possible to equate the positive aspects of the fetish (protection from castration and the primordial mother) with the paternal super-ego, as this aspect of the super-ego that seeks to maintain subjective cohesion. The fetish is negativised by its relation to the negative mother: the phallic and archaic mother, the super-egoic apparition which drives the subject to the jouissance of the Real. Thus the homunculus as fetish for the subject acts as an ideological object that enables access to the jouissance of the Real, under the prerogative of the negative mother. The maternal super-ego pushes the subject to transgression and is thus structurally transparent with the law of jouissance. This is the part of the Disney structure which is representative of addiction as the homunculus itself holds the characteristics necessitated by Loose's (2011) conception of the addictive Thing. Its relation to the primordial is precisely what allows gratification to occur in the absence of the Other and the paternal: the form of the fetish is thus gratifying in itself.

This structure is not able to operate by itself; the subject and the homunculus are not the summation of the Disney apparatus. The consumerist utopia of Disney is not a hedonistic anarchy, it is a perverse structure. This structure is organised by the interdiction of the paternal super-ego. As was the case in Disney propaganda films the super-ego directs the ideological context that enables regressive gratification. The paternal super-ego directs the positioning of the positive mother: the mother as subservient to paternalistic intervention. It is this aspect of the subject's engagement with Disney that is structured symbolically. The paternal prerogative within Disney compels the subject into a relation with their jouissance; it creates a context to access this jouissance. This symbolic structure that enables access to this jouissance of the Real is the essence of addictification: the process that cultivates dependency and produces the addicted subject (Loose, 2011).

In the case of Disney the paternal super-ego is represented by the mythic figure of Walt Disney. It is the ideology implicit in this organisationally internalised voice that dictates the structure of the Disney entity that outlives him to the present day. Thus there is a symbolic position sanctioned by Law under the pretext of capitalist expansion that enables the subject's administration of a jouissance of the Real. While these binary pairs (positive and negative mother, paternal/maternal super-ego, Law of the father/law of jouissance) are mutually exclusive they are able to operate in tandem as a result of the intrinsic disavowal that sutures Disney's perverse organisational structure. It is within this disavowal, fluctuating between mutually exclusive polarities that negate and collide, that we find the subject as the archetypical consumer. And within this structure, this subject is not contented; the process of addictification is socially de-constructive and terminal. The subject as consumer is sick, venal and lost. The archetypical consumer is constructed as a subject pathologized by its artificial prosthesis. Corrupted by external structures, organised and manufactured to suit his basest, most simplified gratification.

Future Research and End Notes

With a structure theoretically established for investigating the place of the consumer within contemporary society there is no shortage of scope for future research, although there are several areas that would be particularly fruitful to expand on. The first of these involves quantitative research regarding audience response to mass media products. While this may appear limited in relation to the abstract arguments within this text, studies such as these have a great potential to establish concepts such as consumer addictification to media. An engaging example of this mode of research is the University of Maryland's study *A Day Without Media*, which asked 200 university students to go 24 hours without any form of media: internet, text messaging, television, MP3 players and so on. Many of the students could not complete the task and most reported being unable to cope without engaging with these commodities, even suffering withdrawal symptoms consistent with those specified in clinical diagnostic criteria of addiction (Mueller et al. 2010). Some research projects have focused on global audience reception, such as Wasko, Phillips and Meehan's (2001) *Global Disney Audiences Project*, which produced a wide-reaching account of Disney product reception across 18 countries using quantitative survey techniques. This research is of great value to critical discussions of Disney as a socio-cultural institution as makes explicit the company's global reach and homogeneous response across culturally heterogeneous audiences. This kind of research is critically important as it provides an anchoring point for more theoretical discussions and dissections of the apparatus involved in consumer gratification.

Regarding areas where the present research project could be expanded upon, there is obviously more to be said on Disney products and media. The creation of Buena Vista should not be underestimated as a major event in the company's evolution. Under Buena Vista, Disney owns a plethora of other media outlets, such as Miramax and Touchstone studios. Thus the company that released *The Jungle Book* also released *Pulp Fiction* (1994), *The Nightmare Before Christmas* (1993) and *Pretty Woman* (1990). An in-depth study of the internal dynamic between Disney, Buena Vista and these other media groups would be fruitful to say the least.

In general there is a great deal more to be said of Disney theme-parks as they have been subject to such a great deal of critical discourse. This would easily form a research project in itself, as the areas of discussion and analysis to draw on are vast. Discussions of Disney live-action films would likewise be productive. As mentioned the studio was successfully able to Disneyify live action as a form; this suggests that there must be a continuum between the visual forms of animation and live action. Plotting this continuum would have greatly expanded on the concept of the hyper-real in the Disney industrial process.

Continuing the analysis of this text of Disney products to the present day would better illustrate Disney's pervasive quality and ideological position within contemporary culture. Although this work was able to synthesise the archetype of the contemporary consumer, it would be of great benefit to demonstrate the resilience of this construction across the decades after Walt Disney's death.

As with any theoretical work, application depends on areas that will facilitate theory's capacity to affect change. It was the project of feminism to raise awareness of gender inequality. It accomplished this in part by informing, instructing and negotiating with the dominant ideological position, until that position was partially altered (Modleski, 1991). It has been the project of this text to collate and unify critical discourse on Disney into a psycho-analytic framework that would provide an account of the problematic engagement the subject has to this particularly regressive medium.

Dissections and explorations of this engagement have been discussed in academic and critical discourse within this text. This work offers is an attempted unification of these concepts and the production of an account of the subject as consumer. For this research to contribute to a hegemonic shift that produces an awareness of these principles and the pitfalls of consumption, it must connect theory to some form of outward expression. A praxis of this text therefore involves connecting theory to cultural mani-festation. Thus the final task of this text is to underline that this praxis already exists. Popular culture abounds with expressions of pathologized consumer-ism and a cynicism of Disney's utopian vision.

The first area in which this cynicism can be seen to be expressed is animated comedy series, paying ironic tribute to Disney as a populariser of the animated form. *The Simpsons* episode *Itchy and Scratchy-Land* (1994) has the

217

family travelling to a theme-park modelled on the cartoons Bart and Lisa Simpson like to watch. The park is clean, authoritarian and seems to hold dangerous secrets. While at the park an army of animatronic Itchies and Scratchies go haywire, threatening to kill the Simpson family.

The animators of *Family Guy* playfully recreate their characters in Disney-style animation *(Road to the Multi-verse,* 2009*)*, who then proceed to frolic while singing along with a musical number. Their gaiety is interrupted by the Jewish character Mort calling to their door as the big bad wolf. They violently murder Mort, parodying Walt's reported anti-Semitism.

A *Venture Brothers* episode, *The Incredible Mr Brisby* (2004), sees the Venture family visiting Brisby-Land. The park is owned by the ageless Mr Brisby who seeks to be cloned so that he may continue his quest of world domination indefinitely, while fighting off the intervention of the Orange County Liberation Front.

Perhaps the most vibrant representation of the place of the archetypical consumer within the Disney apparatus can be found in pop-surrealism: a movement originating on the West Coast of the United States, sometimes referred to as low-brow art. The malfunctioning dynamic of collision and mutual-exclusion can be seen to culminate in this form, which has been dramatically influenced by the aesthetics and ideological position of Disney (Jordan, 2005). While the movement covers a great deal of popular themes, there is a recurring negotiation of Disney iconography within the works of many low-brow artists. There is an uncanny quality to the apparitions of Disney within these forms, a focus on the duality of the Disney animism which expresses a polarisation of paternalistic totalitarianism levied against the archaic hedonism and anarchy of the cartoon form. This is most clearly expressed in Todd Schorr's *The Spectre of Cartoon Appeal* (2000), which sees Mickey fused with characters from other studios as a central apparition, a multi-armed animistic hybrid deity overlooking a sexuated and warped playground of animated forms. It is an image of a leery carnival populated by uncanny mutants and perverted onlookers.

Camille Rose Garcia is a pop-surrealist based in California. Having grown up in the shadow of Disneyland, her work is influenced by unease in regarding Disney and the themes of consumption that underlie its image. This theme she found mirrored in the free-associative writings of William Burroughs and the pathologised utopian visions of Philip K. Dick. In a series of her works entitled *The Saddest Place on Earth* she depicts the collision of consumption with the animated utopian form. Her work expresses the

Creepcake Annihilation Plan
(Garcia, 2004, p20)

Burden
(Garcia, 2004, p21)

brutality of disavowal, embodied in a "fairytale world that is actually an evil, narcissistic wasteland" (Garcia, 2004, p18). Her images display various cute characters riddled with painful sickness and ailments.

Creepcake Annihilation Plan (Garcia, 2004, p20) shows seven dwarf-like characters gorging themselves on a landscape of cream and sweets. They are literally bursting at the seams with the jouissance of their venal addictions. They are shown at different stages of their consumption as it becomes steadily pathological; the three figures in the bottom of the image are sick with over-indulgence. They appear bloated and ill, while a vulture watches them from the side, waiting for the creatures to gorge themselves to death.

Burden (Garcia, 2004, p21), depicts Pinocchio in different stages of a struggle with a malfunctioning phallic disavowal. He cuts at his nose, trying to hide its embarrassing elongation; his shameful reminder of sexuation and lies. The last and largest Pinocchio on the right of the image has sawn his nose off and looks vacantly delighted in his mutilation.

The synthesis of theoretical accounts of consumption has marked the first step in the project of this research. The praxis of this text is to make the second step: to unify theory and its manifestation. Ultimately there are few projects that have encapsulated the dynamic outlined within this research as successfully as the project that inspired its inception: *Hibernator: Prince of the Petrified Forest* (Gilchrist & Joelson, 2007). The problem of consumption is continually addressed in the psychedelic narrative accompanying the films of the Walt chimera. The dialogue is intended to imitate a peyote-trip juxtaposed from the annals of Timothy Leary, whom Gilchrist and Joelson consider the polar opposite to Walt Disney's position in American culture of the 1960s. It is a dialogue of jouissance, a jouissance absent of address and independent of the Other, reminiscent of the floating associative passages of *Naked Lunch* (Burroughs, 1959). It is an exercise in nonsense and narcissism, a domain of radical alienation and solitude:

> "VOICEOVER: 'Follow the light with your eyes'. So says the caretaker. Are you still conscious? The reckoning of your bad dreams is all over. Hexer is gone. This is you now, in person, lying on a slab in a cryogenic vault deep under EPCOT. Clutching your burial goods.
>
> WALT DISNEY: Remember how beautiful it was, how wonderful, when the light came on and shone so brightly that we thought we'd burst with life.
>
> Back spinning of radio dial
>
> ENDS"
> (in Beard, 2007, p24).

References

Adorno, T. (1951) 'Freudian Theory and the Pattern of Fascist Propaganda'. In Bernstein, J.M. (ed.) *The Culture Industry: Selected Essays on Mass Culture*. London: Routledge. pp.114–135.

Adams, P. (1996) 'Of Female Bondage' In *The Emptiness of The Image*, London, Routledge. pp.27–48.

Adorno, T., Lowenthal, L., Massing, P. W. (1946) 'Anti-Semitism and Fascist Propaganda' In E. Simmel (ed.) *Anti-Semitism: A Social Disease*, New York: International University Press, pp125–137.

Adorno, T. and Horkheimer, M. (1944) *The Dialectics of Enlightenment*, Stanford: Stanford University Press.

Agee, J. (1943) 'July 3, 1943' In Scorsese, M. (2000) *Agee on Film*, New York: Modern Library, pp25–28.

Allan, R. (1999) *Walt Disney and Europe*, London: John Libbey Publishing.

Althusser, L. (1971) *Lenin and Philosophy*, New York, Monthly Review.

Andre, S. (2006) 'The Structure of Perversion: A Lacanian Perspective' In Nobus, D. and Downing, L. (eds.) *Perversion: Psychoanalytic Perspectives – Perspectives on Psychoanalysis*, London: Karnac Books. pp.109–125.

Bakan, J. (2004) *The Corporation: The Pathological Pursuit of Profit and Power*, Chicago IL: Free Press.

Barrier, M. (2007) *The Animated Man*, Berkley and London: University of California Press.

Baudrillard, J. (1968) *The System of Objects*, Benedict, J. (Trans.) London, New York: Verso.

Baudrillard, J. (1988) *Simulacra and Simulation*, Detroit MI: University of Michigan Press.

Beard, S. (2007) *Hibernator*, London: Beaconsfield.

Benjamin, W. (1936) *The Work of Art in the Age of Mechanical Reproduction*, New York, London: Penguin Books.

Berger, A. A. (1991) 'Of Mice and Men: An Introduction to Mouseology, Or Anal Eroticism and Disney' In Wolf, M. Kielwasser, A. (eds.) *Gay People, Sex, and the Media*, New York: Haworth Press, pp.155–165.

Berland, D. (1982) 'Disney and Freud: Walt Meets the Id', *Journal of Popular Culture* 15:4, pp.93–103.

Bettelheim, B (1976) *The Uses of Enchantment: The Meaning and Importance of Fairy Tales*, London: Penguin Books.

Birger, D.M. (1984). 'Pinocchio – Géza Róheim', *Psychoanalytic Quarterly* 53, pp155–160.

Bordwell, D., Staiger, J. and Thompson, K. (1988) *The Classical Hollywood Cinema: Film Style & Mode of Production to 1960*, London: Routledge.

Brandes, S. (1993) 'Spatial Symbolism in Southern Spain', *The Psychoanalytic Study of Society* 18, pp.119–135.

Brode, D. (2004) *Walt to Woodstock: How Disney Created the Counterculture*, Austin TX: University of Texas Press

Brody, M. (1976) *'The Wonderful World of Disney – Its Psychological Appeal', American Imago* 33:4, pp.350–359.

Brooker, M. K. (2010) *Disney, Pixar and the Hidden Messages of Children's Films*, Santa Barbara CA, Denver CO, Oxford U.K: ABC Clio.

Bryman, A. (1995) *Disney and His Worlds*, London and New York: Routledge.

Bryman, A. (2004) *The Disneyization of Society*, London, Thousand Oaks and New Delhi: Sage Publishers.

Burroughs, W. (1959) *Naked Lunch,* New York: Ballantine Books.

Byrne, E. and McQuillan, M. (1999) *Deconstructing Disney*, London: Pluto Press.

Campbell, M. B. (2010) 'Artificial Men: Alchemy, Transubstantiation, and the Homunculus', *Republics of Letters: A Journal for the Study of Knowledge, Politics, and the Arts* 2 [Online] Source: http://arcade.stanford.edu/journals/rofl/articles/artificial-men-alchemy-transubstantiation-and-homunculus-by-mary-baine-campbell [Accessed: 23:03:11]

Card, C. (1995) 'Pinocchio' In Bell, E. Haas, L. & Sells, L. (eds.) *Mouse to Mermaid: Politics of Film, Gender and Culture*, Bloomington and Indianapolis IN: Indiana University Press, pp68–71.

Cholodenko, A. (2007a) '(The) Death (of) the Animator, or: The Felicity of Felix Part II: A Difficulty in the Path of Animation Studies?' In *Animation Studies – Vol.2, 2007*

Cohen, K. (1997) *Forbidden Animation*, London: McFarland

Colless, E. (2007) 'Between the Legs of the Mermaid' in Cholodenko, A. (ed, 2007) *The Illusion of Life II: More Essays on Animation*, London and Sydney: Power Publications, pp.229–242

Collodi, C. (1882) *Pinocchio*, London: Puffin Books.

Cousins, M. (1994) 'The Ugly' (Part 1) *AA Files* 28, pp.61–64.

Cousins, M. (1995a) 'The Ugly' (Part 2) *AA Files* 29, pp.3–6.

Cousins, M. (1995b) 'The Ugly' (Part 3) *AA Files* 30, pp.65–68.

Cowie, E. (1984) 'Fantasia' In Adams, P. & Cowie, E. (eds.) *The Woman In Question*, Cambridge MA: MIT Press, pp.149–196.

Creed, B. (1993) *The Monstrous-Feminine*, London: Routledge.

Dadoun, R. (1989) 'Fetishism in the Horror Cinema', In Donald, J. (ed.) *Fantasy and the Cinema*, London: BFI Publishing, pp.39–61.

Davis, A. M. (2006) *Good Girls and Wicked Witches*, Eastleigh, United Kingdom: John Libbey Publishing.

Dean, T. (2000) *Beyond Sexuality*, Chicago IL: University of Chicago Press.

De Roos, R. (1994) 'The Magic Worlds of Walt Disney' In Smoodin, E. (ed.) *The Disney Discourse: Producing the Magic Kingdom,* London: Routledge, pp.48–70.

Dichter, E. (1960) *The Strategy of Desire*, New Brunswick NJ, Transaction Publishing.

Dor, J. (1995) *Introducing Lacan*, New York: Other Press.

Dor, J. (1999) *The Clinical Lacan*, New York: Other Press.

Dorfman, A. and Mattelart, A. (1991) Kunzle, D. (Trans.) *How to read Donald Duck: imperialist ideology in the Disney comic*, New York: International General.

Dyer, R. (1997) *White*, London: Routledge.

Eisenstein, S. (1941–46) *Eisenstein On Disney*, Leyda, J. (ed.) Upchurch, A. (Trans.) Calcutta: Segul Books.

Elliot, M. (1993) *Walt Disney: Hollywood's Dark Prince*, London: Andre Deutsch.

Ellis, J. (1982) *Visible Fictions*, London: Routledge.

Fachinelli, E. (1996) 'Lacan and the Thing', *Journal of European Psychoanalysis* 3, [Online] Source: http://www.psychomedia.it/jep/number3-4/fachinelli.htm [Accessed: 14:10:11]

Freud, S. (1905a) 'Three Essays on the Theory of Sexuality' In *On Sexuality*, Richards, A. (ed.) Strachey, J. (Trans.) London: Penguin Books, pp.33–170.

Freud, S. (1905b) *Jokes and their Relation to the Unconscious*, Richards, A. (ed.) Strachey, J. (Trans.), London: Penguin Books.

Freud, S. (1909) 'Analysis of a phobia in a five-year-old boy' *In Case histories. 1, 'Dora' and 'Little Hans'*, Richards, A. (ed.) Strachey, J. (Trans.) London: Penguin Books, pp.167–303.

Freud, S. (1910) *Leonardo Da Vinci: A Study In Psychosexuality*, Strachey, J. (Trans.) London: W. W. Norton & Company.

Freud, S. (1913) *Totem and Taboo*, Strachey, J. (Trans.) London: W. W. Norton & Company.

Freud, S. (1914) 'On Narcissism' In *On Metapsychology*, Penguin Freud Library, London, Penguin Books, pp.59–97.

Freud (1920) *Beyond the Pleasure Principle*, DuFresne, T. (ed.) Richter, G. (Trans.) London and Peterborough ON: Broadview Press.

Freud, S. (1922) *Group Psychology and Analysis of the Ego*, Strachey, J. (Trans.) London, New York: W. W. Norton & Company.

Freud (1923) 'The Ego and the Id' In *On Metapsychology*, Richards, A. (ed.) Strachey, J. (Trans.) London: Penguin Books, pp.339–401.

Freud, S. (1927) '*Fetishism*' In *On Sexuality*, Richards, A. (ed.) Strachey, J. (Trans.) London: Penguin Books, pp.347–357.

Freud (1930) *Civilisation and its Discontents*, McLintock, D. (Trans.) London, Penguin Books.

Garcia, C. R. (2004) *The Saddest Place on Earth*, San Francisco: Last Gasp Publishing.

Gilchrist, B. and Joelson, J. (2007) *Hibernator: Prince of the Petrified Forest*, Installation in Beaconsfield Gallery, Vauxhall, South London: London Fieldworks. Performance: Installation. (viewed: 27, April, 2007)

Giroux, H. A. (2000) *The Mouse That Roared*, Maryland MD: Rowman & Littlefield Publishers, Inc.

Goethe, J. W. (1832) *Faust*, Bayard T. (Trans.) [Online] Source:http://www.gutenberg.org/files/14591/14591-h/14591-h.htm [Accessed: 12/09/10]

Grimm, J. and Grimm, W. (1857) 'Little Snow White' In *Grimm's Fairy Stories* [Online] Source: http://www.gutenberg.org/files/11027/11027-h/11027-h.htm [Accessed: 12/09/10]

Hansen, M. (1993) 'Of Mice and Ducks: Benjamin and Adorno on Disney' *The South Atlantic Quarterly* 92, pp.27–61.

Hayes, R. (2012) 'The animated body and its material nature' In Pilling, J. (ed.) *Animating the Unconscious*, New York and London: Wallflower pp.208–219

Hartman, J. J. (2000). 'A Psychoanalytic View of Racial Myths in a Nazi Propaganda Film: Der Ewige Jude (The Eternal Jew)' *Journal of Applied Psychoanalytic Studies* 2, pp.329–346.

Hoare, Q. (ed.) (1971) *Selections from the Prison Notebooks of Antonio Gramsci*, Smith, G. N. (Trans.) New York: International Publishers.

Hunt, L. (1993) 'What are Big Boys Made of? *Spartacus, El Cid* and the Male Epic' In Kirkham, P. and Thumin, J. (eds.) *You Tarzan: Masculinity, Movies and Men.* London: Lawrence and Wishart, pp.65–83.

Jordan, M. D. (2005) *Weirdo Deluxe*, San Francisco CA: Chronicle Books.

Kaplan, E. A., (1990) 'Motherhood and Representation: from Postwar Freudian Figurations to Postmodernism' In *Psychoanalysis and Cinema,* London: Routledge, pp.128–142.

Kipling, R. (1894) *The Jungle Book*, London, New York: Penguin Books.

Klein, M. (1952) 'Some theoretical conclusions regarding the emotional life of the infant' In *Envy Gratitude and Other Works 1946–1963*, Cambridge: The Free Press, pp.61–94.

Kolker, R. (1999) *Film, Form and Culture*, New York: McGraw Hill.

Kris, E. (1943) 'Some Problems of War Propaganda: A Note on Propaganda New and Old' *Psychoanalytic Quarterly* 12, pp.381–99.

Kris, E. and Speier, H. (1944) *German Radio Propaganda: Report on Home Broadcasts During the War*, London: Oxford University Press.

Kristeva, J. (1982) *Powers of Horror*, New York: Columbia University Press.

Kunzle (1991) 'Introduction to the English Edition' In Dorfman, A. and Mattelart, A. (1991) Kunzle, D. (Trans.) *How to read Donald Duck: imperialist ideology in the Disney comic*, New York: International General, pp.11–21.

Lacan, J. (1938) *Family Complexes in the Formation of the Individual*, Trans. Gallagher, C. (Online) Source: http://www.lacaninireland.com/web/?page_id=123 [Accessed: 23:01:2009]

Lacan, J. (1953) 'The Function and Field of Speech and Language in Psychoanalysis' In *Écrits*, Fink, B. (Trans.) London and New York: W. W. Norton and Company, pp.197–268.

Lacan, J. (1954a) 'On Narcissism' In *The Seminar of Jacques Lacan Book 1: Freud's Papers on Technique,* Miller, J. A. (ed.) Forrester, J. (Trans.) London and New York: W. W. Norton and Company, pp.107–117.

Lacan, J. (1954b) 'Ego Ideal and Ideal Ego' In *The Seminar of Jacques Lacan Book 1: Freud's Papers on Technique*, Miller, J. A. (ed.) Forrester, J. (Trans.) London and New York: W. W. Norton and Company, pp.129–143.

Lacan, J. (1954c) 'Discourse analysis and ego analysis' In *The Seminar of Jacques Lacan Book 1: Freud's Papers on Technique*, Miller, J. A. (ed.) Forrester, J. (Trans.) London and New York: W. W. Norton and Company, pp.62–70.

Lacan, J. (1955) 'The Freudian Thing' In *Écrits*, Fink, B. (Trans.) London and New York: W. W. Norton and Company, pp.334–363.

Lacan (1955–1956) 'On a Question prior to any Possible Treatment of Psychosis' In *Ecrits*, Fink, B. (Trans.) London and New York: W. W. Norton and Company, pp.445–488.

Lacan, (1956) 'The signifier, as such, signifies nothing' In *The Seminar of Jacques Lacan Book III: The Psychosis*, Miller, J. A. (ed.) Grigg, R. (Trans.) London and New York: W. W. Norton and Company, pp.183–205.

Lacan, J. (1957a) 'La Fonction Du Voile' In *Le Seminaire Livre IV: La relation d'objet*, Paris: Éditions Du Seuil, pp.151–164.

Lacan, J. (1957b) 'Comment s'analyse le mythe' In *Le Seminaire Livre IV: La relation d'objet*, Paris: Éditions Du Seuil, pp.269–284.

Lacan, J. (1957c) 'Les culottes de la mère et la carence du père' In *Le Seminaire Livre IV: La relation d'objet*, Paris: Éditions Du Seuil, pp.353–370.

Lacan, J. (1957d) 'La phallus et la mère inassouvie' In *Le Seminaire Livre IV: La relation d'objet*, Paris: Éditions Du Seuil, pp.179–195.

Lacan, J. (1958a) 'The Signification of the Phallus' In *Écrits*, Fink, B. (Trans.) London and New York: W. W. Norton and Company, pp.575–584.

Lacan, J (1958b) 'The Direction of Treatment and Principles of its Power' In *Écrits*, Fink, B. (Trans.) London and New York: W. W. Norton and Company, pp.489–542.

Lacan, J. (1959) 'Das Ding' In *The Ethics of Psychoanalysis*, Miller, J. A. (ed.) Porter, D. (Trans.) pp.51–69.

Lacan, J. (1960) 'Love of One's Neighbour' In *The Ethics of Psychoanalysis*, Miller, J. A. (ed.) Porter, D. (Trans.) pp.220–234.

Lacan, J. (1962) 'Seminar 3: Wednesday 28th November 1962' In *The Seminar of Jacques Lacan Book X – Anxiety*, Gallagher, C. (Trans.) [Online] Source: http://www.lacaninireland.com/web/?page_id=123 [Accessed: 01:06:2011]

Lacan, J. (1964a) 'From Love to the Libido' In *The Four Fundamental Concepts of Psychoanalysis*, Miller, J. A. (ed.) Sheridan, A. (Trans.) London and New York: Karnac Books, pp.187–203.

Lacan, J. (1964b) 'Position of the Unconscious' In *Écrits*, Fink, B. (Trans.) London and New York: W. W. Norton and Company, pp.829–721.

Lacan, J. (1966) 'The Subversion of the Subject and the Dialectic of Desire in the Freudian Unconscious' In *Écrits*, Fink, B. (Trans.) London and New York: W. W. Norton and Company, pp.671–702.

Lacan, J. (1970) 'From myth to structure' In *The Seminar of Jacques Lacan Book XVII: The Other Side of Psychoanalysis*, Miller, J. A. (ed.) Fink, B. (Trans.) London and New York: W.W. Norton and Company, pp.118–132.

Lacan, (1972) 'Seminar 1, Wednesday 21 November 1972' In *Encore*, Seminar XX Gallagher, C. (Trans.) [Online] Source: http://www.lacaninireland.com/web/?page_id=123 [Accessed: 24/06/11] pp.1–13.

Lacan, J. (1973) 'Love and the Signifier' In *The Seminar of Jacques Lacan Book XX: On Feminine Sexuality*, Miller, J. A. (ed.) Fink, B. (Trans.) London and New York: W.W. Norton, pp.38–50.

Lacan, J. (1975) 'Seminar 5: Tuesday 11 February 1975' In *The Seminar of Jacques Lacan Book XXII – RSI*, Gallagher, C. (Trans.) [Online] Source: http://www.lacaninireland.com/web/?page_id=123 [Accessed: 24/06/11]

Landy, M. (1994) *Film, Politics and Gramsci*, Minnesota and London: University of Minnesota Press.

Le Bon, G. (1895) *Psychology of the Crowd*, Southampton: Sparkling Books.

Lasch, C. (1979) *The Culture of Narcissism*, London and New York: W. W. Norton and Company.

Leslie, E. (2002) *Hollywood Flatlands*, Brooklyn and London: Verso.

Lewis, J. (2000) *Hollywood v. Hard Core*, New York and London: New York University Press.

Long, S. (2008) *The Perverse Organisation and Its Deadly Sins*, London: Karnac Books.

Loose, R. (2002) *The Subject of Addiction*, London: Karnac Books.

Loose, R. (2011) 'Modern Symptoms and their Effect', In Baldwin, Y. G., Malone, K. and Svolos, T. (eds.) *Lacan and Addiction*, London: Karnac Books, pp.1–38.

Mangan, J. (2007) 'When fantasy is just too close for comfort' *The Age* 10, [Online] Source:http://www.theage.com.au/news/entertainment/when-fantasy-is-just-too-close-for-comfort/2007/06/09/1181089394400.html?page=fullpage [Accessed: 02:02:12]

Metz (1974) *Language and Cinema*, The Hague: Mouton.

Metz, C. (1977) *The Imaginary Signifier: Psychoanalysis and the Cinema*, Bloomington: Indiana University Press.

225

McAdams, D. P. (1988) 'Biography, narrative, and lives', *Journal of Personality*, 56, 1–18.

McCloud, S. (1993) *Understanding Comics: The Invisible Art*, Northampton MA: Tundra Publishing.

Miller J.A. (2011) 'The Fundamental Fantasm' In *The Symptom* [Online] Issue 10, Source http://www.lacan.com/thesymptom/?page_id=801 [Accessed: 01:02:12]

Mitchell, A. (2008) 'Introduction: Image – Apocalypse – Desire' In Armand, L. Lewty, J. and Mitchell, A. (eds.) *Pornotopias: Image – Apocalypse – Desire*, Prague: Litteraria Pragensia Books, pp.1–3.

Modleski, T. (1991) *Feminism Without Women*, London, New York: Routledge.

Mueller et al (2010) *A Day Without Media* [Website] Source: http://withoutmedia. wordpress.com/ [Accessed: 23/11/10]

Mollenhoff, F. (1940) 'Remarks on the Popularity of Mickey Mouse', *American Imago* 1:3, pp.19–32.

More, T. (1516) *Utopia*, Turner, P. (Trans. 1965) London: Penguin Classics.

Mori, M. (1970) 'The Uncanny Valley' *Energy* 7, [Online] Source: http://www.android-science.com/theuncannyvalley/proceedings2005/uncannyvalley.html [Accessed: 22/11/10]

Mulvey, L. (1975) 'Visual Pleasure and Narrative Cinema' *Screen* 16.3, pp.6–18.

Neale, S. (1993) 'Masculinity as Spectacle' In Cohan, S. & Hark, I. R. (eds.) *Screening the Male*, London, New York: Routledge, pp.9–22.

Nobus, D. (2006) 'Locating Perversion, Dislocating Psychoanalysis' In Nobus, D. and Downing, L. (eds.) *Perversion: Psychoanalytic Perspectives – Perspectives on Psychoanalysis*, London: Karnac Books, pp.3–18.

Payne, D. (1995) 'Bambi' In Bell, E. Haas, L. & Sells, L. (eds.) *Mouse to Mermaid: Politics of Film, Gender and Culture*, Indianapolis IN: Indiana University Press, pp.137–147.

Pilling, J. (2012) *Animating the Unconscious*, New York and London: Wallflower

Peele, S. (1985) *The Meaning of Addiction*, San Francisco CA: Wiley Company.

Poundstone, W. (1983) *Big Secrets: The Uncensored Truth About All Sorts of Stuff You Are Never Supposed to Know*, New York: William Morrow Paperbacks.

Ramachandran, V.S. (2008) 'The Neurology of Aesthetics' *The Scientific American Special Edition* 18:2, pp.74–77.

Rose, J. (1982) 'Introduction' in *Feminine Sexuality: Jacques Lacan and L'école Freudienne* Mitchell, J. & Rose, J. (eds.) New York: Norton

Rose, L. (2003) 'Interpreting Propaganda: Successors to Warburg and Freud in Wartime' *American Imago* 60:1, pp.122–130.

Roy, J (2012) 'The Body and the Unconscious as Creative Elements in the work of Michéle Cournoyer' in Pilling, J. (ed.) *Animating the Unconscious*, New York and London: Wallflower, pp. 19–31.

Sachs, H. (1933) 'The Delay of the Machine Age' *The Psychoanalytic Quarterly* II, pp.404–424.

Sauvagnat, F. (2002) 'Fatherhood and naming in J. Lacan's works' *The Symptom* 3, [Online] Source: www.lacan.com/fathernamef.htm [Accessed: 26/05/11]

Schickel, R. (1968) *The Disney Version: The Life, Times, Art and Commerce of Walt Disney* 3rd edn, Chicago Il: Elephant Paperbacks.

Shale, R. (1982) *Donald Duck Joins Up: The Walt Disney Studio During World War II*, Ann Arbor, MI: UMI Research Press.

Shortsleeve, K. (2001) 'The Wonderful World of the Depression: Disney, Despotism, and the 1930s. Or, Why Disney Scares Us', *The Lion and the Unicorn* 28:1, pp.1–30.

Smoodin, Eric (1994) *Animating Culture: Hollywood Cartoons from the Sound Era*, New Brunswick, NJ: Rutgers University Press.

Spivey N. (2006) *How Art Made the World*, London: BBC Books.

Tasker, Y. (1993) *Spectacular Bodies*. London, New York: Routledge.

Thomas, F. and Johnston, O. (1984) *Disney Animation: The Illusion of Life*, New York: Abbeville Press.

Tinbergen, N. (1954), *Curious Naturalists*, New York: Basic Books.

Turner, P. (1965) 'Introduction to Utopia' In More, T. (1516) *Utopia*, Turner, P. (Trans. 1965) London: Penguin Classics, pp.7–25.

Watts, S. (1997) *The Magic Kingdom*, Columbia and London: University of Missouri Press.

Warner, M. (1995) *From the Beast to the Blonde: on Fairy-tales and their Tellers*, London: Vintage.

Wasko, J. (2001) *Understanding Disney*, Malden: Blackwell Publishing.

Wasko, J. Phillips, M. and Meehan, E. (2001) *Dazzled by Disney: The Global Disney Audiences Project*, London and New York: Continuum Books.

Wells, P. (2002) *Animation: Genre and Authorship*, New York and London: Wallflower Press

West, M. (2008) 'Pinocchio's Journey from the Pleasure Principle to the Reality Principle' In Rollin, L. West, M. (eds.) *Psychoanalytic Responses to Children's Literature*, Jefferson, NC: McFarland, pp.65–71.

Willemen, P. (1981) 'Anthony Mann: Looking at the Male', *Framework* 15–17, pp.16–20.

Wilson, A. (1991) *The Culture of Nature,* Toronto: Between the Lines Publishing.

Whitley, D. (2008) *The Idea of Nature in Disney Animation*, London: Ashgate.

Zizek, S. (1991) *Looking Awry*, New York, London: Routledge.

Zizek, S. (1992) *Enjoy your symptom! : Jacques Lacan in Hollywood and out*, New York, London: Routledge.

Filmography

101 Dalmatians (1961) [Film] U.S.A: Walt Disney Studios

A Reckless Moment (1949) [Film] U.S.A: Columbia Pictures Organisation

Alice and the Dog Catcher (1924) [Animated Short] U.S.A: Walt Disney Studios

Alice gets in Dutch (1924) [Animated Short] U.S.A: Walt Disney Studios

Alice in Wonderland (1951) [Film] U.S.A: Walt Disney Studios

Aliens (1986) [Film] Dir. Cameron, J. U.S.A: 20th Century Fox

Bambi (1942) [Film] U.S.A: Walt Disney Studios

Cinderella (1950) [Film] U.S.A: Walt Disney Studios

Conan the Barbarian (1982) [Film] Dir. Milius, J. U.S.A: Universal, 20th Century Fox

Country Cousin (1936) [Animated Short] U.S.A: Walt Disney Studios

Der Ewige Jude (1940) Dir. Hippler, F., Germany: Ministry of Propaganda (Nazi-Germany)

Der Fürer's Face (1942) [Animated Short] U.S.A: Walt Disney Studios

Disney Treasure; The chronological Duck (2005) [DVD] U.S.A: Walt Disney Studios

Donald's Better Self (1938) [Animated Short] U.S.A: Walt Disney Studios

Donald's Decision (1942) [Animated Short] U.S.A: Walt Disney Studios

Donald gets Drafted (1942) [Animated Short] U.S.A: Walt Disney Studios

Dracula (1931)) [Film] Dir. Browning, T. U.S.A: Universal Pictures

Education for Death: The Making of a Nazi (1942) [Animated Short] U.S.A: Walt Disney Studios

Family guy: Road to the Multi-verse (2009) [Animated Television Series] U.S.A: Fox, Aired: 09/27/09

Fantasia (1940) [Film] U.S.A: Walt Disney Studios

Flowers and Trees (1931) [Animated Short] U.S.A: Walt Disney Studios

Fun and Fancy Free (1947) [Film] U.S.A: Walt Disney Studios

Gallopin' Gaucho (1928) [Animated Short] U.S.A: Walt Disney Studios

Gulliver Mickey (1934) [Animated Short] U.S.A: Walt Disney Studios

Jazz Singer (1927) [Film] U.S.A: Warner Bros.

Little-Red-Riding Hood (1922) [Animated Short] U.S.A: Newman Theatre Laugh-O-Grams

Make Mine Music (1946) [Film] U.S.A: Walt Disney Studios

Mary Poppins (1967) [Film] U.S.A: Walt Disney Studios

Melody Time (1948) [Film] U.S.A: Walt Disney Studios

Mickey's Garden (1935) [Animated Short] U.S.A: Walt Disney Studios

Mickey's Orphans (1931) [Animated Short] U.S.A: Walt Disney Studios

Mickey's Review (1932) [Animated Short] Walt Disney Studios

Nifty Nineties (1941) [Animated Short] U.S.A: Walt Disney Studios

Nightmare before Christmas (1993) [Film] Dir. Burton, T., U.S.A: Touchstone

Now Voyager (1942) [Film] U.S.A: Warner Brothers Pictures

One Hour in Wonderland (1950) [Television Program] U.S.A: Walt Disney Studios, Aired: 24/12/1950

Orphan's Benefit (1934) [Animated Short] U.S.A: Walt Disney Studios

Oswald the Rabbit; Great Guns (1927) [Animated Short] U.S.A: Walt Disney Studios

Oswald the Rabbit; Rival Romeos (1928) [Animated Short] U.S.A: Walt Disney Studios

Oswald the Rabbit; The Mechanical Cow (1927) [Animated Short] U.S.A: Walt Disney

Oswald the Rabbit; The Ocean Hop (1927) [Animated Short] U.S.A: Walt Disney Studios

Oswald the Rabbit; What A Knight (1927) [Animated Short] U.S.A: Walt Disney Studios

Out of the Frying Pan into the Firing Line (1942) [Animated Short] U.S.A: Walt Disney Studios

Peter Pan (1953) [Film] U.S.A: Walt Disney Studios

Pinocchio (1940) [Film] U.S.A: Walt Disney Studios

Plane crazy (1928) [Animated Short] U.S.A: Walt Disney Studios

Pretty Woman (1990) [Film] Dir. Marshall, G., U.S.A: Touchstone

Private Snafu: Booby Traps (1944) [Animated Short] U.S.A: Warner Brothers

Pulp Fiction (1994) [Film] Dir. Tarantino, Q., U.S.A: Miramax

Puss-In-Boots (1922) [Animated Short] U.S.A: Newman Theatre Laugh-O-Grams

Saludos Amigos (1942) [Film] U.S.A: Walt Disney Studios

Seal Island (1948) [Film] U.S.A: Walt Disney Studios

Secret Lives: Walt Disney (1995) [Television Documentary] Dir. Bullman, J. U.K: Channel Four, Aired: 23 February, 1995

Skeleton Dance (1929) [Animated Short] U.S.A: Walt Disney Studios

Sleeping Beauty (1959) [Film] U.S.A: Walt Disney Studios

Snow White (1937) [Film] U.S.A: Walt Disney Studios

Songs of the South (1946) [Film] U.S.A: Walt Disney Studios

Steamboat Willy (1928) [Animated Short] U.S.A: Walt Disney Studios

Studios

The Adventures of Ichabod and Mr Toad (1949),[Film] U.S.A: Walt Disney Studios

The Army Mascot (1942) [Animated Short] U.S.A: Walt Disney Studios

The Band Concert (1935) [Animated Short] U.S.A: Walt Disney Studios

The Brood (1979) [Feature Film] Dir. Cronenberg, D. U.K: Anchor Bay

The Disappearing Private (1942) [Animated Short] U.S.A: Walt Disney Studios

The Hunchback of Notre Dame (1996) [Film] U.S.A: Walt Disney Studios

The Jungle Book (1967) [Film] U.S.A: Walt Disney Studios

The Karnival Kid (1929) [Animated Short] U.S.A: Walt Disney Studios

The Lady and the Tramp (1955) [Film] U.S.A: Walt Disney Studios

The Lion King (1994) [Film] U.S.A: Walt Disney Studios

The Little Mermaid (1989) [Animated Feature] U.S.A: Walt Disney Studios

The Mad Doctor (1933) [Animated Short] U.S.A: Walt Disney Studios

The New Spirit (1942) [Animated Short] U.S.A: Walt Disney Studios

The Opry House (1928) [Animated Short] U.S.A: Walt Disney Studios

The Reckless Dragon (1941) [Film] U.S.A: Walt Disney Studios

The Seven Wise Dwarves (1941) [Animated Short] U.S.A: Walt Disney Studios

The Simpsons: Itchy and Scratchy-Land (1994) [Animated Television Series] U.S.A: Fox, Aired: 10/02/94

The Three Caballeros (1945) [Film] U.S.A: Walt Disney Studios

The Three Little Pigs (1933) [Animated Short] U.S.A: Walt Disney Studios

The Thrifty Pig (1941) [Animated Short] U.S.A: Walt Disney Studios

The Vanishing Private (1942) [Animated Short] U.S.A: Walt Disney Studios

The Water Babies (1935) [Animated Short] U.S.A: Walt Disney Studios

The Wise Little Hen (1934) [Animated Short] U.S.A: Walt Disney Studios

Venture Brothers: The Incredible Mr Brisby (2004) [Animated Television Series] U.S.A: Adult Swim, Aired: 28/09/04

Victory Through Air-Power (1943) [Film] U.S.A: Walt Disney Studios

Wild Waves (1930) [Animated Short] U.S.A: Walt Disney Studios

Digital Prints

MacDorman, K. and Minato, T. (2005) The Uncanny valley [Electronic Print] Source: http://www.androidscience.com/theuncannyvalley/proceedings2005/uncannyvalley.html [Accessed: 2/10/09]

London Fieldworks (2007) *Disney Chimera*, [Electronic Print] Source: http://www.londonfieldworks.com/gallery.php [Accessed 09/6/07]

Flagg, J. (1917) *Recruitment Poster*, [Electronic Print] Source: http://www.americaslibrary.gov/assets/jb/recon/jb_recon_flagg_1_e.jpg [Accessed 12/02/12]

Disney, W. & Iwerks, U. (1927–1928) *Oswald the Rabbit* [Electronic Print] Source: http://www.cartoonresearch.com/winkler/index.html [Accessed 18/09/08]

Index

101 Dalmatians (1961)   202-203

A

A Day without Media   216
A Night on Bald Mountain   116-118
A Reckless Moment (1949)   71
Adams, Parveen   59
Addictification   26
Addiction   24, 48, 200, 207, 209
Adoring mass   76-77, 85
Adorno, Theodor   51-52, 146, 171, 177, 191
Agee, James   191
Alice in Cartoonland   37
Alice in Wonderland (1951)   198, 201, 204
All Together Now (1943)   175
Allende, Salvador   146
Althusser, Louis   25, 168
Anality   63
Animism   50-51
Apparatus   70
Appeal   214
Archaic   97, 135, 211
Archaic mother/Other   59, 89, 135
Army Navy Magazine   177
Ave Maria   117

B

Baby Weems   152
Bacchus   84-85, 113
Bakan, Joel   19, 22
Bambi (1942)   130-141
Bambi: A Life in the Woods (1928) 130-132
Barrier, Michael   29, 31, 33
Baudrillard, Jean   153-155, 196, 207
Benjamin, Walter   51-52, 130, 181,192
Berland, David   52, 81
Bettelheim, Bruno   73-74, 78
Birger, Daniel   96
Booby Traps (1944)   176
Brody, Michael   63
Bryman, Alan   196, 200
Built Body   138

C

Canadian propaganda   172

Caricature   58
Caricature of realism   91-92
Carnival Kid (1929)   46
Cartoon jouissance   135, 159-160, 187
Castrating father   99-100
Castration   104
Castration anxiety   59, 101-102, 160
Character tropes   81, 83-85
Character types   72
Cholodenko, Alan   6
Cinderella (1950)   201
Clover, Carol J.   185
Cohn, Harry   67
Coincidence of the gaze   189-190
Colless, Edward   112
Columbia Pictures   67
Command to enjoy   174-175
Communism   198
Compulsive consumption   200
Conan the Barbarian (1982)   138
Cousins, Mark   123
Cowie, Elizabeth   50. 70-72
Creed, Barbara   184

D

Dadoun, Roger   59, 140, 149, 214
Daisy Duck   197
Dance of the Hours   118
Das Ding (The Thing)   82-83
Davie Crocket   198-199
Davis, Amy   76
Death Drive   123
Demanding (as character trope)   84-85
Der Ewige Jude (1940)   149
Der Furer's Face (1942)   183, 185-188
Desired (as character trope)   85
Devil   117-118
Dichter, Ernst   196
Disavowal   19, 59, 168
Disney Animation: The Illusion of Life (1984) 90-91
Disney (as institution)
    Audience   10
    Biographers   33
    Merchandise   48
    Studies   33-34, 168

Disney, Roy   36, 166-167
Disney Treasures: The Chronological Duck (2005) 54
Disney, Walt   29-38, 40, 41-44,
                                      47-48, 52, 67-68,
                    146-148, 166-167, 193-194
Disney, Walt, early years   35-37
Disney, Walt (death)   207-208
Disney's Wonderful World of Colour   199
Disneyification   129
Disneyization   200
Disneyland   199
Disneyland (television series)   199
Disneyland (theme park)   35, 154, 198
Donald duck   48,157, 177-180, 186, 197, 209
Donald gets Drafted (1942)   177-178
Donald's Better Self (1938)   174
Dracula (1930)   60
Dumbo (1942)   119, 124-130
Dyer, Richard   139

E

Education for Death (1943)   183-185
Ego   52, 58
Ego ideal   43,162
Ego-libido   75
Eisenstein, Serge   68-69, 110-111, 116, 195
Elliot, Marc   33, 50, 100, 147, 168
Ellis, John   81, 163
EPCOT   206

F

Fachinelli, Elvio   83
Family Guy   218
Fantasia (1940)   71, 105, 107-
Fantasy   17, 39
Faust   57
Feline   131.136-137
Fetish   58, 59, 123, 168, 214-215
Flagg, J. M.   189-190
Fleischer brothers   113
Flowers and Trees (1931)   61-62
Foreclosure   60
Freud, Sigmund
  Civilisation and its Discontents (1930)   130
  Group Psychology   171
  Homunculus   58
  Jokes   150
  *Jokes and their Relation to the
    Unconscious* (1905)   46
  Little Hans   41, 128
  On De Vinci   30
  On Narcissism   15-16
  The Ego and the Id   162
  Uncanny   97

Fun and Fancy Free (1947)   193

G

Gallopin' Gaucho (1928)   44
Garcia, Camille Rose   218-219
Geppetto   134
Goethe, J.W.   57
Golem   57
Good-neighbour policy   157
Goofy   55
Gramsci, Antonio   145
Great Guns (1927)   40
Gulliver Mickey (1934)   48-49

H

Hansen, Miriam   51, 181, 192
Hartman, John J.   149, 170, 189
Hayes Code   38, 110, 112
Hayes, William   38
Hegemony   145-146, 152
*Hibernator: Prince of the Petrified
    Forest* (2007)   14, 219
Hollywood blacklist   166
Hollywood Flatlands (2002)   51
Homunculus
  Conceptual   13, 57, 83
  Illustrative   13
  In Alchemy   57
  Threat to   103
How to Read Donald Duck (1991)   168
Hunt, Leon   140
Hybrid consumption   196
Hyper-reality   154-155, 165

I

Id   47, 52
Ideal Ego   58, 139
Identification 43-44, 81
Imaginers   207
Itchy and Scratchy-Land (1994)   217-218
Iwerks, Ub   36, 43

J

Jazz Singer (1927)   44
Jealousy   54
Jiminy Cricket   94
Joe Carioca   157, 159-161
Jouissance   17, 207, 214

K

Kaplan, Ann   188, 201
Knowledge   114
Kris, Ernst   170-172

L

Lacan, Jacques
  Death Drive   123-124

Demand 79
Desire 16
Family Complexes (1938) 83, 129, 162
Law as symbolic function 94
Little Hans 41, 135
Love 75
Mirror Stage 16, 58
Mirror Stage 85
Name of the Father 102
Other's desire 54
Phallus 20
Pleasure Principle 123
Real 153
Real Father 134
Real, Symbolic, Imaginary 134
The Thing 82
Usufruct 174
Lack 21
Lady and the Tramp (1955) 202
Lasch, Christopher 15
Law 16, 23, 93, 131, 133
Law of jouissance 23-25, 27, 200
Le Bon, Gustav 171
Leslie, Esther 51
Lexicon of regression 89-92
Little Mirmaid (1989) 112
London Fieldworks 14, 219
Long, Susan 18, 21-23, 25
Look of the Other - 50
Loose, Rik 24, 200, 207
Love 75

M
Make Mine Music (1946) 193
Male Gaze 139
Malevolence 84, 86, 99-100
Malten, Leonard 54
Mary Poppins (1967) 196
Mass appeal and regression 68
Maternal phallus 59
Maternal super-ego 98, 108, 191, 215
Mattelart and Dorfman 134, 146, 167
McCloud, Scott 57-58, 111, 113
Melody Time (1948) 193
Metz, Christian 70
Mickey Mouse 43-45, 51, 114-115, 134, 197, 209
Mickey's Garden (1935) 48
Mickey's Orphan's (1931) 49
Mickey's Review (1932) 49
Miller, Jaques-Alain 84
Minnie Mouse 46, 197
Mintz, Charles 43
Miranda, Aurora 158
Mirrors 75, 135
Modernism 195

Modleski, Tanya 122
Mollenhof, Frtiz 5, 45, 46-47, 159, 195
Monstro 103
Monstrous feminine 188
Motion Picture Association of America 166
Motion Picture Producers and Distributors of America 38
Mrs Jumbo 125-126
Multi-plane camera 95
Mulvey, Laura 53, 83
Musculinity 138

N
Naked Lunch (1959) 220
Narcissism Narcissistic society 15-17
National Labour Relations Board 147
Nebenmensch 83
Negative mother 98
Newman Theatre Laugh-O-Grams 36
Nifty Nineties (1941) 197
Now Voyager (1942) 71, 201

O
Oedipus Complex 54
Old Stag 131,135, 140
One Hour of Wonderland (1950) 198
Orphan's Benefit (1934) 49
Oswald the Lucky Rabbit 40
Out of the Frying Pan into the Firing Line (1942) 176, 182

P
Panchito 161, 163
Paracelsus 57
Pastoral Symphony 111
Paternal function 96-97
Paternal super-ego 108, 111, 115, 133, 191, 205, 210, 211, 215
Peak shift 92
Pearl Harbour 176
Perverse organisation 18, 25
Perversion, problem of desire 21
Perversion (structure) 20
Peter Pan (1953) 201-203
Phallic Imagery 53
Phallus 39, 54, 83, 188
Pinocchio (1882) 73, 93-94
Pinocchio (1940) 94-105, 212
Plane Crazy 44
Pleasure Island/Play-land 101
Pleasure principle 94
Pluto 55
Pornography 189-191
Powers, Pat 67
Pre-gendered 57
Pre-Oedipal 69, 86, 122, 124, 140
Pre-oedipal utopia 103

Pretty Woman (1990) 216
Primordial 123, 129
Primordial abyss 60
Primordial mother 96, 104
Private Snafu 176-174
Propaganda 169
Prosthesis 130
Psychobiography 30-31
Pulp Fiction (1994) 216
Pure simulacrum 154

R
Ramachandran, V.S. 92
Real 83, 153
Regression 64, 105, 121-123
Regressive apparatus 65
Riefenstahl, Leni 166
Rival Romeos (1928) 41
Road to the Multi-verse (2009) 218

S
Sachs, Hanns 5, 50
Sadistic gaze 185
Saludos Amigos 157, 158
Schickel, Richard 34, 41, 47, 63, 101, 118, 147, 168, 197, 207
Schorr, Todd 218
Screen Cartoonist Guild 147
Seal Island (1948) 194
Shortsleeve, Kevin 68
Silly Symphonies 49, 61-64
Simulation 153-154
Skeleton Dance (1929) 61
Sleeping Beauty (1959) 202-203
Smoodin, Eric 109, 146, 168, 176-177, 182, 197
Snow White (1857) 73
Snow White and the Seven Dwarfs (1937) 74-87, 89, 173
Songs of the South (1946) 194
Sorcerer's Apprentice 114-115
Steamboat Willy (1928) 45
Stokowski, Leopold 107
Stromboli 100
Super-ego 95, 162, 170-171, 174
Symbolic 16, 153

T
Tasker, Yvonne 51, 138, 179
Taylor, Deems 107
Television 198-199
The Adventures of Ichabod and Mr Toad (1949) 193
The Army Mascot (1942) 180-181
The Band Concert (1935) 49
The Culture Industry (1944) 146
The Disappearing Private (1942) 180
The Hunchback of Notre Dame (1996) 208
The Incredible Mr Brisby (2004) 218

The Jungle Book (1967) 202-204
The Lion King (1994) 208
The Little Mermaid (1989) 208
The Mad Doctor (1933) 48
The New Spirit (1942) 182
The Nightmare before Christmas (1993) 216
The Opry House (1928) 45
The Reluctant Dragon (1941) 149-154
The Seven Wise Dwarfs (1941) 173
The Simpsons 217
The Strategy of Desire (1960) 196
The Three Caballeros (1945) 158-165
The Three Little Pigs (1933) 62-63, 172
The Thrifty Pig (1941) 172
The Venture Brothers 218
The Water Babies (1935) 63
The Wise Little Hen (1934) 49
Thing 25
Threat 138
Transgression 121, 123, 160
Trauma 103, 134-135
True Life Adventures 194
Twitterpation 135-136

U
Ugly 125-127
Ultimate content 171, 190
Uncanny valley 164-165
Unconscious utopia 121
Uniforms 51, 151, 179
Unionisation 146-148, 166
Unquiet pleasure 140
Utopia (1516) 108
Utopia 214

V
Venus of Willendorf 113
Victory through Air-Power (1942) 172, 191-192
Violence 137-139

W
Walt Disney World (television series) 199
Walt Disney World (theme park) 206-
Waltitarianism 68
Warner, Maria 73
Wasko, Janet 33, 147, 194, 216
Watts, Steven 33, 108-109, 197
Wells, Paul 29
What a Knight (1927) 41-42
Wild Waves (1930) 46
World War II 145, 149, 169

Z
Zizek, Slavoj 98, 129, 167, 189-191